brandjam

humanizing brands
through emotional design

by
marc gobé

ALLWORTH PRESS
NEW YORK

DESIGN MANAGEMENT INSTITUTE

Is it design or is it life?

11   10   09   08   07   5   4   3   2   1

Published by Allworth Press
An imprint of Allworth Communications, Inc.
10 East 23rd Street, New York, NY 10010
Copublished with the Design Management Institute

Cover design by Brigitta Bungard
Interior design by Phyllis Aragaki
Page composition/typography by SR Desktop Services, Ridge, NY
Cover photo by Brigitta Bungard
Illustrations pages by Scott Massey and Derrick Lee
Photographs pages by Tiphaine Guillemet
Cartoons pages by the author

ISBN-13: 978-1-58115-468-9
ISBN-10: 1-58115-468-2

LIBRARY OF CONGRESS CATALOGING-IN-PUBLICATION DATA
Gobé, Marc.
Brandjam : humanizing brands through emotional design / Marc Gobé.
p.   cm.
Includes index.
ISBN-13: 978-1-58115-468-9 (hardcover)
ISBN-10: 1-58115-468-2
1. Commercial art.   2. Communication in design.   3. Brand name products—Marketing.
I. Design Management Institute (Boston, Mass.)   II. Title.

NC997.G56   2007
741.6—dc22
2006037021

Printed in Canada

It is only with the heart that one can see rightly.
What is essential is invisible to the eye.

—ANTOINE DE SAINT-EXUPÉRY, *THE LITTLE PRINCE*

contents

Design Is More

Design is more than the vehicle by which brands express themselves and connect with their customers. We know that . . . I hope. At its best, design is a reflection of the human eco-system.

But design is stuck: stuck between the current capitalism of its mid-life crisis and the utopias of its infancy. Trends, fashion, and a certain cynicism—designer jokes abound—are the new pillars of design, replacing the industrial socialism of Le Corbusier and the Bauhaus or the Italian democrat-intellectuals of pre- and postwar Italy. We are reluctant to move forward, so we linger in the current state.

But why do we need change? Why do we need new design? Another chair? Another milk bottle?

More than at any other time, we need designs that are not only new, but that contain a new humanism, that embody the human challenges we face now and those to come. The only thing we have to fear is when, as a species, we don't believe in the future anymore.

There are three areas of opportunity for design that have a special resonance with respect to humanism. We will have to consider these in every design practice:

1. Design for the other 6 billion people. The vast majority of design work addresses the 1 billion populating the so-called developed countries. Finally, designers are getting involved in solving problems around the world, where the other 6 billion live. For example, the One Laptop Per Child (OLPC). This revolutionary product brings learning, information, and communication to children where they need it the most—in developing countries. In a way, OLPC (also called the $100 laptop) accomplishes what the personal computer was supposed to do in the first place: bring information and learning to all.

2. Sustainability. The designer's toolbox now contains this promise: technologies, processes, and materials will allow us to change industry forever into sustainable and renewable sources. Consumers will not wait much longer for the car to become a non-polluting, exciting, and individualized new experience. There is work to do.

3. Emotion. Today we touch on sophisticated emotional needs of consumers. Designers are liberated from the obligation to follow trends and styles, and their expression and point of view wakes us up from the boredom of mass consumerism. They create not only the appropriate functional product, but also a self-expressed statement, depending on what is most relevant to the problem at hand. The Herman Miller Leaf light's minimalism and simple interactivity, for instance, gives way to light's emotive abilities.

Fundamentally, being a designer is a generous endeavor. We embark on a long path of discovery, dig deep into our collective soul and creativity, feel and express the qualities of our backers and clients, and advocate the consumers and their needs. Without this sense of "giving," our job cannot be done well. Humanistic design must tap into that element of our profession. It must be deeply in tune with the needs to create a sustainable future, deeply connected with emotional needs, deeply self-expressive. And we will need lots of it. In this book, Marc Gobé explores compelling ways in which marketers, designers, and consumers can be brought together around a new and inspiring emotional language—the language of design.

—YVES BEHAR

Design Is Jazz

In a century rife with the predictable, the dehumanizing, the dispiriting, Jazz affirmed the fresh, the human, the hopeful and it came to represent humanity at its best.
—*John Edward Hasse*, Jazz, the First Century

Design is to branding what jazz is to music. As people clamor for more emotional brand experiences, the world of branding has been slow to respond to these new demands. Most corporations are managing their brands through disconnected communications departments, which ruptures brand perceptions in the eyes of the public. Often a brand personality comes across as splintered in its offering because broadcast advertising, product design, public relations, promotional strategies, Web promotions, and buzz programs cannot deliver a consistent voice. The desires created by TV commercials often fall flat when people face the reality of unexciting products and the uninspired environments in which those products are sold.

The almost exclusive reliance on a narrow and limited form of communication—broadcast advertising—as the major outlet for communication is failing to engage consumers in a more sensorial and surprising way. Focus group–driven research is the dominant form of relationship made with the market, where unprepared and unsuspecting customers are secretly watched answering important questions about a brand's future in the most uninspired and cold environments. Marketers, customers, advertisers, and communications groups are looking at each other with mistrust and frustration.

Brandjam is the concept that brings all these forces together around a coordinated approach that opens up the dialogue between brands and people in order to bring a new level of consistency, stimulation, and excitement to the brand experience. This new vision promotes a jazzed-up collaborative and trusted partnership between marketers, consumers, and designers as a new element in the marketing process. It shows how a true creative dialogue can exist between people and brands, and how jamming around a brand brings out the best in people, allowing for the creation of the most innovative ideas. Brandjam bolsters the opportunities that are born when a brand communication or narrative is consistent and richer and explores new ways to stimulate people beyond the thirty-second TV commercial.

Transformative Jazz

When American jazz swept across France—where I was raised—and around the world, it inspired its listeners' cultural spirits, their aspirations. It opened the door to a new way of thinking, of being, that not only refused convention, but also made *innovation, improvisation,* and *imagination* their own institution.

Jazz music was transformative, creating new sounds with traditional instruments around a clear understanding of engagement. Then it was pleasure and freedom, exploration and magic, new voices that reached our senses, a music that relied on an organic participation on the part of the player, and that was based on sharing emotions through sound—"jamming," as we call it. As an amateur guitar player, I have participated in jam sessions that began with one tune, evolved into explorations of entirely new sounds, then wended their way back home to the original melody. Jamming is about different people playing in harmony, the sensation of joy when new music starts to emerge, and the elation of coming to the end of the journey. It is an ongoing process, constantly evolving and experiential. The instruments are worked in order to go beyond the norm; the musicians must take risks with the notes in order to explore new harmonies as a group, and they know when it's good. Eyes are shining, hearts are pulsing . . . Yeah! The crowd loves it too. The music resonates with body and soul.

Brands today must shift from "communications" and "commodities" to *emotion* and *inspiration.* We must revive our exhausted, overly familiar offerings. It is time that branding embraces the same philosophy that is at the heart of the jazz culture and starts "jamming," or more exactly, "brandjamming."

Brandjamming is a metaphor that I use in this book to support the idea that brands need to connect with culture and reach people's hearts. Brandjamming, not unlike the musical comparison, relies on collaboration, innovation, intuition, and risk. Brandjamming is about making brands motivating for the players and the audience. Brandjamming is about bringing in diverse talents to build iconic cultural brand phenomena, breaking rules and changing people's perceptions by energizing their minds. Brandjamming is an inspiration for brands and people as it advocates the transforming impact brands have on an audience.

In my first book, *Emotional Branding*, I emphasized the importance of connecting with people's hearts. The book explored a variety of meanings and expressions that reveal how consumers' expectations are changing. I suggested that design could help companies fulfill those changing expectations. Since then, the most potent development has been the emergence of design as a communications tool, as the best "instrument" now out there for jazzing up a brand.

This book is about design inspiration and how it brings a heightened level of excitement to people in a new world of consumer engagement. It is about design's power and meaning, its transformative impact and positive message of progress. Emotional branding needed a new lead instrument in order to build a new "brand sound" that would energize people—heart, mind, and soul. Design is that new instrument, that new tune, the influence, and for some corporate entities it is the expression of an entirely new culture—a culture of innovation and advocacy that focuses on human well-being.

The New Sound of Design

We keep hearing it from the visionaries. Proctor & Gamble's CEO, A.G. Lafley, is transforming the culture at P&G to endorse design as the main product communicator. "Design is a really big part of creating the experience and the emotion,"[1] and his company has embarked on one of the farthest-reaching business transformations by embedding design at the center of its business strategy—a revolution for a consumer goods company. So why beat the drum now, and why is it so relevant to understanding the experiential connection design has with people and its transforming power in a business culture? This is the question I want to answer in this book.

I will explore how brands have become cultural phenomena and individual messages for people, and as such need to build up an emotional soul as part of their message. I will explore how design is the reflection of the true nature and personality of a company and its window to the world. Most importantly, the changes in our world and the postmodern societal evolution that privileges the individual in democratic societies will be at the core of my observations.

As a metaphor, I use jazz to show how a well-designed brand can connect with people in a more visceral way than traditional broadcast commercials and how the instinctive nature of a participative creative process leads to unusual solutions that make people gravitate toward a brand and make brands resonate with people.

Ideas That Are Fundamental to Brandjam

In my first book, I volunteered some of my insight and feelings about the emotional branding theory and its impact on our world. My observations were the results of years of work in the design field, building brand expressions for major corporations worldwide. I also reviewed some of the most insightful global visual research we did that gave me a clear vision of the new expectations people have for brands. Since then, my continued branding experience has been enriched by the numerous conferences and intimate dialogue I have had with leading corporations as the consequence of their interest in my book. Those connections have led me to a new mental process, revealing the fact that people have such tremendous expectations from brands and that brands have transforming powers beyond the simple delivery of products or benefits.

Through my passion for design and the creative process, I suggested a new, more sensorial way to think about branding. I was then, and am now, especially committed to "the designer's way," which mixes instinct, sensory experiences, and visual analysis in a relentless quest to understand the role brand design plays in human culture.

At the core of *Emotional Branding* lie the following ideas, ideas that will be fundamental to this new book:

1. The marketing and service shift: The fundamental change in our economy from a factory-based, capability-driven, production-focused model to a consumer-based model. This leads to branding as a new language, in which flexibility, innovation, agility, and speed to market have become the competitive edge to reckon with.

2. Consumer rule: In an emotionally driven economy, the importance of moving from mass marketing to the marketing of one. We must leverage the power of customization as it applies to different cultural orientations and beliefs. Brands need to acknowledge ethnic groups, gender, age, and other

factors' influence on perception and desire. I was one of the first writers to speak about the gay market as a leading force in moving new ideas and the power of women as the new "Shoppers-in-Chief." However, the consumer never stands still, and the present book will bring the demographics and cultural shifts up to date for today.

3. Design reframes experiences: This is the ultimate provocative expression of a brand. Through experience it escapes commodity and market sameness. Sensory design is the most provocative way to shift in brand expression on the level of emotional desires. Sensory design is the inspiration, the research, the message, and the commercial, a provocative way to bring aesthetics and beauty into our lives.

4. From head to heart and gut: Emotional branding is about exploring more intuitive ways to reach and connect with people. Understanding the subconscious aspirations of people leads to innovative concepts and ideas bringing differentiation and excitement. Inventive and experiential messages emerge here, from within emotions, instinct, and intuition. This requires marketers to think more with their guts and feelings in order to innovate. And it demands that executives learn to trust and support their designers.

5. Brand citizenship starts at home: Corporate culture's commitment to society is absolutely integral to success. Emotional branding is about trust and involvement, commitment and leadership, making our world a better place.

These five underlying concepts have inspired many corporations. Entire books have developed more specific facets of these ideas. However, writing *Emotional Branding* was only a part of the larger goal of seeking design solutions, innovative research methods, and breakthrough creativity techniques in branding. I never looked at *Emotional Branding* as the holy grail of marketing; it was a way to challenge ourselves, provoke our own creative decision-making, and bring richer innovations to our clients.

Writing on branding is never easy: it requires developing theory, but also transcending the clean and neat "ideas" to bring real products to life. Branding is messy! But my relentless passion for advancing the understanding of brands has paid off and is still my focus and my love. When people ask me what I do, I answer, "My job is to make people love brands."

Why Another Book?

This book takes the emotional branding concept further, going in depth to analyze the new languages that have been and could be created to communicate an emotional message—the language of design. This is the most powerful of all languages in terms of business today. It informs and transforms, seduces and reassures. Design brings a human touch to the products we buy. This book is about design and its irresistible message.

Design puts the face on the brand: the curves of the Mac reveal Apple as the thinking, creative brand. The new BMW factory designed by Zaha Hadid expresses that company's commitment to reinventing the culture of car manufacturing. *The Gates* by Christo and Jeanne Claude captured New York City's spirit and optimism in a post-9/11 world. Design permeates all aspects of life, delivering memorable messages that inspire life and fuel emotion.

My goal is to bring you ideas you haven't thought through before. I will show you some of the objects that have inspired my own creative work. I want to bring you closer to the brand innovators who shape your life and your brands and open up your thinking about their vision. My goal will be to demonstrate how designers think and arrive at their conclusions, showing why instinct and gut creativity triumphs over the numbers game. You will discover also how billions of dollars are wastefully spent by brands in research and communication by using the wrong research technique and obsolete media vehicles in an emotional economy.

If I am successful, I will even help link branding to the larger intellectual currents of the twentieth and twenty-first centuries. The concomitant rise of branding and postmodernism is no coincidence. Branding, finally, is not modern, but postmodern. Branding rejects dogma and elitism and pursues a people-driven politics of design. Corporations do not own brands anymore—people do! Brands need to *look* and, most importantly, *feel* the part.

I will let you inside the world of design creation and show you how designers think. You will discover the creative process through the designer's eye and see how the powers of observation and critical analysis complement traditional methods.

I place designers as equal partners and decision makers in marketing and business policy. I show how design impacts and motivates people emotionally.

I will show how visual research is the most inspiring and insightful research possible when done by visionaries and interpreted by designers. Far too little thought goes into the relationship between branding and design today; this book redresses that shortfall.

Some readers will pine for the hard data that has obsessed so much brand management today. Some may cringe, charging me with simply speculating, using intuition and inspiration to shape my "impression" of branding. So be it! I leave such critics to their calculators and slide rules, where they will measure markets but never invent one.

Looking over my years of close work with top executives at Coca-Cola, AOL, Victoria's Secret, IBM, Estée Lauder, Unilever, P&G, Abercrombie & Fitch, and others, I am happy to admit the fragile and tenuous basis that my entire industry builds itself upon: brand design is based on instinct and feelings, it is based on intuition and belief, the curves of desire, the wax and wane of beauty, and the slope of inspiration, because all of these make up the inspiration process.

Shifting Your Vision to Resonate with People

This book is about meeting shifting consumer expectations through new ideas and design language. Brands that are successful will reframe their image through a unique, differentiated visual and verbal vocabulary, in the process crafting original messages that reach the heart. Design visionaries like Starbucks, Red Bull, Apple, Virgin, and even the Bush administration have changed our perceptions through communicative strategies that inspire belief. To understand this, this book will lead the reader through a series of topics, such as:

- How design has become the most powerful communication tool in branding strategies
- How to connect the world of business logic to consumers' emotions
- How you can "imagine" your brand through a better understanding of the world of emotions
- How to bring out your "inner designer" in a collaborative way to create brand innovation
- How the leading designers have successfully changed the corporate cultures and business practices of their companies

Furthermore, this book should not be read as a logical and continuous flow of information but as thoughts that can inspire you and your work. The very detailed table of contents will help you pick and choose, assemble, and make this information relevant to your specific needs in a creative way.

So, here's to inspired reading—and *brandjamming.*

INTRODUCTION

Coca-Cola's New Wave

In 2000, Coca-Cola's Doug Daft (president and CEO), Steven Jones (chief marketing officer), and Steve Crawford (global marketing director) selected Desgrippes Gobé to redesign the Coca-Cola brand with visual graphics inspiring to a new generation of untapped cola enthusiasts. A cynic might have suggested that our task was tantamount to transforming an aging Vanna White into the sex symbol for a generation raised on MTV, *Maxim*, and Internet gaming. Fortunately, we were blessed with a great design team and strong leadership at Coca-Cola, and we discovered branding's closest equivalent to the fountain of youth: the Coca-Cola mythos.

Smart design and good branding never come out of a vacuum: branding requires a commitment supported by a rich corporate culture, a dynamic engagement from top executives, and a passion for innovation. Steve Crawford's presence was a tremendous boon on all fronts. In the cultural partnership between client and designers, there's no substitute for inspired and visionary partners immersed not only in the "numbers" but also the actual affairs that inspire real people. Crawford brought culture in spades: an avid sportsman, an African American, and an intuitive designer, he also understood trends in hip-hop, extreme sports, and youth culture. His extensive worldwide travel infused his perspective with a peculiarly transnational, "wired" sensibility that shared much in common with the so-called MTV generation raised on fast-paced, international fashions and product cycles. Steve brings this rich palette of life experiences to bear on all his work. His famous work on Sprite exudes his hip, urban, "attitudinal" visions. He manages brands from the gut, no two ways about it.

Desgrippes Gobé was awarded the project in a most unusual fashion. Knowing that other competitors would bend over backward to get this plum assignment, we were beating ourselves up over the best way to "wow" this major account. Up until the last minute we were coming up with new ideas, tossing them out, and resuscitating old ones. Since my first book, our group has been known for emotional branding, but how do you translate this into a compelling presentation for the top executives of the number-one soft drink company in the world? It's one thing to sell an idea to the public, but entirely another to sell to a small group of important people. The whole spirit of emotional branding is premised on an intimate, tailored encounter with consumers, not brand managers. Frankly, although the measure of any campaign's success is the public's response, reaching out to the client first may be the hardest step (a dilemma I hope the present book will help alleviate by bringing designers and brand managers into a closer understanding).

Usually a firm lands a job by hosting the client, bragging about its success alongside a slick presentation, and then highlighting the talents of the team working on the job. The routine really has not changed that much since Darren's desperate tactics on the 1960s TV show *Bewitched*. Darren, of course, was married to Samantha, a witch who time and again used her magical powers to land Darren a prize account. Although Desgrippes Gobé's innovative brand vision was strong, and our global network a major asset to help jazz-up the brand, we still hadn't found our Samantha for this one: that magical, supernatural inspiration that goes beyond the rational commodity and touches both client and consumer. We needed something special, something inspired and different.

We worked a full week preparing for this meeting, brainstorming about strategic angles and outrageous ideas, like painting the entrance to our lobby Coca-Cola red. (You don't know how far firms like us are willing to go to win such an account. If someone had argued for Coca-Cola–laden parachuters landing on the roof, I probably would have listened intently!) Indeed, one difficulty in emotional branding is not getting caught up in flashy, obnoxious stunts that can be so in your face that the sensitive, emotional encounters with consumers are neglected. Fortunately, level heads prevailed, and the final decision was to give an international presentation showcasing *who we are*: we would assemble twelve people from our group, including representatives from Europe and Asia, to show our broad-based, personal, and emotional commitment to the project.

Everyone was on pins and needles when the client arrived. Steve Crawford has an impressive presence and a truly sharp marketing mind so we had to be great, unique, and "sans bullshit." After about ten minutes of friendly professional introductions, we prepared to present our work. These presentations are the bread and butter of design firms: full of PowerPoint slides and carefully crafted images, they showcase the firm's strengths in a well-planned manner. If they've done their homework, an agency can put the PowerPoint on autopilot and let the work speak for itself. Design firms love such exhibitions.

However, while sense and formula dictated following this course, my designer's gut abruptly overrode my executive's rational sense of judiciousness. The facts, planning, discussion, expectations, and data called for a sober presentation, but the emotional brander in me realized I had to jazz it up: this encounter needed to be personal, idiosyncratic, and inspired. Emotional branding has always been about inspiration, personality, and connection, and this occasion needed to embody that. To my colleagues' surprise, I pushed aside our presentation and asked for everyone's memorable experiences of Coca-Cola.

What was meant as a brief, unscripted aside led to a spirited two-hour digression. In accounts traversing the sublime as well as the ridiculous, the subliminal, and the rational, my team began recounting what Coca-Cola meant to them. We could not stop talking about Coca-Cola, and even Steve was drawn into what quickly became a brand-loving jam session among friends. Everyone poured out their feelings about the brand in a most revealing fashion. Our account director recalled getting lost in the desert of Morocco, seriously wondering whether she might make it home, when she discerned a Coca-Cola sign in the distance that suggested a mirage but instead provided safe passage home. Others offered up interesting insights, including a designer from Tokyo who told us that the existing graphics—a Coca-Cola bottle gushing cola—suggested decapitation for Asian audiences!

For my own part, I recalled discovering Coca-Cola as a young kid in Brittany, on vacation from my rural village in France. This recollection of the first rush of "coke," that strange American elixir, elicited the whole room's interest and engagement. Desgrippes Gobé had never before had such a personal and broad-ranging conversation, and I wished that everyone from the company could have been there. It was truly intimate, and a tribute to the designers' trust in one another.

And then: the client left for another meeting.

I thought I had blown it. We had presented no work, did not mention anything about the firm, and had bizarrely collapsed under a frenzy of emotional sentiment. Our rigorous approach to brand-building fell entirely by the wayside.

Instead of images of excitement, Steve went away with pictures of decapitation in Asia. Though others felt the meeting went well, I wasn't so sure.

The client had told us they would get back to us in a couple of weeks, and I went to bed that night anticipating two long weeks of stewing over my misstep. But a call came the next morning: Coca-Cola had cancelled its appointments with other agencies and told us that our belief in the brand and our vision for its needed shifts made us the right partner. We were, needless to say, dancing all day and night.

Emotional Design

In this project the important step, from an emotional and design perspective, was to "observe" the audience we needed to communicate with. We had to determine what deep subconscious values young people were looking for. Furthermore, we had to identify and understand what deep subconscious emotional values Coca-Cola was best positioned to respond to. Understanding how young people live, the music they listen to, the sports they like, and the moments they treasure was crucial. With these answers we might begin answering the key emotional branding questions:

• Who are we?
• Are we loved?
• What's our passion?
• Who do we want to share our passion with?
• Are we believable?

From these questions, it is possible to establish an emotional personality that lays the groundwork for an inspired design language.

Coca-Cola's own research data, accumulated from consumers worldwide, complemented and enriched our insights. However, we also relied on our international offices to get our own readings and perception of the brand and its reputation abroad.

We also undertook a *visual audit*, taking stock of the brand's philosophy and personality. The visual audit systematically traces the look and feel of the brand across many sites and platforms. For Coca-Cola, the same graphics were used on the shelves of supermarkets, in nightclubs, at the beach, and in sports stadiums, regardless of the different experiences people had at each venue. The same ubiquitous graphics were displayed universally without any regard for "site-specific" harmony with the environment and its experience.

Coca-Cola's visual narrative was based strictly on the green glass contour bottle, imposing a rigid message that did not make room for people's interpretation or imagination. We thought this was too dogmatic. Furthermore, people's perceptions of the brand revealed that this contour bottle was perceived as dated by younger consumers. Something new, but also consistent with it's rich legacy, was called for. The evolution of the graphics of a brand is not an unusual thing. Logos are updated every so many years. Look and usage varies. Nike famously disconnected its iconic symbol from the logotype.

Our design team knew that our exploration would have to look beyond the famous green glass contour bottle symbol without losing the importance of such an icon. But such endeavors are a sensitive, intuitive affair: the right design must come from the heart, the brand community, the best of the corporate culture. Furthermore, one must keep in mind that that final decision will reshape and redefine the brand expression to the world, becoming a permanent part of the brand legacy.

The right design must come from the heart, the brand community, the best of the corporate culture.

The bold task of shaping a new visual, emotive narrative excited my team. Its brand already resonated with people in an emotional way, and yet it could do so much more. There were so many audiences to whom Coca-Cola was in danger of being seen as another sugary commodity, in a world of refreshment that was evolving toward noncarbonated and healthier drinks such as fruit juices and water. Coca-Cola, we believed, had a premium value and lifestyle appeal that could help shape a new path for the brand; this was our chance to intervene. We wanted to help audiences recognize it as a beacon of optimism, energy, and diversity, and such elusive, ethereal sentiments are best conveyed through thoughtful emotional design. We were there to craft the "feel" of Coca-Cola in a new consumer reality.

Our challenge was to humanize the iconography in new, more powerful emotional ranges. Graphics would be tailored for consumers according to our now famous emotional lens: an emotional need to be reassured (head), the desire to be socially responsible (heart), and the craving for visceral engagement (gut).

Our new emotional model dictated a new design that responded uniquely to consumers' life moments. We recognized and leveraged the way consumers respond to brands differently at different times throughout their lives, and also at

We could shift the brand's iconography from sameness and ubiquity to dynamic, evolutionary involvement.

unique sites. Vending machines, billboards, delivery trucks, blogs, sporting events, beach placement, retail environments: each elicits unique matrices of expectation and engagement. Through meeting these site-specific needs, we could shift the brand's iconography from sameness and ubiquity to dynamic, evolutionary involvement.

What's in a Color?

An interesting aspect of Coca-Cola's design history struck us as we worked. We spent countless days in Coca-Cola's Atlanta archives reviewing libraries of the brand's history. Tracing out the brand's myriad visual iterations, the color yellow kept dancing before our eyes. On delivery crates in the 1930s, promotional materials in the 1940s, even actress's dresses in the 1950s. Coca-Cola was truly a defining and innovative brand by then, but one aspect of the brand that caught our eye and helped change the look of the brand was the yellow wood crates used to carry the coke bottles at the beginning of the last century.

Instinctively and intuitively the team was excited about the idea of bringing yellow back into the visual narrative. We even considered making an alternate yellow can, a promotional bottle. Perhaps yellow coke trucks could speed across highways in the summer! The question was, how far would people be willing to go to enjoy and experience the brand? What bold steps would excite their desires to delve in? Once again visions of parachuters, this time with red caps and yellow cans, were tempting to us. Ultimately, however, we were starting to unlock the energy and fun nature of the brand in ways we would not have thought possible.

But first we needed to focus on leveraging the existing graphic equities. Pushing the limits of a brand expression is a process of evolving the graphic narrative and often leads to interesting discoveries. But at this point, presenting a bold idea might distract the team and puzzle the client. I did not want to get a rejection for an idea that might be more profitably offered later.

Such varieties of "creative flirting" are practiced often, particularly as a way of floating modest ideas before a client before moving to the bigger, potentially disturbing ones. This prepares the right context to eventually showcase larger ideas. We decided to include "Coca-Cola yellow" in a modest way at first. It was used to highlight the brand's packaging, making it more energetic, but also reframing and foregrounding Coca-Cola's "full red." Yellow helped to differentiate and make more inspiring the dominant red. Moreover, the touch of yellow brought a surprising energy and optimism that could enhance the imagery and packaging. Though difficult to measure or demonstrate "objectively," our design team felt its power.

However, the yellow was barely talked about, so as to avoid threatening the client. Instead it was our little secret weapon and insight, embedded in the graphic image. But from our own perspective and intuitive feelings, this little color yellow was a huge step in complementing our other big idea: the return of the "dynamic ribbon."

The Dynamic Ribbon Returns

In evaluating the brand's visual assets, we realized there was a powerful but abandoned icon that emotionally trumped all others: the dynamic ribbon, or "Swoosh"! This powerful, abstract visual icon, created in the 1970s, was truly a brilliant idea; it almost suggested the action painting of a Jackson Pollock in its sprawling, dynamic flight, and was predecessor to the Nike logo. We recommended bringing back this icon but evolving and energizing it to sensually and emotionally connect with today's markets with a new design language, particularly with the addition of effervescent bubbles to enhance its refreshing image.

We recommended replacing the contour bottle displayed on the coke can with this dynamic ribbon. Created in the 1970s, the white ribbon signified the identity of Coca-Cola until the 1990s. When launched in the

The dynamic ribbon became part of an international graphic language that could be understood by everyone around the globe.

1970s, the ribbon was part of the company's growing global brand visual vocabulary. As non-Western characters were introduced onto the Coke cans and bottles in growing foreign markets, there was a concern that its visual iconography and identity would be diminished. The dynamic ribbon became part of an international graphic language that could be understood by everyone around the globe.

Putting the Project into Perspective

The entire project took about two years to complete, including revisions in design as we tested consumer feedback on the new iconography. Coca-Cola worked with Censydiam, a research group from Antwerp, Belgium, that brought a qualitative approach especially suited to and compatible with the insights of emotional branding. Censydiam's approach, as I will explain later in Shift 5, is not based on asking consumers to judge a design, but rather in observing and discovering through in-depth interviews and interactive visual exercises how people *respond* to given presentations. Results are gauged by the *emotions* and *feelings* people experience with a particular design. This is vastly superior to soliciting "design evaluations," which at best provide skewed rational accounts of a design idea.

Design evaluation by consumers is a surefire method to miss out on the best potential of a design. The danger with the traditional qualitative techniques is their tendency to selectively reinforce familiar ideas while downgrading or underestimating the appeal of newer concepts. The unfamiliar is always suspect in these rational, explicit measurement techniques and surveys. In this way, design evaluation is inherently conservative and inappropriate for brands that see their future course charted in growth, expansion, new markets, and expanded imagery. The Censydiam techniques, by contrast, leverage the past while charting new, more promising paths in the future. We wanted a design that would "catch on," that would *come to elicit* more powerful consumer responses.

Censydiam's psychologists believe that the more relaxed the atmosphere, the more conducive it will be for people to share their feelings. Their approach is in depth, and entails spending four hours with individuals, patiently peeling back the layers of emotion and response until a more powerful, unconscious kernel comes to the surface. For this study alone they talked to 160 people worldwide.

On a continuous basis, designs that scored best featured our added yellow color. It seemed to communicate the most energy and vitality even though people interviewed did not relate their comments to the yellow color specifically. Our design was particularly appealing to young people and women. Needless to say, we were thrilled. I am not sure our clients understood rationally the power of this yellow "artsy" touch, but they understood the positive response. The combination of the positive surveys and the client's trust in our design team advanced the project to the launch stage. Yellow, according to Steve Crawford, "communicated globally particularly with Latin cultures; it was the sun, the warmth of a relationship, the energy, the togetherness and the 'we' moments that Coke needed to communicate. This yellow addition was right on."

How Can We *Not* Change?

Then, to our surprise, the company demanded to have a meeting in our New York office to discuss *another set of quantitative results* that contradicted the Censydiam results. If you haven't ever attended a quantitative research presentation, it's hard to explain how daunting and intimidating they are in general, never mind when they generally contradict what you otherwise believe. The complexity of analytical data is so sophisticated that it is nearly impossible to understand, particularly for designers like me who are already suspicious of such highly "scientific" charts and graphs as they relate to emotions.

In a nutshell, after a two-hour presentation, their recommendation was the absolute opposite of the qualitative Censydiam research. "Don't change anything. The market is not prepared to see Coca-Cola change its graphics! The old design will do just fine!" was the new message.

All I could think then was that people are never ready for any disruptive bold changes *if you ask them.* That's why it's called "bold" in the first place; it transcends people's reality! *Emotionally,* people will tell you a different story if you know how to listen and probe deeper into their subconscious to connect with their hidden dreams. But no matter, we already thought we were doomed! There was a caveat that was unveiled in the research by the Coca-Cola marketing team that suddenly gave a new life to the design.

In the quantitative research, the new design was not preferred overall (and therefore the basis for not recommending the new design) but was most preferred with youth, particularly after we had added more refreshment cues such as bubbles and condensation droplets to the white dynamic ribbon. "As we were losing in brand acceptance with youth, we knew what the course needed to be," Steve Crawford explained to me. "We were a bit panicked at first, but the overall quantitative data was minor compared to the more decisive impact on young people. We decided that the brand's future was with young people, and we decided to go for it."

Steve Jones, the chief marketing officer representing Coca-Cola, and Steve Crawford, Coca-Cola's worldwide brand manager, listened carefully, then asked around the table what people thought. After a few minutes of tense conversation it seemed to me that the group just felt better with the change; it was visceral and intuitive. After the two Steves consulted with each other for a few seconds, Steve Jones said, "I appreciate the research but how could we *not* change? We are moving with the new design."

To see a project like this come off was a watershed of relief, reward, gratification, and delight. Suddenly the sweat, blood, tears, and passion came to life in a new brand direction led by a cutting-edge, emotionally compelling design.

The new design had a far greater impact than anticipated. Because consumers responded so well, the new design also helped shift the internal culture. It changed how people there viewed their brand. This bold change opened doors for people to innovate *within the company*. That little bit of yellow backed by a floating ribbon unleashed the energy native to the brand. Good design did not reinvent the brand, but released the latent potential within its image, its audience, and its company. The emotional energy of the brand was brought to life.

Good design did not reinvent the brand, but released the latent potential within its image, its audience, and its company.

I never felt at any point that we were designing a new packaging as much as leveraging the design process to see how much potential for innovation was inherent in the brand. The process helped the company's management team to articulate its belief that Coca-Cola was not fully leveraging its emotional capital and to rethink how to connect the brand with the youth market.

One seminal moment crystallized my impression: when Doug Daft, Steve Heyer (at the time, his groomed successor), Steve Jones, and Steve Crawford, while being presented with new designs, engaged in masterful and consistent brandjamming to determine the brand's long-term future. The team was coming together; they were executives inspired by new visual stimuli.

How That Little Bit of Yellow Jazzed Up the Brand

Less than a year after the new can's launch, I was bowled over to receive a copy of *Vogue Australia* featuring a model on the cover *holding the new Coke can design!* She was wearing the yellow and red colors of the can. The new design had itself become a fashion statement! Inside the magazine, a four-page pictorial featured this same model with yellow and red fashion accessories likewise modeled after the new can.

I cannot convey the excitement we felt at the office when we saw how our new designs had reached the pages of a major fashion magazine—what's more, an edition from the other side of the globe. You can't buy this kind of thing, and you certainly can't predict it through research. In fact, it's precisely this kind of result that ultimately shapes and determines the public's perception of the brand. A huge error in traditional marketing research is believing that consumer response and taste are a fixed target. In fact, they constantly evolve and respond to other cultural changes. Something like *Vogue* designers' picking up on the new design of course is good for the brand, both recognizing and amplifying its design power. But more importantly, it helps cast a new aura around the brand that comes in the wake of its design. These kinds of changes, and in fact most of the important but subtle changes that create design success, can't be anticipated in advance, which is why intuition, emotion, and the designer's sensibility are, at the end of the day, the most promising resources one can have.

Our inspiration had worked. Our visual observation, our designers' sense of magic and the future, found an insight that was provocative. We had been a partner in bringing fashion style to the brand and changing perception. This was one of the greatest moments of my life as a branding professional.

Three months later, I was watching a French news program on TV. Something strange caught my eye: the fall 2004 ready-to-wear collection runway show by John Galliano featured what looked an awful lot like the new Coca-Cola can decorating the hair of at least three of the models. Likewise, the color scheme for the makeup and accessories was coke yellow and red! In this fleeting moment my mind swam with delight. When I looked again I seemed to have lost it, and the models were gone. I turned to my wife and asked, "Did you see that?"

"See what?"

"The Coke cans in the models' hair!"

At this point we both thought that stress had gotten to me and that it was time for me to see some kind of specialist. Obsessive behavior combined with design delusions, even in the branding world, is not a good thing. But, it was too late for me; I was already a casualty of design obsessions. So, I immediately searched the Internet, and there it was: three gorgeous models, each sporting the new can design for the world to see. This was the ultimate consecration of Coca-Cola as a fashion statement and lifestyle brand. It was now up to the rest of the organization to capitalize on this exceptional event.

The Coca-Cola cans on John Galliano's runway.

Brandjamming with Coca-Cola

The success of this brand strategy revealed again the fundamental shifts and attitudes that connect a brand to culture:

- A company where the top management believes in imagination and design
- An entrepreneurial spirit that was not afraid of risk
- An innate belief in the cultural impact design can have on people
- A company culture that is ready to "brandjam"

"Brandjamming" resulted in the creation of Coca-Cola's inspiring new look, intuitively supporting a new identity and relying on the combined talent of the group to make breakthrough decisions. Theirs was a dedication to see the brand reach out for more, connect emotionally to new audiences, and break away from the expected.

A subsequent CD brought this new identity to life with music and liberated the brand to be creative and innovative again. The exercise was not only about that color yellow or the gracious *clin d'oeil* John Galliano gave to the brand; it was about the spirit and emotions that were locked up in the genie's Coke bottle suddenly being liberated and reaching out to people's desires. It was about an identity that transcended the design message to be more about the feeling the brand can convey and the joy that is inherent to it. Design unlocked that potential for people to enjoy.

The Coca-Cola cans on Galiano's runway is the product placement everyone dreams about. Those ideas, those connections can only be found through imaginative and intuitive thinking; the entry door to the world of the unconscious is only possible through the creative mind. The experience taught me that the corporate world needs logic and the consumer world is driven by emotions; this gap needs to be bridged. Brandjamming is the powerful idea that reconnects the business world to people's subconscious desires.

When a jazz band starts jamming on a melody, you recognize the tune and the premise, then it evolves and reaches out to new melodies, inspired by a known music piece but then evolving into a more exciting, transforming, and emotional piece that leads you into a new mental and physical space. Not unlike jamming, design is the basis for connecting emotionally with people, and its most pow-

Not unlike jamming, design is the basis for connecting emotionally with people, and its most powerful instrument.

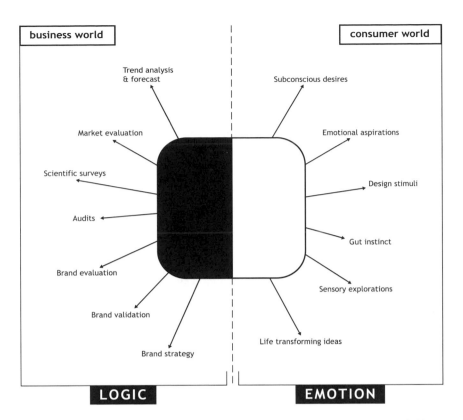

The corporate world needs logic, while the consumer world is driven by emotions and this gap needs to be bridged. Brandjamming is the powerful idea that reconnects the business world to people's subconscious desires.

erful instrument. Emotional design is visibly sensorial and reaches our emotions faster than any other means of communication, yet it is the most under-leveraged of all communications approaches. Design conveys innovation in the most potent way, addresses our social and personal expectations, and builds loyalty for a brand, but the amount of money invested in new products or in the manifestation of a visual identity is abysmally small compared to the budgets spent in broadcast media.

It's More Than Design Aesthetics

Effective branding is about the *emotions design creates*. Brandjam is a perception and a vision, a style and a tone of voice. Brandjam is an innovative concept constantly needing a new, inventive, and refreshed vocabulary. One must use evolving aesthetics and style to forge a sensory language that connects with people's desires to experience life in an uplifting, changing, and positive way.

While brandjamming, here are a few thoughts to remember as you read this book:

THINK ABOUT INTIMACY AND THE DISRUPTIVE POWER OF A NEW SHIFT

People will react to what they don't know. If you see the ocean for the first time, it is overwhelming, awesome, and entrancing. Don't be afraid to show people the ocean, even if you have to start out by limiting yourself to one narrow "ribbon" of it. The enemy of branding is ubiquity and sameness.

RESEARCH FEELINGS, NOT OPINIONS

In doing research, it is important to see how design connects to emotions. It is not about visual like or dislike, but making an impact at a profound emotional level. Research is not the thumbs up or down of innovation but a way to probe people's life experiences and hopes, a way to benchmark and ground the best creative ideas. Research is subservient to the creative process; it does not lead it.

LEVERAGE DESIGN AS A TOOL FOR INNOVATION

By connecting to all the rational, social, and visceral experiences people want to have with a brand, design humanizes it to connect better with people. Design is the emotional touch that stimulates and enhances a consumer's experience. Brandjamming is a process of constant discovery; it must be flexible and engaging. When you leverage design as an inspiration for your brand language, you also invite consumers to redesign their expectations.

PART 1:
FIVE CONSUMER INSIGHTS

Design Inspiration

Brands today must shift from *communications* and *commodities* to *emotions* and *design*. We must *jazz up* our standard, exhausted, and familiar offerings through inspired design. When American jazz swept across France, where I was raised, it inspired listeners' cultural spirits and aspirations. It showed us a new way of thinking and acting that not only refused convention, but institutionalized *innovation*, *improvisation*, and *imagination*. It's time branding embraced this same philosophy.

As a young designer, the goal of "jazzing up" an image, a product, a message, inspired my visions for branding. This book is my attempt to share this inspiration with you.

Remembering Jazz: A Young Frenchman's Perspective

My father first heard jazz when he was an innkeeper and witness to the American soldiers' liberation of Normandy during the Second World War. They were young, and feigning courage and certainty in an uncertain time, but their music was fresh, different, embracing, energetic, and fun. In a time when fascism—the ultimate expression of conformity and sameness—cast a long shadow across Europe, jazz promised an inspiring alternative. Looking back on these times, my father tells me, "I felt a new world was coming into being. The voice of a new generation was being expressed." Although fear and loss haunted Americans and Frenchmen alike, jazz suggested a future that would be brighter and more hopeful. It expressed, and even inspired, self-confidence. "Americans were going to liberate us not only from the Germans but also from our past," my father says today. "You don't know how exhilarating it was emotionally for young people at the time."

Arriving as the first harbinger of American popular culture that would sweep France in the postwar period and then the world, jazz transformed our perception of music. It was emotional and sensorial. Refuting the divisive European nationalism that had mired our continent in conflict, jazz connected people and cultures like no music before it. Blacks and whites, Europeans and Americans, the big band and the blues—the past, present, and future—none of these seemed immutable or nonnegotiable when there was a jazz LP playing. Before the war even ended jazz had won the hearts of young Germans, and then it went on to give youth across Europe a way to feel differently about who they were.

Jazz, Design, and the Brand

For many years now I have been arguing that sameness and commodity-status are the enemy of emotional branding. Our world and economies thrive on stimulation and change. To perform and feel at our best, our brains must be energized and renewed daily. When "the expected," "the routine," and "the standard" takes hold in the work, home, or marketplace, it clamps down on our aspirations.

The great threat of modern conformity played a major role in tearing Europe apart during the first half of the twentieth century. The German sociologist Max Weber recognized this, suggesting early on that the new phenomenon of bureaucratization threatened civilized life. It stultified the mind and isolated the individual. Franz Kafka, another brilliant German, dramatized bureaucracy's threatening conformity and sameness in dozens of short stories that depict overbearing government, professional and societal expectations that sapped the individual's will to live. In spite of these dire forecasts, fascism rose to power in the 1930s.

The taxing effects of modernity also inspired a range of progressive, creative alternatives, such as surrealism and Dadaism. But it was America's response that captured me and proved most influential in Europe: American jazz embodied the most inspiring alternative to stultifying tradition and conformity. Spend an afternoon watching the films of the French New Wave, where jazz is always on the side of the rebel, youth, and the carefree, and you'll see what I mean.

To *jazz up* is to embrace an emotional language that sensually connects and emotionally inspires. *Design* ideas; let your ideas come to fruition through design. Allow the design language to change people's everyday reality—ever in danger of reverting to conformity—and renew their love for your brand. But don't just take my word for it, look at the best commerce has to offer: Apple, BMW, Dove, Motorola, Starbucks, Fiji water, Absolut, Abercrombie and Fitch, Victoria's Secret, OXO. Each has reveled in a success grounded in cutting-edge, jazzy design that tells consumers *this is something different*, and raised the level of brand expectations.

Jet Blue, Target, Callaway Drivers, the Mini Cooper, and Dell, likewise, have dared the public to experience their innovative design language and solutions. Each takes a strong, reliable product tailored around today's market and consumers and clothes it in a visual and linguistic design language that acts as the bold ambassador of their new offerings. These brands have not only reframed their product offerings, but have also recognized that a unique visual identity is central to their agenda.

Designing the Future

Design-driven companies revolutionize their industries, trailblazing the way for others to change the way they do business. Yet their great design is not *sui generis* and does not fall from the sky. Every design-driven company must cultivate its own culture while also drawing from the outside for that special edge, that unique look. Design leadership and design hybridization are one and the same (much as the most idiosyncratic and impressive jazz impresarios created their *own voice* by drawing on the rich culture and traditions of their jazz forbearers and peers). W Hotels took cues from the leading boutique hotels. Virgin's design vision has not only been integral to instantiating its own powerful corporate and client culture, but has also repurposed the visions of its competitors.

In creating a new vision for electronics, Apple opened up a new market in technology for all its competitors in the future. MP3 players and related devices (minidisk players, DAT recorders, etc.) have been on the market for years. Though often superior to their competition, frankly, consumers didn't understand what they were and why they were useful. It wasn't until Apple *redesigned* the MP3 player as a fashion accessory that the technologies really got consumers' attention. By re-branding the MP3 player with Apple design, Apple opened up an entire market segment for this new technology. Yet they also limited their competition's ability to encroach on their market share because, at the end of the day, it's not yet clear that consumers really want MP3 players. It's the iPod they want. A device that merely plays digital music is a poor second best.

The Days of Reckoning

There's a shakedown going on among brands today. There are those equipped to compete with the new demands of consumers, using design, culture, and emotion to be, ultimately, incomparable with their competitors. Falling behind and beneath these are the brands who still think they're selling tangible commodities to rational consumers. These same brands think that product attributes come prior to, and independent of, design. And even the best brands can fall from the top when they forget that they must continue to adapt to their consumers' changing needs.

There are many reasons for the impending and ongoing design revolution: An improved economic climate, and, most importantly, a societal change that has evolved away from modernist theories to postmodernist ways of thinking that privilege the well-being of the individual. Customers are in charge. They *want* and *have* choices. They demand to explore new products. They seek innovation, personalization, and performance. Much of the business world has been caught off guard by this massive social and aspirational shift. The self-inflicted brand-wound of sameness and commodity products languishing in supermarkets, at strip malls, and department stores fails to meet the new expectations of the emerging, and most valuable, consumers (the more discerning the consumer, the fatter the profit margin). Where is the experience? Where is the sensory pleasure? It has fled retail and gone missing at the mall. No wonder consumers are so anxious to snatch up the little bits they find in an Apple iPod or a Starbucks mocha latte. These products are better than nothing, but they are not enough.

Name that liquor

....

Name that pdf

....

Name that fragrance

....

Name that phone

....

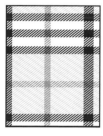

Name that tartan

....

Name that razor

....

Name that car

....

Name that drink

....

Name that soft drink

....

Name that beer

....

Name that orange juice

....

Name that yogurt

....

Name that coffee

....

Name that detergent

....

Name that cheeseburger

....

Name that toothpaste

....

You might start to wonder whether the sea of sameness is the result of research processes that are missing the mark.

5

This situation opens the door for innovators and innovative business ready to build their success through finesse and craftsmanship. The brandscape is ripe for the visionary leaders ready to meet people's higher emotional expectations and contribute to their visions. Brands must be ready to offer up the raw creative materials and emotional artifacts that allow consumers to make their own connections and articulate their own visions of the future. The floor has dropped beneath the functional, processed brands, and it's time for brands to deliver at higher, more ethereal levels of aspiration.

Jazzing Up: For the Brand, But Not Limited to It

The power of jazzing up is that ultimately its truth transcends the brand. It is about lifestyle, about a more universal way of looking at the world we live in, the fact that any familiar and standard idea, product, or image can be transformed into mythos. Not just any mythos, though: What made jazz particularly mythic and powerful was its ability to collect the strands of American multiculturalism, individualism, and traditional expressions, and forge from them a uniquely inspiring expression. Born out of American popular culture, this process is particularly suited to branding, but in no way limited to it.

Consider American boxing: Cassius Clay was a talented boxer among many, striving to survive and thrive within a cutthroat world of brutes. In Cassius's time, boxing was based on raw force and destruction. The likes of Sonny Liston, Joe Frazier, and Larry Holmes inspired interest the way a car wreck inspires rubber-necking. You look, you can't help but notice, but frankly you don't like what you see.

Then came *Ali*. Muhammad Ali, the greatest boxer of all time, changed the whole game. He took the world of brute violence, absorbed its rules, but also rose above them. He took this world of cruel beatings—what you might consider raw commodities measured by punches, muscles, and knockouts—and *redesigned* its meaning with purpose and inspiration. With stunning interviews, cocky declarations, and catchy phrases, he took the commodity "boxing" and replaced it with a jazzed-up and added-value brand: *Ali*. Audiences went to the ring or turned on the TV not to see "boxing" but to watch Ali. The world gravitated toward this *persona* that resonated with the emotions of freedom, spirit, determination, and faith. These were values that America had fought long and hard for, and Ali embodied them in the most idiosyncratic ways. Before Ali, who could have ever imagined America with a

Muslim national hero? A "big, black brute" in the eyes of racist detractors, Ali bravely articulated values, ethics, and commitment for a nation at war with the world and with itself. Ali was not fighting boxing matches; he was fighting for justice. To do this he shifted his message to one that expressed his new vision and reframed his language to express his mission: freedom to choose your name and identity, freedom to believe in your own religion, freedom to reject war, freedom to help your fellow man wherever he is in the world, freedom to make yourself heard with all your heart.

Clay won matches with muscles and fists; Ali won hearts with a jazzed-up message, and it's the latter that we remember today, the latter that transcended commodity and became a brand in its own time.

What Can Design Do for You?

At a time when constant changes in consumer behavior and aspirations impact perceptions of brands, *design rises above the clutter*, delivering a clear and consistent message. Brands that adapt the right design, tailored to the culture of their corporation and consumer, can thrive amidst the forces fracturing the consumer base and multiply consumer expectations.

The following chapters will delve into the most influential currents in branding today from a design perspective.

INSIGHT 1
Postmodern Dreams

It is impossible to avoid a comparison between the separate influences of modernism and postmodernism on individual expression in the twentieth and twenty-first centuries. The architect Philip Johnson, in Paola Antonelli's book, *Objects of Design*, provides a good assessment of modernism: "Today industrial design is functionally motivated and follows the same principles as modern architecture: machinelike simplicity, smoothness of surface, avoidance of ornament."[1]

The modern movement reflected the dynamism of the industrial age and the efficiency of the factory world. It also was inspired by the dogmatic philosophies of the popular elitist intellectual school of the beginning of the twentieth century, which celebrated technology and science above pleasure and visions of a more controlled world over those of a democratic, evolutionary society. In 1984, Arthur Drexler, the famed curator of architecture and design at the Museum of Modern Art in New York, spoke of the pieces selected to be in the museum: "An object is chosen for its quality because it is thought to achieve, or have originated, those formal ideas of beauty that have become the major stylistic concepts of our time."[2] This statement is about purity; it does not reflect the notion of seduction, pleasure, or sensory experience.

This rigorous modernist approach does not get everyone's support. The *New York Times*, for instance, published an article titled "Where MOMA Has Lost Its Edge" by Nicolai Ouroussoff[3] explaining that good taste is not always enough when you are trying to reconnect with the mainstream. He said, "The age of dogmas and manifestos is gone." Modernism also excludes the fashion industry or ephemeral installation work, which include people's experiences in the creative process. For instance, *The Gates*, the remarkable work installed in Central Park by the artists Christo and Jeanne Claude, brought thousands of people together in the winter in a singular location, weaving their way along the same paths.

The Gates, by Christo and Jeanne Claude.

From a branding perspective, dogmatic modernist theories have prevailed in marketing in the last century. The industry has not fully realized the fact that the world has become multifaceted, governed by the wills of the people. The battle between the modern and the postmodern comes to be the measures by which our world is being judged. Modernism is elitist and uncompromising. Postmodernism is evolutionary and innovative.

The modern movement reflected the dogmatic era of communist values and the discipline of the industrial revolution. The modernist industrialists believed they knew what was best for people, with the certitude of their belief anchored in the power of science and machines. The industrial age and the birth of social movements based on Marxist theories influenced a modern and rigid stylistic vision. Modernist theories influenced by communist dogmas took away the freedom that would have supported people's individuality of expression and discovery through sensory and intellectual explorations to create work that was not emotionally connected. Paradoxically, those same rigid ideas were endorsed by free-thinking intellectuals who did not see communist theories as oppressive but as liberating.

Le Corbusier in France and Oscar Niemeyer in Brazil are two famous architects who failed by confronting social issues with dogma. Le Corbusier's "machine for living" was inspiring, but made for miserable housing.

Co-existing side by side in Brasilia, the architectural aesthetics of
the new city and the hard reality of the favelas.

"Beautiful, brutal: but what about the people?"[4] is the title Richard Lapper gave his *Financial Times* review of the book *Brazil's Modern Architecture*, and it sums up this movement.

In 1956, President Juscelino Kubitschek instigated the long-awaited construction of Brasilia (which I visited in 2006), the new Brazilian capital city. The city's architectural landscape, conceived by Oscar Niemeyer with Lucio Costa, brought fame and infamy for both architects. The idea was to bring Brazilians from the coast, where most people live, to the country's mostly desolate heartland. It was a great idea, but a missed and failed opportunity. "The classic modernism of the 1940s and 1950s was also flawed. For all their social idealism . . . the modernists could be elitist and dogmatic," says Richard Lapper.[5]

During its construction, housing was built a few miles southwest of Brasilia for workers building the city and was supposed to be demolished after construction was complete. Known then as "La Cidade Livre," or "Free Town," it could barely house people then, demonstrating that the human factor was not integrated into the creative process. Sadly, it was never torn down, and today is a veritable "favela" or shantytown, known as Núcleo Bandeirante.

Brasilia is a good example of modernist theories—they knew what was best for others with "certitude," regardless of what people believed. It has led to devastating executions. Those theories started with the best intentions and ended up missing people's expectations for a better life. In contrast, in Shift 4, "Think Retail as Advertising," I will talk about how new postmodern urban-renewal projects are succeeding in integrating the total population's aspirations into a new urban experience.

The Postmodern Revelation

The mainstream is really what was lacking in the modern movement, the connection between art and design and culture, the democratization of taste and inspiration, and the popular appeal of work that not only informs but also inspires people. Maybe this is why postmodernism does not have a particular style per se, as the aesthetics reflect the various experiences people are seeking.

Today in Bilbao, Spain, you can enjoy culture at the Guggenheim Museum just as you enjoy it by sitting and eating at a café. It is impossible to overemphasize how many rules the museum has broken to change from what could have been an uninspiring cultural institution to be a concept that resonated with the public. The impact the museum has had on the town and the fervor with which the local people participate in the life of the museum is now one of the most glorious successes of that museum.

The postmodern movement challenges the status quo and focuses on the emotional experiences, decorative opportunities, and the technology that make up our lives. It is about the evolution of society and about people and their senses. Postmodernist culture reinforces human movement and discovery.

Postmodern Deconstruction

The theory of deconstruction, developed by Jacques Derrida, is controversial on many points and can be interpreted to fit a lot of "absolute" theories, but it also reflects on the world in which we live as a world in *movement*, a world that keeps changing with our evolving ideas and perceptions, because people themselves are constantly changing within an environment of democratic freedom.

This postmodern theory also emphasizes the nature of words as being unfixed, with meanings that have been arbitrarily attached throughout years of usage. This notion, I believe, can be extended to objects, whose forms don't entirely reveal their meanings at first sight but keep on giving off interpretations exponentially.

Ultimately, all objects and experiences are really just recipients of the meanings we want to attach to them. At certain points in time, those meanings could change to fit our existing emotional state of mind. A car could at times be a status symbol, but at others a means to arriving quickly at a destination or even a way to seduce a lover: same car, different emotional meanings. The biggest misunderstanding in the modern approach versus the postmodern one is that the modern theories have failed to understand that meanings attached to a particular idea or design are created by people, not brands or designers. In the business world it could be interpreted as the following: manufacturers and designers propose; consumers dispose.

There is always more than what meets the eye, more to experience, though we can never know the whole of anything, because there is no way to know what that "whole" consists of.

In his *New York Times* op-ed, Mark Taylor could be an inspiration on how deconstruction relates to art making:

> The guiding insight of deconstruction is that every structure, be it literary, psychological, social, economic, political or religious that organizes our experience is constituted through acts of exclusion. In the process of creating something, something else inevitably gets left out.[6]

This brings the notion of void and transformation, and in brand design it clearly shows that people will migrate toward the new by rejecting the old, will change their lives by disposing of the past. In modernism, what was getting left out of art and design was how people change. In order to hold up modernist dogmas and absolute truths, people and their individual quirks and preferences had to be sacrificed.

Now, the opposite is true. Think of the ability we have today to download music from the Web and carry it with us in the most personalized music system to date, the iPod. This pocket-size device represents a revolution in the business and distribution of music. At first there was an enormous criticism within the music industry to the fact that consumers could download individual songs and even entire albums without going through the record labels. Now the concept is embraced as an advancement of our freedom of selection and our power to personalize our lives, from the clothes we wear, to the food we eat, to the music we listen to. At the same time, it forced a major music distributor, Tower Records, to file chapter 11, and could permanently eradicate the manufacture and sale of music CDs.

In the branding world, postmodernist theory has generated approaches that are different from what we have known in the past. But in some ways, branding theories are still stuck in the modernism's industrial age. Certain consumer goods companies that have always delivered their products in cans will not consider any other form of packaging. In an extreme example of the modernist theory, or arrogance, Mr. Ford proposed, "you can have any color on our cars as long as it is black." Wine companies in France will not change the shape of a Bordeaux or Burgundy bottle even if the iconic meaning escapes most consumers around the world. As France now is poised to find markets for most of its wine production (excluding the prestigious wine labels), the country has a hard time adjusting to the fact that wine branding now is less dogmatic, and more about lifestyle, fun, and pleasure. Beringer Blass has just come out with a reduced-calorie, less-alcoholic white wine called White Lie designed to meet the needs of women wine drinkers, who make up the overwhelming majority of wine buyers. By providing them with a wine they can drink at lunch or after work without the unwanted side effects of weight gain and tipsiness, Beringer is tailoring this traditional product to give pleasure to a specific audience.

Because many marketing strategies are still created for a world that stands still—same brands, same distribution, same research techniques, same approach, same old, same old—some companies are quickly learning the meaning of postmodernism. The impact of innovators can change their business reality. Dell has impacted the PC dominance of IBM by going online. From a postmodern perspective Dell has given people the freedom to customize and the empowerment to choose. Now Dell is being challenged by Hewlett-Packard for missing out on the most important element of postmodern marketing: service.

Fiji water, through a more sensorial bottle design and name, has usurped some of Evian's market share among high-end water offerings. By showing up in most prestigious restaurants in America with a very distinctive presentation, Fiji has connected with bottled water drinkers in a more personal way.

Postmodern philosophies took time to develop and gain in popularity but they are a driving force in the twenty-first century. What intrigues me most about the postmodern phenomenon is that it puts people at the center of experience and challenges any rigorous dogma in the branding world. Artists like Christo and Jeanne Claude, for example, create nonpermanent work for people to enjoy. Philip Stark's work is surprising, fun, and accessible. Frank Gehry's architecture is emotionally compelling and approachable. Consumerism is not dogmatic. It is postmodern; it is about choice, freedom, and the individual. Exceptional experience is the new rule of law.

This is what designers are good at, sensing changes and trends in the world to bring pleasure and joy to people. We have come a long way from the elitism of modernism and its caricature of what life should be. We are now reaching society in a more emotional way, bringing a new and richer engagement to others, as well. And that is the most interesting shift of all.

We have come a long way from the elitism of modernism and its caricature of what life should be. We are now reaching society in a more emotional way.

Postmodernism forces critical judgment and risk. For one person who does not care about the aesthetics of a car, there are thousands who will gravitate toward it with pleasure. For the thousands who will snub the new Mini design, hundreds of thousands will want to own that little bullet of a car. For the hundreds of thousands who will not care about a new Internet offering, millions will move to get in on the excitement. Branding in an emotional economy is not about what you can't do, but about the endless possibilities.

Reframing the World through Brand Impressionism

By painting outdoors, the Impressionists followed people in their leisure activities. The rediscovery of nature by thousands of urban employees and factory workers in their newfound free time allowed for by social progress and the industrial revolution compelled a new generation of artists to leave the studios and paint on location.

But the bigger shift and innovation was the fact that this new generation of painters left behind centuries of dogmatic themes—royalty, military triumphs, or religious iconography—and started to paint not what they saw but how they felt about what they saw; they transcribed their emotions through painting.

From a branding perspective, the Impressionist movement is such a great inspiration to me. People want to *feel* something about their brands and expect that design will help them escape their reality to enjoy a new experience. Vincent Van Gogh was the catalyst of a new aspiration, a newfound freedom by a new society; his work was about a new beauty, a personal touch, and an inspiring style. He also represented his generation and how they saw their world. A new age of leisure and free personal time was becoming the norm and this new generation needed a new language. The Impressionists found it through their art.

What this means: *The modernist movement was about head, intellect, dogmas, and certainties translated in the ubiquitous, imperialist brands that are not flexible enough to respond to people's emotional needs. The postmodern movement is about heart and gut, about life and its reality in a personal way, its unconscious and emotional dilemmas. It is about people focusing on their destinies and their eternal reach for well-being, freedom, and prosperity.*

Emotional designs are postmodern in their conception, keeping people first in mind and creating partnerships of shared interests that benefit everyone in our ever evolving world.

Innovation Comes from the Margins

Globalization was understood in the 1980s as *standardization*. A brand's function was to create a relatively uniform product that could be sold worldwide with few changes. Levi's jeans, McDonald's, and Marlboro were the perfect dream brands in this regard. Today, however, globalization is about design *hybridization* and *personalization*. Again, jazz offers an instructive design inspiration.

Once upon a time, jazz grew up in smoky clubs and backroom rehearsal sessions, often among musicians who'd never had a day of formal training in their lives. It was a personal affair of close-knit, working-class African Americans who labored in the shadows of America's prosperity. During the 1970s and 1980s, jazz became an international and professional affair, taught and practiced in great conservatories worldwide. Today, the most obscure and exciting recording, no less than the most popular and banal, is only a few clicks away from Web-surfing aficionados. Does jazz have anything left to teach us about "innovative" design?

Innovation always comes from the margin, not out of the established, dominant voice. Case in point: Jazz Jamaica. This group, made up mostly of African American musicians, works and records in London, and they are one of the hottest groups in contemporary jazz. But their success is rooted in their innovative mixture of international jazz cultures organized around their local, idiosyncratic British experiences. They stir in American jazz, swing, Caribbean rhythms, and

Such is the spirit of *brandjamming*—to recognize a transcultural expression and ground it in the expressions of an absolutely local and singular idiom.

British working-class tunes to forge a new sound relevant to today's audiences. Although well-trained in white, British jazz and European-based jazz, Jazz Jamaica creates its own sound by listening through the ears of its background in Caribbean culture. In this way, these most "globalized" musicians create a dynamic, intercultural expression that is at the same time firmly grounded in the local English communities they live in. Such is the spirit of *brandjamming*—to recognize a transcultural expression and ground it in the expressions of an absolutely local and singular idiom.

Likewise, global brands seeking to "jazz up" their offerings must learn to be at once international and absolutely idiosyncratic. Like Jazz Jamaica, they must draw on their international reach, networks, and knowledge, but at the same time channel their product or service through the most local and distinctive designs. These designs must be organized at the level of local experiences if they are to resonate with consumers. In this way, globalization is *localization.*

Skateboarding as Design Inspiration

When branding strategies fail, it is because they don't make a *grounded cultural statement.* A few contours are added here, a few colors are added there, and it's thought that this will "distinguish" the product at hand. It's not enough to look at the contemporary trends and simply apply an element the competitors lack. Branding has a *design voice* that defines its own language for the world, crafted by a poet-designer to convey a particular experience and culture to its users.

How does this happen? Well, for a good example, take a walk to the nearest skateboard shop, and look around at what you see. Look at the shoppers, the workers, the colors, the words on the walls, the surfaces of the myriad skateboards. In the past three decades, skateboarding has gone from a foreign activity only teenage delinquents in California took part in to an international, multimillion-dollar industry sporting robust growth in the pre-teen set. This is not simply a story of commercial success: it is a design example and allegory.

Having visited the skateboard shop, now go out and see two films: *Lords of Dogtown* and *Dogtown and Z-Boys.* Usually, these movies are watched for the story they tell about early skateboarding culture, but I suggest looking for a story about how unique design cultures emerge. In the mid-1970s, this was an edgy, sometimes violent, but usually high-intensity and good-spirited "underground" sport for rebels, a way for outcasts to apply surprising uses to empty in-ground swimming pools. These people were guerilla designers operating in the trenches, unauthorized. The smooth holes where skaters practiced their sport became the crucible for design revolutions. As the skaters' tricks became more flamboyant, and they became better and more widely known, other accoutrements emerged: newly designed boards, shoes, and clothing, not to mention language, gestures, and swagger. Together these elements expressed skaters' unique culture. From precisely such a unique, daringly idiosyncratic and bold emotional culture emerged an industry today worth hundreds of millions of dollars.

The press soon followed. Popular magazines full of daring pictures and an array of skateboarding products cultivated a loyal base and provided entrée to fans far and wide. These magazines also developed their own visual language and narratives. Here we can see why design is so important: though there was a unique skating culture among the dogtown boys, it required physical artifacts to express it. For those who were remote and wanted in, it wasn't enough to see pictures and hear stories: the language, gear, and clothing made the lifestyle emotionally real. This is what emotional design innovation aspires to.

Nearly all the rebels from the Z-boys are today somehow involved in the marketing and distribution of skating goods, often with lucrative results. Although

The Vans brand visual narrative reflects the cultural vitality of its customers.

their skills and attitudes remain the amorphous, elusive stuff of legend, through design almost anyone can get a small piece of it.

By the mid-1980s skating became a nationally known preoccupation for edgy, angst-ridden youths. Millions bought boards: few ever showed the skills and inspiration of the Z-boys, but the unique fashion sense spawned by skateboarding encouraged an aura of participation nonetheless. When ESPN began broadcasting the X-games in the 1990s, the sport officially went mainstream. Today, expensive skating shoes and shirts bring in more revenue than skateboards, and most skating shoes probably never set foot on a board. This did not happen because of a few guys making catchy and attractive sporting goods: rather, a robust culture took root among skaters in the 1970s and provided the material for compelling design statements.

"I See Everything through the Pop Culture Lens."—Tommy Hilfiger

From the few professional contacts I have had with Tommy Hilfiger, I can understand how his brand has become one of the most powerful fashion icons in the world and a business success from a branding and design perspective. In Tommy's book *Style*, he mentions that, in the 1960s, when the American flag was used on stage and in fashion items such as shoes or scarves, the question was "is it protest and desecration or a rebellious way to reclaim that flag around a set of new values for a new generation?" The meaning is profound when you think of brands and what they mean: Change might be less a rejection of values past as it is each generation's way to appropriate a symbol by bringing a new meaning to it. This is the hardest thing I find in explaining emotional branding to brand directors: The importance of understanding the different appropriations people of different generations create around a brand. That changing meaning across generations is what brands feel uncertain about.

The Tommy Hilfiger brand started with a great logo design—the famous red, white, and blue flag designed by George Lois, a dominant adman and designer in the twentieth century. That design not only launched the brand but also helped make it one of the best-known brands outside the United States, along with such other ubiquitous brands as Coca-Cola, McDonald's, Nike, and Marlboro.

The first advertising that launched the Tommy Hilfiger brand is now part of the best advertising ever created: "The four great American designers" the copy said, and you could read the initials R.L., P.E., C.K., T.H. (nobody missed the reference to Ralph Lauren, Perry Ellis, and Calvin Klein) so T.H. for Tommy Hilfiger established the brand's instant notoriety in a provocative way.

The ad was so bold that it did not go unnoticed; it also showed how great ideas can build brands. This unique and provocative approach and breakthrough thinking in building a fashion brand was not unlike the rebellious way rock celebrities build their fame. Tommy Hilfiger's connection with the music world might have been an inspiration for the launch of his brand and its uniqueness. His passion to see his brand live in culture, by understanding the drama of wooing a public crazed by the need to stimulate their lives with new experiences, led him to make his mark from the start. Not unlike rock bands going onstage with innovative fashion statements, Tommy understood that the first order of the day was in creating a new graphic dress. Having the right "branded outfit" would build the uniqueness of his fashion statement.

Being inspired by and connecting with the music culture was radical thinking at the time Tommy started his business, and he loved to say that the "hip-hop connection" he was able to create had helped initially sell his clothes with "cool white kids wanting to show their rebellious side." The connection between his fashion and music gave the emotional credibility to wear his brand and the creative energy that made it cool. He is the only fashion designer that has been able to expand his brand relationship with youth by understanding the evolving rebellious spirit of their music world.

Tommy's clothing today has a preppy, hip, classic New England sportswear style to them. So what is the connection between rock, rap, and its revolutionary disruptive reality in the context of selling this brand today?

The answer, I believe, is that one must delve into the emotional perception people have of Tommy's brand to understand why the brand is still cool. Fashion "apparent" style is only a narrow definition of who a person is from an appearance perspective. A person who prefers a preppy classical look might be a big fan of rap artists or find a safe emotional digression in rap that allows him or her to express a rebellious side. In the nuances of a brand personality people find personal meanings that enhance their buying pleasure. Tommy Hilfiger provides them with the prestige of a known brand and the emotional adventure that is inherent to its heritage. It allows people to feel as safe as they want, but also as provocative as they want, keeping the brand discovery always open and evolving.

Fashion and music are interesting areas to look at, as they help one understand what it takes to build and communicate emotional messages and meanings, sometimes in a very contradictory way. Military clothes, for instance, can say "anti-war" or the opposite, "military dominance." Jeans could mean work clothes or make sexy body-tight statements. Lingerie is either seen as provocative or hidden and suggestive. Often rebellious messages, such as standing up for what you believe in, are not just an outgrowth of left-wing politics. The emotional complexity of people's aspirations is what brands need to open up to in order to match people's changing moods. Tommy Hilfiger's brand strength lies in how it can connect to many groups around a set of cultural values, not just fashion styles.

Music labels since the Second World War have been the most defining brands. Jazz liberated music with its new rebellious sound and opened up opportunities for new generations to make individual statements and jazz up their lives. Looking at the music scene, it is interesting to see that the definition of a star is not far from the definition of a star identity. An artist is not only the product of his music but also his visual identity onstage and his lifestyle offstage. The lesson there for brands is that the success of a brand is not only based on the clarity of its message but also on how its total identity is inspired emotionally by culture and in turn moves people's desires. Tommy Hilfiger is a great example of that strategy, because of its:

• Powerfully recognizable design dress
• Commitment to creating brand experiences
• Clear brand definition: an inspired American brand
• Continued connection with cultural inspirations
• Evolving and continued cool factor

Design Inspires Communities:
New York City and the Margins of an Impossible Dream
Tom Wolfe captured the new spirit of design that shapes the great cities today in his editorial "Pleasure Principles." As he wrote of New York City, "None of Gothamland's stocks in trade are tangible. Rather, all offer the sheer excite-

ment, even euphoria, of being 'where things are happening.'" This attention to designing the intangible, he observed, inspires all of New York's added value enterprises:

> Humanity comes to New York not to buy clothes, but rather . . . fashion. . . . Not to see musicals and plays, but to experience "Broadway." If the traffic on Broadway should ever lack congestion, if the people ever stop spilling over the sidewalks and out into the street, if they ever stop hyperventilating in a struggle to get to the will-call window before the curtain goes up, the producers and theater owners should hire hordes of the city's unemployed actors to serve as extras and recreate it all.

> Millions roam New York's art museums each year, not to enjoy the artwork but to experience the ineffable presence of . . . Culture. People throng Yankee Stadium game after game, season after season, not to see the Yankees play, not this year's Yankees, as the fellow might say, but to inhale . . . the Myth.[1]

Design doesn't just transform products—it can transform entire communities. In recent years there was major praise for Gehry's Bilbao Museum, but there has been surprisingly little talk about New York's 1964 World's Fair. *This was a design event that reimagined an entire city!* All but forgotten, the most prominent memory of the fair event hangs over Queens, New York: the New York State Pavilion, two flying saucer–like discs hundreds of feet in the air, held aloft on long steel columns. Even less remembered than the fair is what was there before it—a veritable wasteland of filth where thousands of pounds of coal ash were dumped daily. Author F. Scott Fitzgerald called it the "valley of the ashes."

This wasteland was reinvented by Robert Moses, one of New York's greatest designers (which is no small feat). Moses, best known for designing Jones Beach on Long Island, spearheaded two massive events: the 1939 World's Fair and the 1964 World's Fair, using both occasions to reinvent the Flushing Meadows area of Queens. With the first fair, he leveled out the mountains of ash, replacing them with parks and the breathtaking towers that remain today (perhaps they are a little less breathtaking today). For the second fair, he erected the inventive buildings and facilities that remain standing. Without Moses' tackling the unimaginably huge project, the remnants of the dump, and the dirty Flushing River that abutted it, would surely still be in its place.

Instead the area is today home to New York's second largest park, a bevy of thoughtfully designed multipurpose structures, and festival grounds that continue to be regularly used by the thriving border community that has taken root in the decades following.

More recently, New York debated putting a New York Jets stadium on Manhattan's West Side—and rejected it. Never mind the political wisdom or folly of this decision: what about the design prospects? The proposed building was uninspired, lacking the bold design necessary to rally support behind it. The Jets' president explained to the *New York Times* that one could not expect the building to revitalize the community because "One building can't do it on its own."[2] Indeed, if they were looking for a building to play football in, then, yes, this is true. However, a truly exciting and imaginative design *can* inspire a community, and its reach goes far beyond the functionality of a football field. What is missing is breathtaking design of the sort that Moses pursued, of the sort that elicits puzzled stares with its fantastic and improbable visions. When I talk about brands and "jazzing them up," I'm talking about creating these unexpected visions, seeing beauty where beauty does not exist yet.

These projects are part of a grand American tradition of transforming the landscape and communities through bold artworks: Since the early settlers arrived in North America, Americans have shown an almost perverse commitment to rolling back the existing environments in favor of environs of their own design. In one of the moments of great design vision, in the midst of the Great Depression, Franklin Delano Roosevelt authorized the Works Progress Administration, an organization meant to provide employment to the public. Perhaps the greatest legacy of this program is the fantastic art it produced, which we have today in thousands of prominent locations around the country. Particularly in libraries, post offices, and public squares, distinctive 1930s realism abounds. Just recently, Harlem Hospital restored and recovered its own murals, part of a rare trove of 1930s works by African American artists. The hospital is currently contemplating how best to exhibit these works as the cultural treasures they are. (America found the resources to beautify the country during a time of such immense hopelessness. Imagine if we had undertaken a similar effort in post-Katrina New Orleans.) The legacy of the WPA suggests that perhaps there is no shortage of talent, only bold vision to support stunning work. The spirit of transformation that "brings the Euphoria of being where things are happening" is at the core of the most successful branding strategies.

From the margins of culture to the margins of dreams lies the challenging science of human emotion and experience—what I believe to be at the core of great branding strategies.

- New ideas are found outside of the mainstream, in the emergence of new cultural expressions.
- Music is the barometer of social changes.
- There is a rebel in every one of us.

What this means: *In a postmodern emotional world, brands must embrace and leverage both the corporate cultures into which they are born and their consumers' idiosyncratic cultures, and draw on these two fronts to create unique, compelling designs that inspire. Ultimately, innovative design does not come out of a vacuum but always relies upon engaged and emotionally powerful cultures.*

Emotional Design Is Feminized Design

The fact that there is such a thing as "emotional design" today implies that design in many ways is being feminized, if we hold to the assumption that women are more emotionally expressive than men. Whether or not this is occurring because companies are increasing their efforts to connect to this new consumer (80 percent of today's buying is influenced by women), it is without question a sign that our culture is shifting, that women now have more influence than ever before on the way we see the world. As a culture, we are getting more intuitive, more spiritual; we are learning more about and looking at the world from a woman's point of view.

The Woman Consumer Is Leading the Design Trend

Women are stepping into place next to men as chief engines of design. Martha Stewart and Oprah are only two of the prominent women who represent a wider cultural passion for design. Stewart's and Oprah's magazines lavish attention on design, bringing an expertise that updates the design interests long maintained in more traditional women's magazines. Furthermore, these celebrities reveal that branding is not about "better functioning" design. Rather, it is all about lifestyle, culture, emotion, and aspiration. Too many brands still believe that designing for women means painting a hammer fuchsia. Instead, brands need to learn to take into account the lifestyle paths and changes that confront the postmodern woman and design products that mesh with that culture.

This is also the age of the *makeover*. Americans, both male and female, are obsessed with programs that add a new style to old goods: reality shows feature plastic surgeons, the *Queer Eye for the Straight Guy* revamps the lives of homely heterosexual men, *The Daily Show* jazzes up the tired current affairs program, *The Simple Life* explores what happens when style queen Paris Hilton goes cavorting in the country. Americans can't get enough of programs that challenge our tired old formats.

What this means: Everything that is old will be new. Rather than reinventing the wheel, unleash your designers and visionaries on the existing world to revitalize the world at hand. In a brandscape as crowded as our own, we don't need totally new products so much as we need better and more relevant design for existing products that have otherwise already proven themselves. As designers revamp these goods, they must keep women in mind; the woman consumer is the one who is leading the makeover charge, and she is the main decision maker when it comes to choosing what to buy.

What Women Want

Today, more than 22 million women live alone, reflecting a resounding 87 percent surge over the last two decades.[1] The increase in single-woman households has empowered more women everywhere to make purchasing decisions, which now account for about 90 percent of all apparel purchases, 80 percent of purchases overall. Among their purchases have been first-time homes. In interviews, focus groups, and polls conducted for their book *What Women Really Want*, Celinda Lake and Kellyanne Conway found that more than anything else, women value control in various aspects of their lives—health, finances, time, what they wear. This is an important statement about the way consumers in general are living their lives. People are favoring independence and control, and product innovation and communications will have to reflect this.

Hotels as Homes Away from Home

Hotels are having to adapt to the rising number of women who bring their children with them on business trips in an effort to put family first. Because of this, more hotels are offering child-care services and proper attention to women and children. Kimpton Hotels, based in San Francisco, has launched a Women InTouch program, which infuses the accommodations and services at its many hotels around the country with care specifically tailored to women traveling professionally or personally. From smartly chosen interior design for each of its locations to child and pet care services to mind and body wellness experiences, Kimpton Hotels stays true to its COO Niki Leondakis's special commitment to women visitors. "The Kimpton Women InTouch [program] is inspired by my experiences on the road as a traveler," she says on the group's Web site. "I travel a great deal both personally and professionally and appreciate hotels that take the time to plan for a woman's specific needs. Our goal at Kimpton is to create warm and inviting hotels that tell their own unique stories while at the same time, striving to provide our women guests with comfortable and safe environments, caring service, creative travel packages and high quality amenities."[2]

What this means: People are doing it their own way, putting their own lives first. Service industries must learn to "jazz it up," providing comfortable, convenient accommodations and services adapted to meet the living habits of individuals. If a woman arrives at a hotel with a baby, it is not because she is a housewife who has given up her career, and it doesn't necessarily mean that she is a downshifting executive. Rather, she is part of a new class of workers who continue to take their lives into their own hands, and expect to have services provided that are tailored to their specific needs.

Closing the Generation Gap

E's popular reality program *Gastineau Girls* is about a baby-boomer mother and her teenage daughter who party, shop, and live the best of life together, like two sisters. As a matter of fact, many mothers and daughters do make similar kinds of outings. "Shopping together" is an idea that is sometimes missing in the services retail brands provide. Imagine Macy's department stores, which have resonance across generations, capitalizing on the popularity of the *Gastineau Girls* program through promotions that encourage mother and daughter to shop together. The new youth, always resuscitating some retro design, could even be attracted to designs that evoke a pleasing nostalgia for mom. Other offerings ranging from wine tastings to lingerie shopping (for the more daring) could make these outings something outrageous, different, and emotionally charged in a way that department stores have not done for so many years.

A good friend of mine, an executive I consider to be in the top tier of well-dressed women, does not buy anything without her twelve-year-old daughter's supervision. Imagine their discussions on home decoration!

What this means: There's no shortage of generation-aimed feel-good promotions. However, the best branding will not just solicit a community, but help it feel bigger, better, larger, and more robust. When thinking about women, brands should not only think about one "generation," but should learn to identify, distinguish, and then unite generations according to promotions that have unique added value for the various participants.

Expressing Who We Are

When a pregnant Demi Moore famously appeared naked on the cover of *Vanity Fair* fifteen years ago in a photograph taken by Annie Leibovitz, she announced that pregnancy and motherhood are beautiful. She was part of a wider movement in the 1990s that embraced the diverse challenges facing women and their lives. The traditional arts are changing to meet these new expectations of women. A recent breakthrough has been the acceptance of pregnancy in ballet—long a bastion of anti-maternity sentiment. At one time ballet was foremost in a wider range of cultural prejudices that expected individuals to fit a single body type, lifestyle, and career path, often at great cost and punishment to the individual. But today even that great bastion is learning to redesign its expectations, culture, and perhaps dances to recognize a wider range of individuals' needs and expectations. This is precisely the kind of change that is likely to reverberate elsewhere in the consumer market.

Revealing a different kind of body (a pregnant one), exhibiting another kind of lifestyle (the sexy pregnant professional woman), or simply contesting popular norms—each of these demonstrate the spirit of affirmation and the tremendous influence women have in transforming culture.

Recent interest in maternity photography reveals how the momentum in celebrating pregnancy is real, and growing. Jennifer Loomis, a prominent maternity photographer, explains that "the message I am trying to communicate is one of strength, transformation and beauty"[3]—a powerful statement in itself for many women-centered brands. Understanding a woman's pregnancy means understanding her relationship to her children, as well as her psychological identity. This also translates on a different level to the opportunity brands now have to participate in home design, from children's bedroom furniture to the toys they play with, in a much more considered and open fashion. Emotionally, this kind of design can be viewed as a celebration of one of life's greatest miracles.

What this means: *The fact that a woman's body, even in pregnancy, has become an acceptable image for consumers in the media points to a changing relationship between design and life. Designers who tap into the natural course of life and its many transformations will strike a chord in consumers' hearts and break into promising new market territories that are only just beginning to come to fruition.*

Nike's Reality Anatomy

Nike Women has launched one of the first major ad campaigns to feature "real" women and their bodies, openly celebrating "big butts, thunder thighs, and tomboy knees."[4] Dove's breakthrough "Real Women, Real Curves" campaign by Ogilvy & Mather (see also Shift 6) posed real women, not models, in their underwear to promote its new cellulite-firming body lotion. Since then, the trend toward emphasizing women's natural bodies and appearances in advertising has gained momentum. The Nike ads, designed by the company's Portland agency, Wieden & Kennedy, show six different images representing six different parts of the body and highlight text that talks realistically about women's anatomy. One ad, featuring a woman's large behind, says: "My butt is big and round like the letter C, and 10,000 lunges have made it rounder but not smaller. And that's just fine." Other ads talk about "thunder thighs," legs that "were once two hairy sticks," and shoulders that "aren't dainty."

"In the 1990s we finally got smart and said, 'Hey, let's talk to women,'" says Nike's U.S. ad director, Nancy Monsarrat. "But we never talked specifically about women's bodies, and that's a hot topic right now."[5] In terms of branding, the hot topic is that women are getting in touch with what their bodies naturally look like, not what they *should* look like. If a brand connects with this need in women to be represented honestly in the media, showing women who look more like them in ads, then that brand will be more successful at attracting buyers. "Women come in all shapes and sizes, which is no surprise," said Ms. Monsarrat, "but when you talk to women in an honest way, they respond."

It is this drive to meet the changing needs of women that has proved to be one of the biggest agents in promoting new design.

Women have been wishing for their natural selves to be represented in the media for decades now, and finally, perhaps permanently, businesses are listening. Our culture's greater movement toward self-awareness has most likely shaped this trend toward naturalism. The growing and still-dominant market power of the baby boomer generation is a huge factor, as is our expanding multicultural awareness, especially toward African American and Hispanic communities. This is evident in the women of different ages and ethnicities represented in Ogilvy & Mather's ad campaigns for Dove. It is this drive to meet the changing needs of women that has proved to be one of the biggest agents in promoting new design.

Back in the Kitchen with a Vengeance

The kitchen, the bastion of the pre-feminist era, is once again becoming the privileged territory of women and an arena for expressing a woman's personality. Kitchens in our postmodern world exist more for show than for function. Their size has increased as they have conquered part of the dining room to dominate the house in the most impressive way. The message now is different and more emotional; it is not about pâté and gourmet dishes but conviviality and the promise of sharing. Kitchens may be there to garner compliments from the neighbor, but they also set the house's tone and style—a boring kitchen means a boring home.

A bane seems to have struck many an American kitchen: polished metal and brushed steel as far as the eye can see! Home kitchens have been engulfed by polished metal covering refrigerators, handles, stoves, blenders, chairs, toasters: any day now I'm certain those steel prison toilets will become the new hip accoutrement in SoHo. Now don't get me wrong: once these metal-surfaced kitchens were chic, utilitarian, and post-industrial.

Rick Marin of the *New York Times* recently recounted how rewarding it was when he went to great length to forge a kitchen of color. He sought out custom and vintage designs. Though many of us enjoy the hunt, it should be made easier for the design-savvy family: you shouldn't have to scour Brooklyn for a factory that can create attractive, colorful knobs for your cabinets.

The new spirit for breaking out of the plain, brushed-steel look as a next step appears to be somewhat influenced by Frank Gehry's recent work. Long an icon of the postindustrial, all-metal look, the architect has recently tried something different. His fantastic new museum for Panama (planned and designed but not yet built) boldly surrenders his signature silvery steel in favor of undulating eruptions of red, yellow, and orange on the metal panels.

Proving once again that art imitates good brand design, Gehry's work is attended by similar explosions in American kitchens and households. Although they are still relatively few in number, we should expect the

These new kitchen products beg the question: What other parts of the kitchen are waiting to be transformed from common commodity to design delicacy?

future proliferation of new colors, surfaces, and materials. The new line of Kenmore HE4t dryers, for example, jumps with stunning colors. It suggests that even a standard appliance can be extraordinary. The new kitchen can't accept anything less than good product and accessory design to populate it. These new kitchen products beg the question: what other parts of the kitchen are waiting to be transformed from common commodity to design delicacy?

Likewise, Illy Espresso has brought in bold design to stir up emotions in the kitchen. Espresso, of course, has never been simply a commodity among others. When someone drinks espresso at home, she wants the feeling, the associations, the cultural meaning of espresso, not just the drink. Recent ads by Illy feature the brand's elegant cans of espresso, which themselves already embody the aspirations that come along with drinking espresso: a touch of European sensibility, smooth lines, elegant colors. But this is all stock-and-trade for any espresso vendor.

What distinguishes Illy are the *design elements* now offered along with its product. Those who become members in the Illy espresso "club" get regularly delivered, fresh espresso. A whole set of gracefully designed matching cups are included, and a flamingo-pink espresso maker cut with retro modern lines is thrown in. What was before limited to the luxury and expression of a can and a good drink here becomes an entire experience, spread across design elements that jazz up the kitchen and ally the consumer with a lifestyle club that marks him or her as special, different, and *discerning*. A commodity—espresso—is hereby transformed into a vehicle of design and aspiration. This is particularly appropriate for a delicacy such as espresso; the passion for the process and culture of the drink seem to rival if not exceed the dark liquid that steams in the cup.

A very similar feat is accomplished in recent ads for Starbucks' exquisitely designed coffee liqueur, which comes in a dark, elegant bottle that's a cross between a drink mixer and a coffee canister. It's the type of product one buys simply out of the desire to hold it in one's hand. Surely innumerable brand extensions could attend this product as well. After all, Starbucks' main line of business is not simply good coffee, but also an entire *lifestyle* of coffee drinks they customers never knew before or desired. Starbucks provides first and foremost a program of *cultural design and initiation*; its role as a purveyor of coffee is a closely following second function. The more it can expand its cultural offerings and aspirations across myriad designed goods, the better it will serve its customers and the more successfully they will be able to immerse themselves in the cultural encounters they've long turned to the brand for.

What this means: *In Emotional Branding, I talked about the rising importance of color, fashion, and design sensibility in all spaces of our domestic life. Intimate and mundane sites may even be the places more ripe for reinvention. As the trend continues, more and more of our surfaces, from computer exteriors to blenders, are going to meet consumers' demands for bright coloring and inspired design.*

From Kitchens to Babies' Rooms

What about the products designed for children; don't women have influence over those? How do parents look upon ugly gifts designed for their children? Is utilitarianism and safety enough? No, of course not. Anyone who has ever decorated an expected baby's room, or watched parents do this, knows that color, atmosphere, taste, and other elusive design aspects not only matter to parents, but can even become points of obsession! Parents kept awake all hours of the night, driven to the verge of insanity by a teething child, will throw away all concern for personal appearance before they allow their child to look ugly and unhappy. Parents seem to suffer from a temporary madness when, even as their own lives are going to hell, they insist that the design of their child's room, clothing, and toys be just right.

Recently, a crop of young entrepreneurs recognized this and brought stunning designs to children's clothing and furnishing. Their design leadership and entrepreneurial attitude exemplify the best in jazzed up design techniques. Children's furniture has been a particular growth area. As the owner of one children's furnishings shop explained to journalist Marianne Rohrlich, "The baby industry took a long time to catch up with other design industries. . . . It took small entrepreneurs to answer our prayers for cool baby furniture."[6] As is often the case with great design, it takes small, culturally rich, inspired producers to create a new aesthetic. The women and men who went into designing children's furniture and clothing were parents themselves who used the experience of their own families, as well as their passion for design, to create attractive—and lucrative—designs that would serve a new generation of families. Their designs interpreted and expressed the new passion and desires generated through the smaller more intimate family that has become the norm in recent years. As family size has dwindled and a general taste of fashion has been popularized in the past two or three decades, more and more parents have become interested in lavishing style upon their children.[7]

This trend is amplified by the growing demand for careers and lifestyles that accommodate both women's and men's desire to spend more time with their family. As more people are working from home, and improving their home offices, it has become natural to extend these luxuries to other parts of the home. This is particularly the case when two parents work and one works from home to better provide for the family: these women and men are already bold leaders in "designing" their own improved, more modular families. But these changes in lifestyle will also demand new, more luxurious and reassuring designs, from children's rooms to high chairs to rec rooms. In turn, families will support products whose designs reaffirm their choices. Amidst social change, designers often assume the role of expressing in embodied materials the new values and choices of society's members.

Amidst social change, designers often assume the role of expressing in embodied materials the new values and choices of society's members.

The Workplace Welcomes Women . . . Gasp!

The move toward colorful expressions and sensory materials has already hit office fashion: casual Fridays marked by dowdy, saggy khakis are losing popularity in the business world. Cold, crisp, dark suits that long dominated Monday through Thursday are also in recession. More and more, businessmen and women are coming to work with bright pinstripes, pink shirts, and neon ties or stylish dresses and blouses. Not just whimsical fashion, but rather with a touch of the earnest peacock and the dandy for men, and for women a way to dominate the territory by expressing their true choices and personalities.

Perhaps in a tribute to *Queer Eye* (the TV show I spoke about earlier), fashion sense—and more than that, being bold and outrageous, and, of course, colorful—is becoming more popular in the business world.

The Paris runways, likewise, have shaken off smooth and functional lines in favor of ever more exquisite and formal fashions with robust shapes and lines. Recalling the not so long ago 1980s when design was *in*, more designers are asserting themselves and more retail lines, anxious to distinguish themselves, are turning to bold designs. Extravagant cuts, assertive colors, and other forms of "designer expression" (or even "designer aggression") are making their way onto the runways.

Technology Takes on the Feminine Touch

The job of good design is to make our experiences manageable *and* meaningful, taking a bland or messy experience and giving it poignant elegance and distilled power. Nowhere is this more in demand than in technology. What people say to each other, and their sense of aesthetics, is influenced by the vast impact technology has had on our world, how it has transformed it.

Design is the most important part of technology; the more things are changing or improving, the better the design needs to be to allow consumers to understand, appreciate, and apply the technology.

Though innovation is rampant—microchips become smaller and more powerful, features become more numerous—most of these "advances" languish due to inattention to design. How can industries so obsessed with "innovation" ignore the only part of the product—the design and handling—that consumers actually see, touch, and feel? It is design that takes all these features and actually puts them in the hands of users. The curve of a phone tells a consumer more about it than the numbers of pixels and gigs the phone has. Design is the most important part of technology; the more things are changing or improving, the better the design needs to be to allow consumers to understand, appreciate, and apply the technology.

As women embrace technology as a means to have more control in their lives, the way technology products are designed will become critical to their survival in the marketplace.

HOME COMPUTERS

Our multimedia universe, driven by innovation in computers, gaming, and home entertainment, has brought home a look and feel that is more colorful, more innovative, and more sensorial than any other products we have been familiar with, either at the office or at home. This has raised the bar of our expectations to be stimulated by similar innovation in all the products that we buy. Well designed technology is an important theme in a market that changes faster than consumers' learning curves. Good design makes the difference by helping the consumer assimilate these changes, and brings the ability to relate goods to users and their environment. Apple's candy-colored computers brought a sense of relief to the scary, all-black and gray technology world. The feminine touch is everywhere. Ours is the age of designed experiences, and it is the technology that is made for young people that is on the cutting edge of advancing this agenda.

Apple's candy-colored computers brought a sense of relief to the scary, all-black and gray technology world. The feminine touch is everywhere.

Many designers of computer hardware are responding with improved design, but most technology continues to scream "office" and "work." It's like designers of computers, phones, and the like want to remind users that we're stuck working on a computer when we'd rather be at the beach. Designers need to reinvent these machines. They should look at products like the Xbox that are raising consumer expectations (particularly the emerging consumers of the future) not only of computer hardware, but also film, fashion, and advertising. Dynamic stimulation allied with harmonious design is the name of the game. Retailers and manufacturers must decide whether to treat their goods as functional commodities competing on the basis of price alone, or instead to treat their products as *vehicles for designed experiences*.

While Apple surged ahead with beautiful hardware and veritable pleasure boxes like the iPod and the Nano, Hewlett-Packard, IBM, and other major manufacturers continued to produce reliable business machines. As these companies continued to purvey "computers," well designed for computing and data processing, Apple offered up community, experience, and emotion in the form of savvy design.

DIGITAL PHOTOGRAPHY

The proliferation of digital photography has consumers awash in more images than they know what to do with, and scrambling for ways to manage, personalize, and better design their memories. There are plenty of memories, but no design sensibility to them: how many families today have dozens of CDs filled with several thousand images, in such abundance that it's doubtful they'll ever be able to casually and pleasurably view them with friends? Film imposed economy on our family photos, and offered up the well-designed family album. Today, with thousands of images clicked off and downloaded per week of vacation, consumers' freedom to produce is cutting back on the capacity to design an experience.

Many photo shops are offering a cure for this—and women especially are responding—by offering comfortable environments where consumers can relax and easily design, produce, and manage their photos. Michael St. Germain, owner of Concord Camera in New Hampshire, created space in his store for customers to relax with friends and drink coffee while they review and print their images. "Customers bring friends and show them how much fun it is to make prints."[8] Not only is business good, he also observes that such services offer a much higher profit margin than his traditional lines in film and selling cameras. In effect, St. Germain took a technology and a need—digital cameras and image printing—and redesigned it as an added-value *experience.*

Cell Phones

"How Much Is Too Much?" So proclaimed the heading of an article lamenting the glut of cell phones crammed with innumerable and proliferating design features.[9] What's the problem with this? Shouldn't more features mean more design? No! Design is about taste, elegance, proportion, and experience. However, journalist Steve Lohr pointed to an exception: Motorola's Moto Razr, designed for "fashion and simplicity of use." Its sleek outer design complemented by a few well-executed features: large screen, Bluetooth communicator, and other basic but essential features.[10] Rather than offer an abundance of impossible-to-navigate features, the Moto Razr offered up a few key and easily navigable components.

One thing to think about is that, like the Moto Razr, most of the best cell phones today are similar in look to the make up compacts women carry with them in their bags and use every day. Whether the design inspiration came from the compact or not, it is interesting to see how experiences developed in one category can inform another. By reaching out to women and their experiences, a cell phone designer can integrate the ergonomic relationship a woman has with her cosmetic compact, a product she is familiar with and comfortable using.

Cars by and for Women

If there is one place where women have more influence these days it is the car industry. In terms of both security and family use, the industry has honed in on women's sense of community and their busy sched-ules to create designs that better fulfill their expectations. The soccer mom image may still be around, but new design concepts have shifted from the minivan for the mom who spends her days shuttling kids and groceries to the ultimate car for the working woman who desires the flexibility of a roomier vehicle as well as a cool-looking design that reflects and respects her pro-gressive lifestyle.

Automakers are spending more time culling input from women drivers when designing their cars. This is because, according to CNW Marketing Research, women today have just as much influence when buying a car as men do, making about 48 percent of all car-buying decisions in the United States.[11] The car industry is catching on and engineers and designers alike have got their ears, and minds, wide open.

At the 2004 auto show in Geneva, Switzerland, Volvo showcased the YCC (Your Concept Car), a brand-new concept car designed by and for women.

From the initial proposition to the finished product, all design decisions were made by an all-women team, shattering ingrained stereotypes about women's adversity to cars and driving. "We were very focused on who our target customer was and used that profile as a filter for all ideas," said Dr. Elna Holmberg and Tatiana Butovitsch Temm, members of the YCC design team, in an online interview. "Only solutions that fitted our target customer's needs went into the car."[12]

The two-door sedan features a large console with room for a handbag and compartments for keys, coins, and a cell phone, adjustable pedals that have a specially shaped heel support bar underneath, and voice-activated sensors that help drivers parallel park. The driver's headrest even has a split to fit a ponytail, so the driver wouldn't have to lean forward while she is driving if she is wearing her hair up.

Volvo is taking this new design concept one step farther and developing what it calls "Ergovision," which would customize vehicles to the individual driver to ensure the safest and most comfortable ride. At the dealership, a driver would have his or her body scanned and the measurements would be relayed to the car when the key is inserted into the ignition. The car would then reposition the seat, pedals, shoulder seat belt, headrest, steering wheel, and mirrors so that the driver has the optimum level of vision while driving.[13]

Because it is a concept car, the YCC will never be built, but many of its features are sure to find their way into production car designs. Automakers already use test drivers and focus groups to gear their designs toward women's needs, but projects like Volvo's are making that even more of a priority. Female drivers and designers are spearheading innovative improvements such as a storage space for a purse so that it doesn't flop around on the passenger seat, a belt clip for a cell phone that can be plugged into the stereo, vanity mirrors in the back seat, added room for umbrellas, a flashlight and a first aid kit, and washable floor mats and seat covers. Not only do these ideas provide simple solutions to problems in cars that divert drivers' minds and eyes from the road, they also improve the livability of a car while you are driving—they seek to optimize the driving experience through design.

Lena Ekelund, deputy technical manager for the YCC, assured car companies that tailoring a car to meet the needs of women should not repel male car buyers. "This is a bold statement," she said. "If you meet the expectations of women, you exceed the expectations of men. And it's true."

World Feminization

The feminization of our world is an idea that philosophers and writers such as André Malraux have expounded upon in the last half century. But the entry and growing number of women in the workforce and of single women in the home-buying market is a shift that is real and tangible, and which is now showing viable effects in gradually changing expectations and desires for our work and home environments. With women's unparalleled influence in all purchases made today, and the powerful, proliferating presences of women like Martha Stewart and Oprah in major media positions, it is evident that more and more women are defining their lifestyles in their own terms, expressing them along their own "taste" lines. Not only are they the Shoppers-in-Chief (as I pointed out in *Emotional Branding* and make clear here), but they are also fast becoming the Designers- and Decorators-in-Chief, and our democratic world will soon be "remade" in their image. The feminine influence on designed experiences is becoming more common as women step up the ladder and take part in the design decisions made internally by companies today. Look at the example set by Claudia Kotchka, VP of Design Innovation and Strategy for Proctor & Gamble. Women are leading the charge and bringing the true meaning of the designed experience to life.

Personalization is a key step in making a product fit its user, and businesses that follow the personalization trend will cater better to their customers. Women like Martha Stewart are leading the movement, inspiring millions of consumers to snatch up their offers by infusing their businesses with a sense of intimacy, emotion, and care (see Shift 7, "Think Emotional Customization").

From the kitchen to the workplace to the fashion show runway, color, expression, and bold designs are becoming more prominent. Bold design statements are an area women have always been comfortable with, and those brand designers who are creating with an open eye to a woman's sensibility have an opportunity to expand and capitalize on this trend.

What this means: *Women drive design choices in the context of our lives. Women understand the language of emotional design as it applies to their families and the quality of their lifestyles. When designing for women, brands need to understand this often forgotten reality.*

INSIGHT 4

Welcome to the
Twenty-first Sensory

It is difficult to talk about design from just a visual perspective and not review the idea that makes design such a wonderful brand communication tool: design's ability to connect with all of our senses. In my book *Emotional Branding*, I spend a full chapter on the importance of the senses and what they mean, how brands can connect more powerfully with people if they stimulate all their senses. I would like to share even more of that discovery in this book and expand on one particular if not the most powerful sense: *smell*.

Restaurant Jean-Louis

Jean-Louis's reputation in the greater New York area as one of the finest French tables is already well established, but for this book I was interested in meeting with him because he is one of the first chefs in the world to believe in marrying food with scent to create the type of mood that would enhance the total dinner experience.

Jean Louis's vocabulary exists in the mystery of cooking as it makes us discover with our taste buds sensations that we can't experience anywhere else and in most cases certainly not at home, regardless of how hard we try. With products that everyone can buy (we are still talking about meat and potatoes here), we discover the creative twist of this *haute cuisine* chef that elevates the cooking innovation and visual presentation of those products to the level of art and creative flair. Jean-Louis loves those kinds of challenges. For instance, he was asked recently to create hors d'oeuvres that looked like precious stones for Van Cleef and Arpel, the famous jewelry house. It took him three months to find the right solution, but everyone was amazed by the craftsmanship and imagination that went into the final presentation.

Jean-Louis's creativity does not stop there. Designing the most beautiful cooking he says could be so much better if he could also affect the mood of the people having a dinner experience at his restaurant. "For instance, if I serve a roasted chicken to someone brought up in a farm and include the smell of hay at the same time, it can bring that person back to his or her childhood experience or maybe mom's cooking. This discovery will be able to enhance my clients' experiences. There is so much more we can do to stimulate our senses."

This type of search led him to speak with Jean Pierre Subrenat, a notorious fragrance nose who also had been thinking about ways to make even a great meal more memorable. After more than a year of serious trial and error—particularly on how much of those natural pure "essential oils" you needed in a particular dish, or how those essential oils activated their odors in warm or cooked food—they finally resolved the challenge, to their delight. Jean Pierre invited some of his best clients in the perfume industry for an evening dinner at Jean-Louis to see and smell for themselves the result of their work.

"The connection with food is emotional and sensorial," says Jean-Louis, and he is right, as research and science have proven that the sense of smell has of all the senses the longest memory, it can take us back to our childhood, as we won't forget the scents that surrounded us then. "Ylang Ylang is one of the ingredients used in the Chanel 5 fragrance but it could also be added to chocolate," says Jean-Louis, who recalls women having a chocolate dessert at his restaurant and telling him how they felt so sensuous while eating chocolate only to find out later that those women most likely wear Chanel 5.

The opportunities to customize a dining experience obsess the restaurateur and the chef as well. Imagine a couple where the man would be proposing to his future wife—wouldn't it be great if he could create for them the mood through scent that would make the moment even more romantic?

With Jean Pierre's help, Jean-Louis developed the idea of spraying a small amount of select essentials oils, the purest form of a fragrance, under the warm plate of a customer, just enough for them to discover new sensations but not strong enough to bother the next table.

"I want my customer to travel through their senses, create memorable emotions that belong to them," says Jean Louis. I realize how great a designer he is. Not only is he a chef but he also works to make people's experiences in life more interesting and sensorial in ways that create memorable moments. The importance of sensory experiences is a great new field to explore, and there is no place like the fragrance houses to discover the impact of olfactory research on people's behavior and moods.

International Flavors and Fragrances: The Love of the Flower

To be at the forefront of olfactory discovery and understand how it could influence branding, there is no better place to visit or work with than the fragrance houses. International Flavors & Fragrances (IFF) is one of the multi-talented fragrance houses that has created unique approaches to discovering the rich sensory and emotional experiences that will win the hearts of consumers. "Our role," says Nicolas Mirzayantz, senior vice president of Fine Fragrances and Beauty Care at IFF, "is to help give permission for people to explore their senses and fantasies. We are the Disneyland of the sensual world."

> **"Our role is to help give permission for people to explore their senses and fantasies. We are the Disneyland of the sensual world."**

IFF is a public company that creates and manufactures flavors and fragrances for virtually every leading company in the beauty and food industry. It has embarked on a search for the emotional meaning in the products that it creates to help clients better understand the impact flavors and fragrances will have on people and their brands. For a manufacturer that is in a business-to-business mode, the move was quite innovative.

I met with several executives of IFF's fragrance division. I was intrigued to see how they managed the relationship between their artists, "the fragrance designers" who operate in a very emotional and sensorial world, and their business and marketing people, their customers. I also wanted to find out about the house's well-known, emotionally driven discovery techniques, an expertise it first used as a way to develop fragrances for its clients that has now become a source of inspiration for major fragrance brands as well. "The key to market success today is not to sell more products but to create brand and fragrance experiences that resonate compellingly with people's deep-seated desires," says Alex Moskvin, vice president of BrandEmotions, an in-house agency at IFF. "We need to create fragrance stories around new and unique emotional experiences. It is about making strong emotional connections in a market flooded with many undifferentiated 'me-too' launches."

To accomplish this, IFF is one of the only business-to-business companies I know that has hired a chief marketing officer, Joe Faranda, with experience in consumer goods at such diverse companies as Avon, M&M Mars, and Home Depot, and a planner from the advertising world (Moskvin) to create narratives to express the emotions inherent in a fragrance as viewed by consumers. IFF clearly recognized that a consumer who uses a fine fragrance is the same consumer who will use a fabric softener or drink a certain beverage. Therefore, the company values the importance of understanding consumers' needs from a more holistic point of view. In creating the CMO position, IFF is now poised to leverage and cross-fertilize all of its insights about consumers across all flavors and fragrance categories.

In their limited edition "Visionaire," IFF collaborated with contemporary artists to create scents that stretch the sensual boundaries of the imagination.

IFF's belief that people respond better to scents that are extracted from plants that were lovingly cared for has led them to create their own, unique botanical gardens where they can understand, protect, and observe the more than 750 species of flowers and plants. Nicolas Mirzayantz believes that "consumers are not rational beings." He says, "There is an unconscious collective out there that is far beyond what we see in the marketplace. We barely understand the depth of the emotional vocabulary at our fingertips and people's relationship with our natural environment."

"There is an unconscious collective out there that is far beyond what we see in the marketplace. We barely understand the depth of the emotional vocabulary at our fingertips."

When you first meet with this group, you really feel that you are entering a different world, a place not unlike Dorothy's Oz and Alice's Wonderland all in one. You might think, What are those guys doing acting like creative gurus in what might inappropriately be labeled as a manufacturing company? Their language is different; the company speaks the language of emotional branding, a language of innovation and sensorial experiences. When chatting with them, as I did for this book, they often trip over each other's conversations, so passionate are they about what they do and uncover every day. I thought for a minute that I was in my office during a brainstorm session! But then, they are the leader in their industry, and they line up some of the best fragrance successes in the world (such as Happy for Clinique, the first truly emotional fragrance that came out of their profound belief in emotional experiences).

It Starts with a Flower

Dr. Braja Mookherjee is one of the most revered persons at IFF. He passed away a few years ago, but his legacy is seen in the way IFF looks at their business. With a PhD in chemistry, his role was to find the best source of scent in flowers and natural products. That's why he encouraged IFF to build botanical gardens: to grow, study, and extract the molecules of those beautiful scents natural flowers provide us every day.

What differentiated Dr. Mookherjee from everyone else is that he believed that flowers had emotions and that, when cut, they lost some of their vitality and olfactory richness. Scientifically he had proven again and again that in order to keep the richness of all the precious olfactory vocabulary flowers could bring us, we needed to respect them, and he searched for another alternative to extract their precious value. He created a technique that allows some gas to be inserted in a glass dome that covers a particular flower, a gas that helps the flower release its richest scents. The gas then is retrieved with the olfactory print of the flower to be analyzed and recreated for commercial purposes. The botanical garden was a way to bring flowers in a loving environment so they could manifest themselves in the richest way.

In the case of Dr. Mookherjee, the flowers gave back to him the respect he deserved; he was able to find the molecules in plants that allowed him to create, among others, the now-famous Gardenia or Lily of the Valley scents we are so enamored with.

Dr. Mookhejee did not stop there; he found that flowers that are fighting gravity when growing, if planted in a water (hydroponic) solution with a lot of light, grow naturally faster and stronger. Also if you put two flowers from different species together, such as Jasmin and Osmentus for instance, they will create olfactory molecules that do not exist otherwise. Consumers respond better to fragrances created from living flowers in general, says IFF. They are more emotionally accepted by consumers, an idea that I find incredible and inspiring.

IFF even sent a rose into outer space with John Glenn, which was an expansive and brilliant PR coup. The leaves of the flower grew faster in space and the olfactory molecules of the flower changed. (If you want to get a feel of that fragrance, you should buy Zen by Shiseido.) And we all thought that fragrances were only about the stuff you are being sprayed with in department stores!

KNOWING MORE ABOUT EMOTIONS AND SENSORY EXPERIENCES
IFF feels that the high level of emotions people experience in products—video clips, electronic games, shows like *Sex and the City* and *Desperate Housewives*, as well as the rabid focus for youth on anything that is "X-treme"—is not represented in most brands. "We are superficial in the way we express our brands and fragrances emotionally, when people are about richer and more complex dreams and desires," says Nicolas Mirzayantz.

Women are not buying fragrances for rational reasons, believes IFF, but for inspiration and transformation; the opportunities are endless and the magic without limits. Still, some fragrance businesses keep focusing on past experiences, for lack of innovation, when people are looking for new ideas. This accelerates the trend for many fragrances ending up in the graveyard of discount stores or black-market distribution, literally destroying the brand capital along the way. That's the reason why IFF is spending time and money trying to understand the emotional and sensory connection that exists between people and fragrance products. The goal is to create fragrances that will leave an indelible mark on consumers and brands that will have sustainability in the marketplace.

THE RIGHT SIDE OF THE BRAIN

When speaking with Alex Moskvin, the first thing you sense is his uncompromising attitude toward finding new ways to get out of people feelings they don't even know they have. His most revealing experience while he was in the advertising field was his discovery that marketing professionals were listening to people telling them that what they wanted in a major chewing-gum brand was long-lasting taste, when in reality

"You can't ask people what they want; most people don't know or can't or won't say how they feel."

what they desired was an explosion of flavor in their mouth that would stimulate the brain and bring about new emotions. "We needed to understand the spaces between the words in order to reveal what consumers were getting at," he says. Since then, he has been relentless in probing human psyches, and he found a home at IFF, the ultimate playground for emotional branding. "You can't ask people what they want; most people don't know or can't or won't say how they feel. Brands and fragrances are processed in the right hemisphere of the brain, and we need new ways to listen to consumers and tap into their innermost needs and desires."

Alex is working constantly on research that connects fragrances to emotions. His job at the end of the day is to make sure his clients (fragrance marketers, fashion designers, and celebrities) understand the fragrance creations they are presented with from an emotional perspective. He supports the work of the company's fragrance designers by creating visual narratives that bring to life the new olfactory concepts. To help chart the emotional profile of the fragrances, IFF has developed a proprietary, global database that identifies the emotional responses people have to almost 5,000 scent ingredients and fragrances. This rich palette of sensory associations and emotions can be drawn upon to inspire designers and consumers.

BrandEmotions specializes in brand development using "right-brain" approaches to reveal consumers' emotional connections with brands and fragrances. Alex and his team identify and build narratives in support of new fragrance creations. The exploration of people's psyches is through a creative visualization process that Alex Moskvin has developed to connect with people's embedded desires. The process takes people on a narrative-building journey that ultimately reveals their innermost feelings on new fragrance projects. "This helps us to discover the psychological tension between the public and the private, the hidden truth and the superficial image, the socially acceptable and the darker desires. We like to get deep down into the fears and hopes, into the most provocative, deep well of human emotions," says Alex.

His dynamic approach shows how limited we have been in developing brands via traditional consumer research methods. Through this dialogue, IFF also discovers the fundamental differences in philosophy and lifestyle in different cultures; for example, Europeans are often intellectualizing, while Americans are more direct and pragmatic, says Alex.

Could the IFF research techniques and their discoveries be an inspiration for the creative industry and brands in general? The answer to this question is actually revealing of the type of company IFF is. It is a company that operates around a new set of values where the passion for innovative ideas is matched by the passion to understand people's motivation. This group works together and creates together. Fragrance designers and sales and marketing people have only one thought in mind: how to help their customer develop and grow successful brands by pleasing consumers with rewarding products. The new research that they have built, the emotional mapping that they have created, gives everyone a set of tools and language that helps the company speak the same creative language, the same innovative approach.

Could the fragrance industry's research techniques and discoveries be inspiration for the creative industry and for brands in general? The answer to this question is yes. IFF, like any other company, is a manufacturer that operates around a new set of values, where the passion for innovative ideas is matched by the company's passion to understand the motivations of people, the end users.

IFF is also breaking new ground that could be of interest for other industries. I have always wondered why we couldn't breathe in a nice fresh scent when opening an Apple computer box or use scent strip in regular ads to promote a brand image. To top this, Lenovo, the Chinese company that has acquired the Think Pad business from IBM, has launched a cell phone in China that "holds a few drops of perfume, enhancing the quality of a conversation with sweet smells as the battery heats up."[1] This phone is already successful with

Chinese women. The possibilities are endless and could make a difference in how people view brands. This use of scent is a great inspiration for brands that want to find new ways to reach consumers.

Brandjamming Sensorial Experiences

In the branding industry, visual boards are used to arouse and uncover subconscious desires. The fragrance industry, however, has realized that the quality of people's responses will be determined by the innovative nature of visual stimuli. They need to be so unexpected they disturb you. If you show fruits or flowers, they should be crushed, rotten, or stale. Show the gooey and the sexually suggestive—the messy lipstick on women's lips, the gender bending, and the darker colors that bring mystery around a photo. Disturbingly provocative pictures can be *beautiful and artistic*. Those visuals help you get people's deepest emotions out. In probing emotions, you can't hold back; it is a challenging process that will bring the best insight for a brand. You need to know: is it about the orgasm or the foreplay? Is it about the anticipation or the kill? The suggestive or the intimacy? You want people to rejoice in this relentless process of profound self-discovery.

The fragrance groups have only one thought in mind: how to please people with rewarding products. But their innovative success is based on creating new emotional experiences for people. The new research that they have built and the emotional mapping that they have created help fragrance designers, sales executives, and businesspeople speak the same creative language and develop the same pioneering approach. Innovation comes from the depth of the human heart, the places where no one can go through traditional research methodologies! You'll find out, for instance, that people can associate colors to fragrances, an important insight when designing packaging.

You might be thinking, okay, this works for fragrance brands, but they have license to do the stuff that can't be done anywhere else. Wrong! Brands are about the story, the narratives. When they are fully fleshed out, colors emerge and materials are celebrated; you get what people really mean. It is not about the like or dislike, not about the words; it's about the fundamental emotional truth. When you are in the emotional discovery trenches, you should not be afraid to see the good, the bad, and the ugly. Don't be afraid to see life as it is.

Design companies, or brand-driven suppliers like the fragrance houses, become the keepers of the past, libraries of consumer data and product experiences that are rich but often ignored. Many of the executives I met while researching and writing this book have told me that it sickened them to see the lack of ownership some brand executives have for brands; they leave when projects are not completed and make sure that their sweet ass is not on the line. In a world that is changing rapidly, corporations can't retain executives and they lose the continuity that is necessary to build long-lasting plans. The short-term "hit" is really what drives people, as it will help them get a better job elsewhere. Great ideas potentially fall through the cracks or are never brought to fruition. We have in our files, for example, hundreds of ideas we developed for certain clients that were never explored by their successors—a missed opportunity.

Listen to the Brand

A common misperception in the branding world—mostly among supermarket goods, pharmaceuticals, health and beauty aids, the automotive industry, the fashion industry, and airlines—is that musicians like the Rolling Stones, David Bowie, Michael Jackson, Elton John, Bruce Springsteen, Madonna, Puff Daddy, Lenny Kravitz, or Marilyn Manson are brands that operate under a different branding paradigm. Many in the design world won't even try to understand the huge efforts those brands have made to craft the visualization of their own personalities. Those "brands" understood that, besides creating quality music, they had to present distinct personas that would inspire the most profound emotions in their audience.

This has led those celebrities to join with fashion designers to create the look and feel of who they are. Tommy Hilfiger's book, *Style*, is the most compelling documentation out there of the association of music and fashion as a brand-building relationship. Designed around an exhibition on the role of fashion design in rock and roll music that he sponsored at the Metropolitan Museum of Art and at the Rock and Roll Hall of Fame and Museum in Cleveland, the book shows how the rock and roll industry quickly understood that their presence on television and in mass media helped build their persona and that it was critical to reinforce their identity through the fashion statements so they could connect with their audience beyond the concerts. We witnessed the King's sexiness that started the sexual revolution, the Beatles' long-haired early rebellious look, Motown's glamour, the operatic Elton John, the bondage message of KISS, the transgender image of David Bowie, the decadent surrealism of Prince, Madonna's religious and sexual agony, gangsta rap, and even designer hip-hop.

It always amazes me that while music can transform itself to appeal to the emotional aspirations of one generation to the next, consumer brands are just frozen in their history. A can of Campbell's soup is still almost the same and Tide has pretty much the same packaging since inception. What is it then that the music industry understands that other brands do not?

It is this: Most of those musicians worked with cutting-edge designers to enhance their image and they went out on a limb to create memorable brands. Tommy's connection with the hip-hop crowd is now vastly known but few understand that Madonna's stage dresses, or sometimes underdresses, were the work of French fashion designer Jean Paul Gauthier or British designer John Galliano; that the Rolling Stones hired fashion designer Steve McQueen; and David Bowie, Vivianne Westwood. Madonna, in the book *Style*, is actually quoted as saying that she would not go onstage if her outfit was not right for every song: "If you have the greatest music in the world but are boring on stage, it's like a dead balloon." This statement rings true for me when I think about some consumer products "onstage" in supermarkets.

Those artists that have expressed a new emotional reality and changed our way of looking at life have imprinted our memories with indelible ink and challenged us to go out of our shells to stimulate our senses in ways unknown before. After half a century, the Rolling Stones still rock for younger and younger generations.

Design a Soap That Feels Like an Ice Cream

Lisa and Benjamin Nissanoff have invented a bath line that looks exactly like Dryers' ice cream. The idea is the same: how can you successfully change the perceptions people have of a product that is generic? The packaging is fun, and the products are named with such monikers as Shower Sherbert, Land of Milk and Honey, and Peppermint Whipped Cream, bringing to life a sensory component that transcends the generic offering of fruits and flowers scent. The overall concept is about sensory experiences connected to food, a trend that has started to bridge the gap between our senses and varied our perceptions of products.

The new dimension in emotional design is design's connection to all five senses, its ability to stir up emotion and help us relive forgotten sensations.

The new dimension in emotional design is design's connection to all five senses, its ability to stir up emotion and help us relive forgotten sensations. If these sensory feelings are slightly unexpected, that is, if the design is jazzed up or adapted to uncommon categories, it can bring about entirely new sensory discoveries for the consumer.

This idea has not been lost on advertisers. An ad in the 2005 *New York Times* advertising supplement promoting baths and kitchens was titled "Sanctuaries for the senses, indulge yourself in opulent baths and kitchens." Another for Supima towels characterizes their products as "luxurious, lustrous, lasting." Origins has launched a Ginger line, calling it "a warming herb long known for stimulating the body and increasing energy," a new way to connect to an experimental and curious customer. The line also offers "ingredients such as orange, mandarin, and grapefruit for our continuously evolving palate." (It is interesting to note here the connection with food characteristics.)

Westin's new sensory advertising includes a scent strip.

In Westin Hotels and Resorts' new print advertising, they use the scent strip technique favored by the fragrance industry to help you smell white tea, "the calming new scent of Westin" as the headline claims. For a hotel that prides itself on helping you discover how you should feel, I thought that this campaign was extraordinarily powerful.

The Flavor of a Wine Fragrance

O Boticario, a Brazilian cosmetics company, has combined the art of wine making with that of perfumery. Malbec, a famous Argentinian wine, is now a partner in a venture to create a fragrance based on Malbec wine. The new fragrance, aptly named "Malbec," is being targeted toward "metrosexuals"—a term used to describe heterosexual men who share an uninhibited relationship with the beauty and fashion industry in hip metropolitan areas. This group is considered more adventurous and always in need of new stimulation. They like to show their knowledge of what's "next" before it even exists. And a brand based on one of the most popular wines of the moment—the wine is even included as one of the notes in the fragrance—is bound to catch on quickly.

What this means: Brands need to connect with all five senses, but in a disruptive and sometimes "explosive" way. Sensorial research leads to emotional states that help bring a new set of communications on how people experience brands. There is loyalty to a brand when the brands connect with our senses. A richer, more compelling message can connect profoundly if discovered through all of our senses in a positive way.

INSIGHT 5

Design Democracy

I was looking forward to speaking in Istanbul for Marka, a Turkish organization. I arrived, along with some of the other speakers, at the Istanbul airport, where we were met by two Marka representatives. It was about seven in the evening, already pitch dark. On the way to our hotel, we were often slowed by heavy traffic, which gave me an opportunity to observe the city's architecture and its extraordinary sense of vitality. While traveling through Istanbul you could feel like you were in any major European or American city, with the usual signage glowing in the night and advertising billboards lined up along the way. The only difference was the silhouettes of mosques that indicated a predominantly Muslim country.

Halfway to our destination, I spotted an enormous red and white sign on the side of a building, much like the way billboards are propped up in major metropolitan cities in the United States. The sign was so intriguing I asked the van to stop so I could take a photograph. There in front of me, printed on this gigantic poster in the middle of Istanbul, was a soft drink can designed around two dominant colors, red and white, and labeled "Turka Cola."

In Turka Cola Country . . . Aspiration!

My first thought was that this was some kind of protest against America and American brands. Not so, I was told by the Marka representatives. During my stay I realized that by buying Turka Cola, Turkish people have the sense that they are acquiring the sense of freedom, vitality, and optimism that is associated with leading American soft drink brands, only in a product that is culturally relevant to them. Turka Cola borrows the emotions of the "real" Coca-Cola brand, as well as Pepsi's "rebellious" advertising, and enhances it with the local flavor, which makes the proposition irresistible. From an emotional perspective, then, Turkish consumers were not interested in the product per se but in its emotional significance.

To the Turks, Turka Cola testifies to the fact that their country has reached a level of progress that allows them to create brands as "big" as the American brands. I would describe the message as one of "We have arrived!" Perhaps it is a message of hope that things are changing, a symbol that signals that it is okay to stand up to authority—even if it is "brand" authority. The brand in this case becomes the vehicle for a deeper cultural message and takes on a life of its own.

The association of one's country, particularly a Muslim country, to the brand values of a leading American brand is a marketing coup that demonstrates that the company standing behind the brand has a keen understanding of its country's pulse, its relationship with American "parent" brands, and the meaning of the brand itself. Turka Cola is not marketed or sold by the Coca-Cola organization. It is an independent venture. But the colors, graphics, and obvious naming connection to the famed soft drink, underlined by a patriotic message, shows how much emotional connection people have with the American brand. One could ask the question, Is the Turka Cola brand a means by which Turks can embrace a sense of pride in their country and in their identity?

From an emotional perspective, one cannot overlook how sentimentally involved people get with certain brands that have clear positive values. In some corporate circles, this would be viewed as a negative development for a brand, when in fact it is a tremendous opportunity for brands to convey a message. Why didn't the major American soft drink brands think of it themselves first, coloring their offerings with a local message?

Obviously, young people are the ones who would be most interested in buying Turka Cola, to signal a form of rebellious activism and independence. But the message is not necessarily a message of resentment or hate but one of dialogue, a way to tell the major cola brands that by recasting their promises in a local language they can be even more appealing.

A point that helps to validate this theory, and the irony of it, is that the spokesperson for the Turka Cola brand is none other than Chevy Chase, an actor known for his hilariously quirky roles in many of the most popular American comedies. At a time of heightened anti-American feelings in the Muslim world, choosing humor as an emotional platform is quite appropriate.

"You are drinking America, not a soda," says Serdar Erenar, the CEO and Creative Director of WPP Group's Young & Rubicam, Istanbul, the ad agency responsible for the Turka Cola spots for the campaign "Touch a Nerve" in Turkey. In light of the recent strain between America and Muslim countries, the commercials, which were shot in New York, are intentionally funny and reverse the concept of transformation through branding in a playful way. By drinking Turka Cola, the ads imply, Americans can become Turkish. The positioning of the brand as the symbol of two countries overlapping and blending is humorous and downplays the real-life tension between the two cultures.

For example, in one TV spot, Mr. Chase walks through Times Square and comes across a car wrapped in the Turkish flag and full of Turks celebrating a soccer victory. He enters a diner to grab a cup of coffee and a cowboy sitting next to him begins to speak in Turkish, after drinking from a red and white can of Turka Cola!

In another commercial, Chase is seen parking his Griswald-style station wagon outside his suburban home, where his wife is preparing a Turkish meal for her parents and the children. At the dinner table everyone sings "Take me out to the ball game," until they take a sip of Turka Cola and break into a Turkish-language Boy Scout song from the 1970s, a song that is part of Turkey's national identity. At the end of the spot, Mr. Chase even sports a bushy mustache.

The ad agency is American born, British by acquisition, and operated by Turks in Turkey. Given the high percentage of people speaking English in Turkey, more bilingual spots can take a really hilarious bent. The blending of cultures is something that has happened historically there, where in the past the Orient met the West, and as the confluence of two powerful cultures, Turkey can successfully mix them both to its advantage. What is the message here? The message is the "emotional" story: more fun for the Turks, less fun for the American soft drink companies that had to lower their prices and saw their market share drop!

Design to Survive

Not unlike humans, brands also go through life stages: birth, growth, maturity, old age, rebirth for some, death for others. The Darwinian principle of survival of the fittest is ineluctable: only the strongest survive, only the adaptive win. Businesses have to foresee the opportunities that will help them to prolong their success. P&G's entry into the male shaving business by acquiring Gillette has added tremendously to its success. Victoria's Secret's investment in the beauty industry has also changed that business's future. Coca-Cola's entry into the water business is proof that you have to adapt to consumers' tastes, and the acquisition of MAC Cosmetics with the creation of Clinique by the Estée Lauder company has strengthened that company's offering to younger women.

Compaq was absorbed by Hewlett Packard, and IBM's PC business has been unable to compete with Dell's model of distribution and cost proposition. Who remembers Pan Am Airlines? What will happen to Sears and K-Mart? How is Boeing going to compete with the larger Airbus model? For every successful incumbent brand there is always one maverick competitor.

Different challenges await different companies at different levels of their growth. The bigger the brand gets, once it has reached critical mass, the more challenges there are to keeping its leadership without losing the energy to innovate. Some brands lose the impetus that made them great in the first place. They are compelled to deliver on financial goals under a high amount of scrutiny. Predictability and solid return are required—precisely those expectations that generally stifle innovation and risk. Those companies are the Colgates, Kodak, Sonys, IBMs, Kraft, Xerox, Sears, Levi's, and Disneys of the world.

All of these tried-and-true but often tired brands keep plowing away, carrying their enormous destinies in order to keep stocks rising, sometimes regardless of a lack of traction. They are the admired ones, but also the ones the press and the public love to make fun of. They are the greatest targets for lawsuits as well, given their wealth and size. They serve, but they do not inspire. They grow, but they do not excite. They survive only as long as they have the power to buy their space on the evolutionary ladder, and they lose to others that come along with a more relevant form of business.

THE MAVERICKS

Every mature brand has a maverick nemesis. Small startups have nothing to lose: they thrive on risk and innovation, their investors are adept at financing those risks, and everyone speaks the same language. They stir things up and shift the business paradigm by breaking the rules. They are the enemies of the status quo, the troublemakers, but they are also the agents of progress that will challenge everything larger corporations are comfortable doing by making new offers that are more efficient, pleasurable, and fresh. Most importantly, they are adept at delivering new and better solutions to people because they understand the shifts in people's expectations.

Charles Branson of Virgin Airlines was a college dropout, an iconoclast fed up with the British Airlines establishment and bad service who created his own airline in order to show them how to do it better. Michael Dell started his business in college and has since created one of the most powerful technology delivery systems in the world. Steve Jobs wanted to bring power back to the people through technology by creating user-friendly, affordable computers. Donald Trump has made real estate sexy. Estée Lauder trumped Charles Revlon by believing that American women were ready for an American luxury beauty brand, which the Revlon brand was not.

Maverick brands are a virus, but a good virus, one that pinpoints the weaknesses of a system and forces other players to adapt. Intel, for example, had to change from microprocessors to chips in order to be competitive, transforming in that one move the culture of a company of 200,000 people. Darwin was right: you can't stay at the same place forever, in your personal life or in your corporate life. Security provides a false sense of well-being, another way of escaping reality. For every IBM, you will have a Dell. For every Pan Am, you will have a Howard Hughes. For every Microsoft, you will have an Apple. For every Wal-Mart, you will have a Target. For every Coca-Cola, you'll have a Red Bull. For every Folger's or Nestle, you'll have a Starbucks. For every Delta Airlines, you'll have a Jet Blue or a Southwest. For every Harrah's, you'll have a Steve Wynn's Mirage and Bellagio. For every SUV, you'll have a Mini. For every global brand, you'll have a Turka Cola. For every Goliath, you'll have a David, and every giant has an Achilles' heel. The nimble always trumps the mighty. That goes for politics, economics, sociology—and branding.

> **Maverick brands are a virus, but a good virus, one that pinpoints the weaknesses of a system and forces other players to adapt.**

FREEDOM OF COMPETITION

In this competitive brand evolution, consumers are the winners: fairer competition brings economic progress and social advancement opportunities. It fuels progress and discovery. For consumers this means more choices, more stimulation, more fun, better ways to improve their lives, and simply better living.

When this does not happen—when commerce, distribution, financial institutions, manufacturers, even politics halt in their tracks, unable to change—you find yourself in a state of inertia that stifles innovation and has a negative impact on people, who are always looking for the next stimulating experience. Supermarkets today are a clear indication of the lack of innovation that has accrued over the last fifty years. Brands have literally shut off the excitement that people need to feel when purchasing a product. By relying on flawed consumer research, brands have taken on a look of ubiquity and sameness that has led to a generic perception of products. This approach has emotionally disengaged consumers. By incapacitating our sensual desires, brands have evoked resistance, even anger, from consumers looking for, more than just functional benefits, freedom to choose products that will bring them joy. Supermarket aisles are now overwhelmed with even more private-label, generic products that provide cheaper versions but which drop the ball when it comes to innovation and renewal.

Today's Design for Tomorrow's Pleasure

The recent outpouring of product design is one sign of how much people are looking for innovation in their brands. After years of "plain, expected offers," people are finally revealing their emotions and desires by acquiring the new "design-minted" products. People are beginning to find innovation and more choices through new design expressions.

In this world of uncertainty, "we might as well enjoy it now," as the latest Apple campaign suggests. Big brand marketers, however, are not finding this all that inspiring. They think in past terms, while consumers are way ahead of them, expecting a recovery. These marketers are frightened of change, but what will they change into once new marketing models that have not yet been invented come on the scene or enter their midst? They begin to doubt their research and the consulting they have been getting over the past fifty years. They are in desperate need of a new vision for their brands, watching helplessly as a new sensory design revolution takes place before their eyes.

That's where designers come in: to mend the broken relationship that exists between brands and people. Designers try to mix and match human sciences and intuitive innovation in order to understand market realities and bring a level of inventiveness back to the marketplace. By leading change and redefining its mission, not simply following another brand's lead, a product can reinforce its position in the marketplace as well as its dominance in a category, giving people one more choice to choose from.

That's where designers come in: to mend the broken relationship that exists between brands and people.

Designers have their own research recipes for evaluating the cultural pulse and the emotional touch points that allow brands to compete beyond their obvious physical benefits. Designers are uniquely fit to grasp a corporate personality and then create strategic growth from an innovation perspective.

P&G's Freedom Brands

P&G is a marketer worth noticing at this point. Under A.G. Lafley's leadership, P&G has not simply reengineered its products to better meet consumers' needs, it has *redesigned* its culture to introduce a pleasurable, above all human, touch to the products it sells.

"I've been in this business for almost thirty years, and it's always been functionally organized," says Lafley. "So where does design go? We want to design the purchasing experience—what we call the 'first moment of truth'; we want to design every component of the product; and we want to design the communication experience and the user experience. I mean, it's all design."[1]

Lafley, with the help of Claudia Kotchka, P&G's VP of design innovation and strategy, is determined to make design an integral part of every step in the product-development process, from the research to the store shelves. Since Kotchka joined the company, she has tripled the number of designers and planted them in every business unit, resulting in P&G products that are decidedly more design driven.

For example, the design team charged with building a new cleaning tool that would suit professional house cleaners and bachelors alike spent hours observing consumers clean their bathrooms. The outcome? Mr. Clean Magic Reach, a bathroom cleaner on a removable stick whose design details, such as the blue color of the foam head and audible "click" when its handle is snapped into place, help all types of consumers understand and use the product.[2]

P&G's consumer-inspired, redesigned bathroom cleaner.

P&G is allowing its designers to discover what it is that motivates people in their never-ending quest for escape, seduction, success, and innovation in their ongoing lifecycles. Design research and innovation allow for a better understanding of the complex psychological territory brands must navigate in order to answer an audience with the products it wants by connecting to them emotionally. P&G's strategy is generating more freedom, more choice through innovation, and the payoff can clearly be seen in people's positive responses to those offers.

"Design is a really big part of creating the experience and the emotion," says Lafley. "If you stay focused on experiences, I think you will have a lower risk of designing something that may measure well in the lab but may not do well with the consumer. . . . We need to be able to make [consumer design] part of our strategy. We need to make it part of our innovation process."[3]

In Mexico . . . Brand Democracy!
In September 2003, I was invited by TEC University in Monterrey and Guadalajara, Mexico, to speak about emotional branding in Mexico City. To my surprise, the number in the audience neared twelve hundred people, including five hundred students who had traveled long distances to discover the secret of brand magic.

Students came from all over the Mexican states—by car, plane, and bus—to listen and learn about the power of branding. Until then, I had been speaking mostly to Ivy League MBA students well versed in current marketing practices and to savvy corporate executives polished in the best business schools in Europe, the United States, and Canada. I had presented in Japan to professionals who had built some of the most recognized and powerful brands in the world.

My presentations—though I try to deliver them with passion and wit, and are generally perceived as inspirational—are received mainly by mature audiences in mature countries that are looking for new ideas from a tactical perspective. Branding, yes; emotional branding, maybe; bottom line, absolutely; and, please, not too much risk. No rocking the boat in this room!

In Mexico, as I was coming onstage to give my keynote speech, I could feel that the mood of this crowd was different. I sensed a tremendous energy and restlessness in the audience. I felt that what was critical was to deliver not the tactical side of branding but my personal passion and love of branding as I experience it every day in my job, and my belief that branding can be transformative.

From my first conferences, I have learned to avoid a still, static position on stage and to avoid reading my speech from a podium. I like to walk freely around the stage. New remote control devices allow me to change slides as I go, pacing, jumping, articulating my movements in order to make my point . . . emotionally. This meeting took place in a theater, and for the first time I felt like an actor, bound to deliver my best work to a demanding audience. It was exhilarating, transporting, and certainly adrenaline fueled. The audience would clap, stand up, cheer on only the slightest hint of a brand favorite; I responded, I felt the energy, the passion, and I gave back all I believed in.

"This is not about money," I said in closing. I had been improvising for the last thirty minutes. "This is not about money: branding is about life, it is about respect, it is about success, it is about love, freedom, and hope. It is about building bonds everyone can trust."

I got a rousing standing ovation. I suddenly realized what branding meant to them. It was about freedom, about coming out of a challenging past, it was about hope for their future. Brands are the first signs of a democracy. They crystallize and express what is good about the life people want to make for themselves. Brands are the opportunity and proof that their society is changing and their future is unfolding before them.

After the show, I talked with twenty students who had been selected to spend an hour with me to further discuss my book, *Emotional Branding*. I could sense their passion for branding, all the hidden emotional messages we take for granted in the United States or Europe that mean so much to them. MAC cosmetics was a way for them to tell their families that AIDS was something everyone should be concerned about. Body Shop was an indirect message for women to express their frustration with the lack of support against domestic violence. They viewed Coca-Cola as a message of optimism and freedom; Nike as a symbol of infinite possibilities. Brands were their way to fight back, to tell a message. Brands were part of the solution, a statement against privilege and poverty. I was completely inspired by their desire to succeed.

My only fear is that brands themselves sometimes do not understand the real emotional connection they have with people and their expectations. There is an economic and psychological divide that exists between societies. If brands are the great equalizer, shouldn't they then inspire, motivate, problem solve? Shouldn't brands be part of the solution, not the problem? Shouldn't brands continue to foster freedom of choice?

Brands have become a source of reference, a visual, verbal, sensorial language that helps to communicate our feelings, beliefs, and emotions. People will go a long way to get the brands they love. Branding has become culturally connected.

Activism Is Standing Up for the Brand

When people fight against brands, they say they are fighting against ugliness, both moral and physical. They fight brands with new powerful tools like films, television, the Internet, and the street. A new genre of "reality" film-making—*Supersize Me*, which exposed McDonald's, or *The Firm*, another visual essay on the cynical side of the corporate world—is another way for people to scream out with displeasure. Through all these media we realize how much people want things to change.

People organize in order to have their voices heard, or they write books that are for the most part satires on their world. Why should brands be concerned with social and human movements? The answer is that, unless we look at branding in terms of its reality as a *transformer* and *solution provider*, it is almost impossible for it to be relevant or successful, to be "a brand of the time." One needs to make humanistic messages that resonate with people.

I once spoke at a conference where an activist anti-branding group was demonstrating in the street in front of the building where the conference was held on the "evil" manipulative techniques of marketing. After telling me that their group was "Brand Free," I observed that most protesters were wearing Birkenstocks, a famous anti-brand brand for people who do not like brands . . . except this one! Understanding major shifts in the way people relate to brands is a critical step in comprehending the public. People gravitate toward brands that speak to them in a very clear, honest, and uplifting fashion.

When Steve Jobs makes a presentation on his new products, it only takes a moment to realize that he is talking to you, not the retailers, not the financial guys! You get excited, emboldened, enlightened, and you love that brand magic. But his presentation is all about a language of innovation and beauty, a language of new experiences and discovery. Really listen to what he says and you'll see how he integrates people into his story.

Design is the glue between people and corporations; style is the message that makes the brand special and true. But brands can sometimes give splintered messages and forgettable offerings that don't excite people. Between advertising, packaging, product design, public relations, Web communication, and the look and feel of their company's workspaces, every message must fit together; nothing can be left to interpretation. Designers' best asset is not the ability to be brand specialists, but their instinct to see the interconnectedness of the world in a humanistic way. For designers, a logo is a shape, a smell, a color, a product, a message. The best work my company has done has been where our impact on graphics, products, and store design created a unified "voice" for a retailer that excited customers.

People want to stand for something; we want to volunteer. We are no longer passive but activists in our lives and in our beliefs. We stand up, we protest and let our voices be heard. Ralph Lauren's ads on activism reflect this new approach. Target's support for breast cancer research is powerful and innovative. Understanding the consumer environment and a brand's social responsibility are causes corporations need to endorse. We want the freedom to make an impact. We want brands to give us the freedom to get involved. We want to be free: free to choose, free to experience, free to discover even more.

What this means: *Global brands lack the sensitivity that could make their message memorable and esteemed, one of hope. People are waiting for brands to adapt to their own life reality. The aspirations people have for brands transcend the normal functional and practical approach most corporations see for themselves. People want the freedom to choose, to discover, to experience, and to get involved.*

PART 2:
SEVEN BRAND SHIFTS

Design Exploration

The following seven brand shifts unveil the most important opportunities that help humanize brands. By creating more integrated sensorial and emotional worlds, brands reconnect their products and their communications with people. This means that as a new mindset takes root in corporations around the emotional bonds and experiences people want to share with their brands, marketing dollars are moving from broadcast and print media to seek consumers on the Web and around new forms of experiences.

These seven shifts address those new opportunities to connect brands with people in a more powerful way by integrating all forms of communication around one consistent visual and sensory message. A global revolution is taking place in how people interface with brands in a postmodern world, and it brings to the forefront the realms of psychology, ethnographic understanding, and consumer empowerment. The role of design then becomes the overarching language in fostering innovation. Not unlike "jamming," design will bring about the participative nature of marketers and consumers around a new set of rules that privilege intuition, risk taking, and emotions.

If in general the biggest question is "What is the meaning of life?" then the biggest question in the marketing world today is "Why do people buy what they buy to bring meaning into their lives?" These seven shifts will make you think about the question and help you discover innovative design strategies that will make brands compelling. You will also get a sense of what creativity and innovation feel like and how far it can take your brand.

SHIFT 1
Think Emotional Identity

We had to honor those tickets. Our word was at stake . . . our commitment, too.
—Jeff Glueck, CMO of Travelocity, on honoring $2 million worth of plane
tickets to Fiji (even though Travelocity was not legally required to) after a glitch
on their Web site promoted $100 round-trip flights.

Defining the Soul and Gut of a Company

When you meet Jeff Glueck, you are immediately taken by his passion. He is the type of guy who is driven by his job, and at the same time there is a spark in his eyes that shows he truly enjoys what he does. There is a sincerity and a commitment to his work that goes beyond the normal expectation. This kind of sincerity from Jeff and the whole team at Travelocity has helped fuel the rejuvenation of their brand.

Emotional identities are just that, the expression of an internal passionate corporate culture motivated to serve. The public perception of brands is directly linked to the human factor behind the brand, whether it is a person, a country, a service, or a product. Brandjamming—or the emotional connection Travelocity has recently built with their members and guests—is about a company's ability to commit. Jeff can see his company both in light of the business reality, but also in terms of its impact on people's lives. What I had forgotten and rediscovered about Jeff during my interview with him were the fulfilling experiences he has had in life, his years in public service helping countries in South America and the Middle East to build economic development, where he focused on alleviating poverty through job creation and sustainable development.

Jeff wants to help, period. So after the bug to be an entrepreneur bit him, he could not think about any other business but one that would solve people's anxieties, a way to preserve his commitment to society and hone in his entrepreneurial talents. That's why he joined with his friend Michelle Peluso and a handful of others in starting an Internet company: Site59.com, a New York–based travel Web site specializing in last-minute travel packages, a concept aimed at alleviating people's traveling angst.

Travelocity, a division of Sabre, acquired Site59 in 2002. Soon after, the founding team changed from "entrepreneurs" to people's advocates within a new organization. Their passion led them to the top managerial spots, with the responsibility of turning the business around. This challenge perfectly fit a group eager to make their mark in the online traveling world. "We were in a business that was technology and pure-price driven, with no commitment to make people's experiences more complete. Our business was technical, trans-actional, and disconnected from their complete trip experience—and our guests treated us like a commodity; we did not have any loyalty in return." Indeed, Travelocity had lost their pole position to competitors and their new services were not even known or considered. This was the state of the brand when a new management team, including Michelle as CEO and Jeff as CMO, took on its leadership in 2003. Travelocity was up for a serious makeover: the brand needed to connect emotionally with people again.

Michelle and Jeff had a year to figure out what the brand was about and how they could infuse their love of traveling and their passion for people into an organization that could make a market difference and stand for something. Their first thoughts were for the employees. They found a demoralized staff that needed to be reenergized, empowered, and fueled by a spirit of entrepreneur-ship in order to bring back optimism in online travel booking. "Our gut was telling us that we needed to be about 'optimism' and all we were hearing was same old, same old." The change needed to be "inside out," as Jeff likes to say.

Getting people together to be emotionally engaged with each other around a brand promise was critical. Desgrippes Gobé was retained by Travelocity to find out what emotions would motivate the team and what emotions would inspire their own dreams and those of their guests. Our visually based brand-building process Brand Focus (which I explain later in Shift 5) helped us craft the proper emotional platform and narrative for the brand's future.

An Emotional Identity Must Affirm or Reclaim Its "Emotional Focus"

To humanize a brand so that it resonates with people, it is critical to "jazz up" the emotions that drive the passion of a company's internal workforce as well as customers' aspirations. For Unilever, the commitment to society is the basis of its corporate values and influences its operations around the world. Nike is more about the thrill of the performance. Emotional identities help to create and balance the proper *sensory and visual stimuli that will awaken people's feelings*. As emotional brands connect unconsciously with the soul of their intended audience as well as inform a company's value and brand vision, they need to have a clear emotional personality.

There are universal "emotional drivers" that reflect most corporate personalities as they are perceived in the world. In this chapter, I will show how those "emotional drivers" can participate in building a powerful culture of believers that will help a brand stand out among others.

The Five Primary "Emotional Drivers"
• Citizenship
• Freedom
• Status
• Harmony
• Trust

EMOTIONAL DRIVER	CITIZENSHIP	FREEDOM	STATUS	HARMONY	TRUST	
CONSUMER ASPIRATION	"love of the world"	"love of thrill"	"love of class"	"love of tribe"	"love of ethics"	
EMOTIONAL PROMISE	ENGAGEMENT	ESCAPE	GLAMOUR	CONVIVIALITY	SECURITY	archetype of emotional identities
CONSUMER MOTIVATION	**doing good** sustainability justice equality humanity	**breaking out** stimulation survival risk change	**shine** recognition predictability craft pleasure	**sharing joy** connection celebration renewal family	**stewardship** knowledge solutions heritage support	

An understanding of these emotional states is critical when differentiating a brand with certitude and focus. Emotional drivers help a brand take off from the ordinary, to reach out and connect with people's emotions through a branding language that is personal, convincing, and relevant. They are positive, optimistic emotions that have proven to be the most compelling propositions in commerce. And they are also metaphors for brand narratives and innovative discoveries.

I do not include negative emotions such as jealousy, panic, power, revenge, or greed, which are sub-elements that influence the emotions most used in marketing. Giorgio Armani, in the special WWD edition of his business's twenty-fifth-year anniversary, is quoted as saying that "advertising should be uplifting and provide a positive experience. It should enhance instead of detract," and I agree with that. Negative emotions are used in communications but always in a humorous context in order to be successful long term.

These five emotional drivers connect the emotional identity of a corporation or a product with people's aspirations, meeting their subconscious desires to achieve more fulfilling lives.

1. Our drive for hope and engagement: citizenship
2. Our drive to escape: freedom
3. Our drive to achieve glamour: status
4. Our drive for conviviality: social harmony
5. Our drive to be secure: trust

Those emotional drivers can be the inspiration and foundation of a brand's character or personality, internally and in the outside world. They can also be used as benchmarks for naming and product extension, as well as visualizing people's subconscious aspirations.

CITIZENSHIP

A brand personality defined by *citizenship* is known mostly for its social commitment (like Starbucks, Body Shop, MAC Cosmetics). Citizen brands will connect with people who aspire to *love the world*, who are committed to building a better environment. The emotional promise is *engagement*, and the consumer motivation is to create progress by *"doing good."*

• Emotional driver: citizenship
• Consumer aspiration: love of the world
• Emotional promise: engagement
• Consumer motivation: doing good

FREEDOM

Brands defined by *freedom* are known for valuing risk and transformation (like Virgin, Dell, Apple, or Diesel). Freedom brands will connect with people who aspire toward *the love of the thrill*, and their need to explore. The emotional promise is *escape*, and the consumer motivation is to *break out*.

- Emotional driver: freedom
- Consumer aspiration: love of the thrill
- Emotional promise: escape
- Consumer motivation: break out

STATUS

Brands known for quality and exclusivity (like Vuitton, Prada, Burberry, and Coach) are defined by the *status* emotional driver. Status brands will connect with people who aspire toward upper-class badges of success, their "*love of class*." Their choices are validated through recognized brand symbols. The emotional promise is *glamour*, and the consumer motivation is *to shine*.

- Emotional driver: status
- Consumer aspiration: love of class
- Emotional promise: glamour
- Consumer motivation: to shine

HARMONY

The emotional driver *harmony* characterizes brands known for sharing, support, and optimism (like Disney, Coca-Cola, and eBay). Travelocity clearly turned out to be primarily a harmony brand for its sense of community and a freedom brand for the discovery it brings to its guests. Harmony brands will connect with *people who aspire to belong to the tribe*, as a springboard for celebrating life, exploring new horizons, and sharing joy. The emotional promise is *conviviality*, and the consumer motivation is to *participate in life, share joy*.

- Emotional driver: harmony
- Consumer aspiration: love of the tribe
- Emotional promise: conviviality
- Consumer motivation: sharing joy

TRUST

Brands that are part of the foundation of the democratic system (such as banks, accounting firms, pharmaceutical companies, food businesses, insurance and financial organizations) are characterized by the emotional driver *trust*. These brands also include age-old, established firms with a history and heritage that provide products and services you can trust, such as certain food companies, for instance. Trust brands will connect with people who aspire to and privilege a "*love of ethics.*" The emotional promise is *security*, and the customer's motivation is *stewardship*.

- Emotional driver: trust
- Consumer aspiration: love of ethics
- Emotional promise: security
- Consumer motivation: stewardship

These emotional drivers not only connect a company's mission with a consumer's emotional need, but most importantly they help humanize brands and foster the inspiration for unique visual images and brand aesthetics. From the naming of the company to the tone of the advertising and the flair of a retail space or Web site, a brand's emotional personality must reflect a tight set of emotional values deployed in a consistent way. This approach helps, from a marketing perspective, to define opportunities for brand expansion in a more relevant way.

From the naming of the company to the tone of the advertising and the flair of a retail space or Web site, a brand's emotional personality must reflect a tight set of emotional values deployed in a consistent way.

Some brands, like people, do not fall only under the context of one emotion; we experience them at different times in our lives. Sometimes we feel "citizen" and want to save the planet; other times we want to selfishly show our discerning taste through "status" symbols by buying an outrageous luxury brand. A lot of liberal-minded people watch the conservative Fox News channel, and many conservatively minded people let off steam in Las Vegas. We all need to find brands that will help us experience and express our emotions sometimes in contradictory ways. When brands are copycats of each other, or "cookie-cutter," as the retail industry likes to say, they do not represent the vast array of emotions people want and need to experience. Then there is a rejection of the "expected" until new ideas appear in the marketplace.

Therefore, brands need to be very clear about which emotions they want to emulate, since that clarity will be a huge competitive point of difference. In a blurry world of brands, clear emotional strategies inform strategic planning, consumer segmentation, design expressions, internal motivation, and consumer's partnership. The construct of an emotional identity is being able to define a brand's two or three dominant emotions and their order of importance. For Travelocity, for instance, the dominant emotional footprint is *harmony*, a feeling of being part of this tribe of travelers, with a second being *freedom*, always bringing opportunities of reaching new destinations, and a third being *trust*, a promise to be there for its guests at all times.

The Truth Builds People's Loyalty

It is one thing to create an emotional identity, and another to deliver on the promise of the identity. Travelocity had already taken major steps toward its commitment to travelers, even before launching the new visual identity. It was, for instance, the only online company in the business that makes electronic reservations with hotels; the leading competitors used to fax all their reservations, which led to errors and losing up to 10 percent of reservations. (Competitors have begun migrating toward electronic connections, but still fax the majority of bookings.)

Travelocity focused on the "taboo" car reservation problem that we all encounter when a $30-a-day reservation after taxes and hidden local fees comes to a $50 rate once you arrive at the counter. Travelocity created "TotalPricing" to clarify this tariff and bring transparency to the transaction, promising their quote will be within a few cents of the final total price. Travelocity was also the first major travel Web site to allow real travelers to write and post independent reviews of hotels and cruise ships.

In May 2005 they launched the "Travelocity Guarantee," a commitment to stand behind the customer not only during the good times but also when problems arise. "Everything about your booking will be right, or we'll work with our partners to make it right, right away," they pledged. Travelocity backs that with a team of 2,000 professionals, on call 24/7 in case of any problems on a trip. They bring a human touch and the ability to problem solve on the fly. If, for instance, you book a hotel with Travelocity and you arrive to find the swimming pool is closed or ocean view you were promised is not available, you can call Travelocity toll-free and they will re-book you immediately in a comparable hotel that meets your needs—and Travelocity pays the difference, no questions asked.

Now, here comes the challenge and the reason why I am spending so much ink talking about Travelocity! Imagine that a small human error causes your company to briefly offer round-trip airfare to Fiji for $100 (normally a ticket worth $2,500 or more) and the travel blogs are red-hot transmitting the information? As a harmony brand with a just recently launched brand guarantee, what do you do?

Two days had passed before the problem was fixed. Travelocity did not have any legal obligation to honor those tickets; still a big question was: what is the right thing to do? The brand promise is suddenly faced with a moment of truth, with everybody watching, including the travel blogs, waiting for an answer.

"Are we about our guests or are we propagating fluff?" was certainly one of the thoughts that crossed the Travelocity management's minds when faced simultaneously with its responsibility to its guests and to its shareholders. But Travelocity is so serious about their brand promise and guarantee that instead of canceling their customers' dream vacations, they saw a unique opportunity to send a defining message that millions of dollars in advertising never would have accomplished. They decided that this mistake was their responsibility and that by honoring those tickets they would show how far they would go to respect their pledge to their customers.

Beyond the fact that they got tons of free publicity and kudos from the blogs, guests, and the press, the biggest benefit and the one Jeff is the most proud of is the pride the employees showed in their company. One hundred of them wrote personally to him and to the CEO to tell them of their proud feelings about this commitment. "The commitment of the company needed to be uncompromising. We cared about the brand and its reputation."

I will never know how agonizing the time spent thinking about their decision must have been or the pressure they got from "above." But the brand's emotional values that they had all agreed upon, when tested, held true, and such a clear vision led to the right decision. The great news is that emotional brands do make a difference. The tough news is that there is a serious commitment that needs to be made when building emotional brands. Don't go there if you are not ready for a commitment. Emotions can be volatile and powerful, particularly when trust is broken.

The Travelocity culture is winning both emotionally and financially. Travelocity in 2001–2002 was a company losing market share and with stagnant revenues. By 2004–2005 Travelocity had posted eight consecutive quarters of revenue growth over 25 percent, and gained share quarter after quarter. After launching the Guarantee in May 2005, Travelocity grew sales 31 percent in the last six months of the year, more than double the growth rate of its major competitors—all while being hugely disadvantaged in marketing spending. "We only spend $100 million in advertising a year roughly, while Expedia has spent as much as $300 million a year, our biggest competitor, and our communication is more fun and positive," says Jeff. When the new Travelocity advertising and brand identity launched, Expedia had for several years run a series of TV commercials about the nightmares of travel. "Expedia's very funny campaign," said Jeff, "focused on the nightmares of travel: you sit next to the jerk from the office on a long flight, the bugs might attack your tropical paradise, the surf instructor might try to steal your wife. We wanted Travelocity by contrast to stand for the life-expanding joy of travel."

Instilling positive emotions through a motivating "emotional identity" and brand advocacy does work. The most underused strategy lies in mobilizing the troops and employee culture. Most importantly, emotional strategies based on a sincere promise cost less than others, since you build a loyalty with your guests that helps to avoid larger communications dollars. So what does Travelocity do with their extra money? "We just put the money we save in advertising back where it has an impact: our guests' love of travel," says Jeff. If corporations have karma, as some believe, it will be influenced by the law of cause and effect. With all those good causes, Travelocity might keep on retaining its momentum, as its logo's promise foretells: Travel well.

So, What's in a Logo?

A logo becomes what we put into it emotionally. Jeff Glueck can talk passionately about his logo as communicating "optimism and humanity." When Jeff took on leadership of the Travelocity group in 2003, he wanted to express the company's new passion to the outside world and he recognized that changes needed to be made. It led to an articulation of an inspiring emotional brand narrative, which in turn led to a new logo described by Jeff Glueck as "a logo that plays well with our humanity. The hand-drawn stars in three different colors are aspirational and our new typography is approachable. The new graphic identity communicates a feeling of optimism and approachability we feel good about."

What Jeff does not know is that he might owe this logo to Antoine de St. Exupery and his book *The Little Prince*. Traveling is indeed something bigger than the destination: it reveals who we are and our need to renew our love for life and our appetite to discover ourselves through the stimulation of different cultures.

Weight Watchers is a company also under the leadership of a brand visionary. "Our name is a message, a meaning, and a promise," says Linda Huett, Weight Watchers' president. "Our logo needed to reflect the profound emotions attached to the brand by our guests and the life-changing experiences people have with us. The symbol conveys a feeling of hope with the colors moving from darkness to light, from dark blue to light green and yellow in a circular movement. It says also that you are never finished. The typography is genderless and friendly in a blue color that is positive in every market."

Linda can say that without reading any promotional material, it is so clear in her mind. Emotional brands such as Weight Watchers favor powerful logos that will be the iconic representation of their commitment. For this global organization, the logo is not just a marker or a recognizable signature but also the expression of a passionate effort by the leadership of the group to find the type of visual symbol and typographic expression that has a sense of optimism and pride that can be appropriated by both staff and guests. Not unlike Travelocity, the logo was again an "inside-out" job motivated by the company to show the true essence of who and what they were about.

A visual exercise helped to unearth one visual among many that inspired the logo: a hand opening a white curtain in an unlit room. Showing through the window was the green color of a lawn outside on what appeared to be a sunny day. This visual attracted all members of the Weight Watchers team because of its powerful visual metaphor of darkness versus light, and a sense that there is always a possible solution.

Weight Watchers is not a beauty company. It does not sell firming creams; it isn't a toothpaste company promising a whiter smile. Most Weight Watchers customers, upon entering the door, have already recognized that they have a weight problem and a history of failure with other dieting approaches. Weight Watchers offers a new chance to solve a problem and change their lives. For the message to be understood, every aspect of the Weight Watchers communication needed to represent how the company feels about what it does. To be successful, the company has to care more than any business; it has to accept its mission with great integrity and love. The Weight Watchers brand is a trust brand in its purest form, a brand based on the values of safety, ethics, and stewardship.

This identity helps the brand overcome one of its biggest challenges as a business: denial. As encouragement toward the self-realization that can overcome denial can only happen in a trusted environment, the identity helps to reinforce the message as well as a sense of hope. The nature of Weight Watchers, an organization that leverages the power of connection through group meetings, must always reinforce its commitment through a profoundly caring approach. The emotional identity, as expressed in the Weight Watchers' logo, offers relief and a message of hope.

What this means: *A logo is not just a neutral marker for a business but the profound revelation of all meanings associated with a brand. It is a lighthouse, a promise, and a comet at the same time. A guide, a vision, and infinite future dreams tightly crafted around a visual expression of the brand that inspires to be memorable.*

Daring to Stand Out: AOL in Focus

I first met with AOL through its international group, as I was invited to give a speech on "emotional branding." I immediately loved the company and wanted to work with them. I sensed that they were trying to see how they could change and reconnect with people in a more personal way. But I could also see that a lot of challenges lay ahead and I wanted to hint at those during our meeting.

In my presentation, I put up three slides saying, "I am a brand doctor" and then proceeded to show that the "symptoms" I was seeing (lack of visual meaning, lack of graphic coherence, unfriendly logo, and some negative stories in the national press) were sure indicators that the brand needed some serious brandjamming. I think those comments made the presentation more fun and started a dialogue between our company and AOL.

Embarking on the design of an emotional identity for a powerful brand such as AOL forces you to ask tough questions: What kind of emotional identity did AOL own? What is the role and impact of a powerful brand in society? How is the image perceived, particularly by women? The beauty of an online business is its ability to connect with members. At last, AOL asked 10,000 online members of AOL what they wanted, and they wanted the brand to change its look. Emotionally, AOL members wanted the brand to care. A leader in the Internet world and a forerunner in cyberspace communication—to the point of being the inspiration for a successful Hollywood movie, *You've Got Mail*—was in need of a new relationship with its guests. AOL was perceived as a business that privileged technology more than people, and it showed. They dared to ask, people answered, and it worked.

In auditing the visual persona of a company, you quickly get a sense of what the company is all about, what they care about, and where they think they are going. Not unlike people's appearances, the brand's graphic dress—from the logo to the Web look and feel to all printed communication—is a sure indication of a brand's personality. Visual audits, when interpreted through the eye of the designer, can reveal hidden messages and emotional motivations. It can show anxiety or lack of focus, hope, pride, or even fear. The AOL identity looked and felt more like Wal-Mart, Blockbuster, or Home Depot, a mass look that spells price promotions and acquisitions, not representing the vastly rich emotional territory they were about. It was an emperor with clothes but the wrong clothes, and the consumers were confused by this sloppiness.

For AOL, we helped clarify the persona of the brand tremendously. Negative terms such as *arrogant, generic,* and *lack of sensitivity* were believed to express who they were by users; *lack of product differentiation* and the *dated look of their image* was clearly prevalent in the internal discourse. Those negatives are important to talk about before a solution can be found. Without a visual process, a frustrated internal team could not turn those negatives into positive opportunities. Our visual process also revealed a great passion and courage on the part of the team for the brand to change and the recognition of its huge opportunities to create value in people's lives.

Concerns about customers' safety online made security a responsibility, as well as more robust customer service, entertainment, and connectability. Broadband was also revolutionizing cyberspace and AOL, who had been at the forefront in developing this technology, wanted the world to know that the technology would deliver content that would make AOL a richer experience.

The dialogue evolved toward profound human values and the immense role AOL could play in people's lives. The dialogue was transforming itself along emotional lines. The opportunities became the focus, the technology the asset.

A MULTIDIMENSIONAL IDENTITY
A new identity was needed to connect with people in a different way, bringing a message of change, innovation, and leadership. When looking at the visuals selected by AOL during our visual process, you can see visuals that express intuitive and effortless discoveries, colors that are bold and fun, a spirit of independence, and a sense of security. The future of the brand in people's minds was a bright and imaginative one.

One visual for me was emblematic of the subconscious personality of the brand as seen by the AOL executives. It was a very clean and simple photo of a woman's hand, fingers extended, with letters painted on the nails. From a visual/emotional analysis, you could see the desired attitude of the brand: individualized, personalized, everything-comes-from-the-hand, global, fun, fresh, and modern. The hand pointed toward the future, but with fingers extended, a visual metaphor of the brand's future identity: the meaning being the future in the twenty-first century is not just one way or one path but many directions for you to choose from. You could see that the brand was ready to move and jump into a new future of discovery and excitement with consumers powerfully in control and exhilarated.

"Our new logo transformed the familiar blue triangle along those lines into a multidirectional arrow pointing to the future. With softer letterforms to convey warmth and a more modern typeface, the logo announces that AOL is committed to being an advocate now and into the future," says Russ Natoce, AOL's brand director. The people's response was truly positive, acknowledging the changes but also looking forward to participating in new experiences with the brand. The brand moved from being a techno geek to a people's advocate.

One of the most interesting ideas that came out of this program was AOL's demand that we work in parallel to create a retail expression of the brand to bring a heightened level of sensorial experiences to the program. This idea now brought to life has fueled our imagination and communicated a tremendous understanding of the power of technology in a human way. (I explain the store design concept in Shift 4.)

AOL is clearly a harmony brand, and the brand strategy as expressed in AOL's new "10 Commitments" clearly emphasizes how it is a brand of the community first. The first commitment is very compelling in that way: "AOL will always help our members feel safe and secure."

What to learn from AOL from an emotional perspective:

• People connect with the meaning of the brand; a logo is not forever, and even a well-known logo will fade if the meaning attached to it is irrelevant.

• Bringing an identity in three dimensions brings it to life. The brand is sometimes the most powerful message to convey.

• Every brand needs to be built from a visual and verbal narrative to understand fully its emotional connection with an audience.

• The robustness of a Web-based connection with your members or guests is a powerful way to engage in a benefiting dialogue for the brand.

What's in a Star?

In *The Little Prince*, Antoine de St. Exupery writes, "We only see truly with our heart," an interesting thought on the limitation of our physical perceptions. As the Petit Prince shows a drawing of what appears to be a hat to a grown-up, he asks the question, "Are you afraid of my drawing"? The grown-up responds that it would be odd to be afraid of a hat. "But," says the Petit Prince, "this is not a hat, it is a snake that has just swallowed a goat."

What we project onto a drawing or symbol is what we see in our own minds. It allows our imagination to engage in a deeper way as our mind is stimulated. Then a true dialogue starts to happen with a brand and with the ideas behind it. In the debate for or against symbols, the cultural factor is critical. There are brands that are known and others that are also emotionally connected. Interestingly enough, the most powerful emotional brands have developed their perception of a logo as not just a marker but as an iconic, visibly emotional tool used in their communications program. Target, Apple, and Nike have reached a high level of positive recognition in leveraging the emotion behind the brand through their graphic identities. Still, there is a tendency to stop short of supporting a great logo for fear of ubiquity, pure lassitude, or just a shortage of imagination. The logo then becomes a static, limited expression of the brand. The worst happens when the brand has nothing to say or has a crisis of conscience about what it should be saying. The challenges in evaluating or creating emotional graphic identities are these:

1. Do I want a logo that will express my culture?
2. Do I want a logo that will signify my culture?
3. Do I deploy my logo's sensorial identity to be the basis for a richer vocabulary?

A logo that *expresses* a culture is multidimensional and flexible, full of life and meanings. On the other hand, a logo that *signifies* a culture will not be weathered by time and does not respond to changes. So, the philosophical debate starts there. As discussed in Insight 1, modernism is based on the dogmatic concept of "mind over matter," which leads to the rigid intellectualized version of an identity. The postmodern approach celebrates the progress and people-driven experiences of a fluid world.

In the quintessential postmodern emotional identity, the logo can be "it," the message and the philosophy, the inspiration and the motivation. The Target logo is probably the best expression of this. Even Nike and Apple have limited themselves too much in the expression of their most celebrated icon, forgetting to leverage their most important asset when facing a changing world and evolving cultures. The emotional dimension that a logo can convey is still unexplored by most brands for technical, legal, and logistical reasons, corporate issues that do not take into consideration the emotional engagement people want to have with the brand.

Federated Department Stores, Inc.—the large retail holding that owns Macy's, Bloomingdale's, and Marshall Fields, among others—realized that through all their recent acquisitions and mergers, their portfolio of brands could not be sustained from a business perspective, much less as a branding proposition. There are two major brands under Federated, Macy's and Bloomingdales, and it makes a great deal of sense to invest in building these two brands. Within the Macy's brand, however, there are some major differences in the way its divisions go to market; Macy's East and Macy's West were culturally and historically different. The plan to bring one national brand program for both did ruffle a few feathers.

For Macy's West, the superstar of the company and a favored luxury brand on the West Coast, this new integration needed some serious explaining. An annual meeting of the Macy's West leadership team was organized to bring everyone in the loop, so they could understand the benefits of a powerful and unified national branding program. I was invited by Bob Mettler, the chairman and CEO, to be the keynote speaker for their annual meeting. I knew Bob from his days at Sears and always admired his third eye for merchandise. He really "gets" his customers and is a strong believer in the importance of an emotional dialogue with his guests. My role was to open up the debate to position the brand as one they could all be proud of, explaining that the regional concepts were not as great as the power of a unified national brand built upon the same set of values.

As part of their new effort to reach their associates and customers alike, they brought back the famous but clearly under-leveraged Macy's star. Through the press I had followed their branding strategy changes and was pleased at this decision. Everyone knows about the traditional Macy's identity, but when you see those red stars in a mall on hundreds of bags, you get goose bumps, even if you are not yet a Macy's customer (yet!). This identity alone was already bringing a new sense of partnership and belonging to Macy's West. The visual identity crystallized everything the brand was about, regardless of the geographical differences. I had the feeling that this star was a catalyst and motivator in bringing a real sense of renewal and energy to the group.

Again the power of a graphic symbol came through for me. Furthermore, Macy's had prepared a group exercise that encouraged the audience to create a thirty-second "brand message" using the new emotional identity, revealing the aspiration the team had for the brand. Seventeen teams of ten executives each were given a camera, two minutes' training on how to use it, and three hours to come up with a branding film on Macy's that would be judged by management and me. The top three teams would receive an award.

The results were fascinating to me from a "brandjam" perspective, as the most powerful message for all teams centered around the new shopping bag decorated with the Macy's star. The star had become the starting point and inspiration to release their imagination. I thought one of the winning films to be a very professional and creative idea. It showed hands coming together to form a star, then as the hands moved away they revealed a red star that unexpectedly appeared on the screen.

That star best encapsulated the new brand strategy, its emotional excitement and optimism for the future. The star was the message and the emotional badge that everyone was proud of, regardless of their previous affiliation. Ideas about the star's potential on various products to be sold in a stand-alone shop within the store were flowing around. When people buy T-shirts just for the logo on it, it shows how much people care for that brand—and is another source of revenue for the company.

Travelocity's three stars, the Weight Watcher's wave, and Macy's bold red star represent a new breed of brands that don't mind showing their emotional stripes to the world. It is therefore not surprising that all of them have strong citizenship programs as part of their business priority. Macy's commitment is one of the most active in giving back to the community, with programs that are stunning in their size and dedication. Macy's giving is not only corporate but driven by each individual employee. Bob Mettler himself and his staff can be seen every year giving food to the needy. This is why those brands are building a truly iconic image for themselves, one that makes a winning corporate culture the soul behind the brand.

Naming

Naming is one of the most important parts of a branding strategy. Finding a new name is always challenging and it's the horror story for branding organizations or advertisers: where do you start, and where do you find the inspiration and the relevance for a new name? And how do you find a name that is available?

When approached by Steve Case's marketing group to invent a name for his new venture in cable television, a health and well-being channel, the task was quite challenging. Names with "well-being" or "health" or any combination of those two words had already been created and taken. From a functional perspective, it was impossible to innovate with a new name; from an emotional perspective, we had more opportunities. Our writers and designers came up with a flurry of options but one stood out as the most powerful one: Lime.

Lime was not the direction one would expect, but emotionally, lime expresses freshness, bite, and purity. The meanings behind lime are active and transforming, an added positive element to something else, a memorable refreshing taste that adds some bite to life. Emotionally it was right; the program wanted to cover the transformative aspect of a balanced life as well as an active participation.

Names historically are falling into different strategic buckets that reveal—when dissected along emotional lines—interesting insights on what could be the naming strategy or creative focus.

In the case of Lime, we did not use this chart, but one could say that the name falls in the freedom camp, a name transforming enough by itself that it would convey a unique and revolutionary way to see one's health and future well-being.

Emotional Identities Are the "CEO" Essence

Emotional identities show that you are in the game and trailblazing; they are the credibility and the platform behind the brand promise and message. They need to inspire and convince. The engaging message of an emotional identity is led by a great visual language and supported by an imaginative sensory experience that meets people's aspirations and helps to build a culture of engagement.

At the end of the day, the emotional identity must come from the dream the CEO has for his or her employees and, more importantly, his or her customers. CEOs can bring the emotional identities of their companies to life by remembering the following concepts.

EMOTIONAL IDENTITIES START WITH A WELL-COMMUNICATED PERSONAL DREAM

How can you make people dream if you are not a dreamer yourself? How can you be convincing in delivering on a new promise? Emotional identities reframe the dialogue to be less corporate and more humanistic. CEOs and the top management of corporations sometimes need to go deeper into their feelings and past experiences, back to the freshness of their earlier business motivations and dreams to find new solutions and be convincing with their audience.

To best illustrate the power of these feelings, one must only look at Phil Mickelson struggling on the last day of the 2005 PGA Tour at Baltusrol, his ball deep in the most unforgiving rough on the eighteenth hole—a presumably impossible shot. He had struggled with that shot all week, and with his last chance to make a difference, at this crucial moment, he went back to the feelings of joy he had as a kid, practicing that shot in his backyard. Forget about the teaching pros, the professional training, and the mechanics of the swing. He won because he went back to an emotional time when he dreamed of being a champion. Remembering the feelings of doing those shots as a kid won him the tournament, the coveted trophy, and a place in golf history.

Most executives don't often remember the feelings they had when they made a difference in business. The adrenaline that leads to creation and growth through innovation certainly beat the cost-cutting and supply-chain strategies. Company leaders must reach out to the feelings and experiences that are at the core of the human life and share those emotions. To communicate this passion, an organization must develop its personal dream. This is the first step and most important effort in rebuilding trust and confidence in people. A new emotional identity can help do that in the most compelling way.

People do not understand scientific research data or terms such as *brand nomenclature*, *brand identity manuals*, or *corporate guidelines*. They understand and trust, love, beauty, and surprising ideas—poetry. Poetry is about beauty, interpretation, imagination, crafted words, and profound human messages. Jazz is a poetry of sorts as it connects through people's hearts.

The challenge is for top management to assemble the troops and make the company culture one of emotions and shared creativity with consumers. Companies must ask themselves: how do we revisit our image and face our consumer world with confidence? How does the message get executed? In a culture of paralysis where people don't communicate, there is no model for getting people together to clean up their act, leverage an asset, or climb the ladder. For weaker companies, how do we fix it? For successful ones, how do we build it? How do we go to the next level? If you look at any logo book, you will come upon a sea of sameness. Even worse, the "swooshing" of the logo industry is amazingly ubiquitous as everyone tries to look cool. Even our office is an offender! The reality is that 90 percent of the time, corporations today are buying obsolete brand consulting when they should be buying emotional design. It's time for corporations to dream again about what their image means for people in an emotional way.

That's what this chapter is all about, understanding what it means to have a great company, how it feels to have those breakthrough ideas that launch most people's careers and change people's lives. Focusing company culture on those transformative dreams— building a brand language that will sound, taste, and look like a dream—is crucial. Starbucks titled a recent ad "Owned and operated by human beings." The copy then starts with the following: "High ideals don't have to conflict with a bottom line." Their logo? I'll

wear it on a T-shirt. The Cirque du Soleil logo is an element of the company's entertainment strategy and innovative spirit; the Harley Davidson symbol reinforces the heritage and badge status of the brand; the Rolling Stones tongue is reflective of the quirky rock band; and the Tivo logo character looks like a little troublemaker, which fits Tivo's disruptive business identity well. The logo often is the inspiration for the brand language as well as a sounding board.

For Unilever, their desire to change their marketing approach to be emotionally driven meant changing the famous (but cold) logo to reflect their more humanistic values. Their new symbol conveys the reality of that brand's consumer dedication. Then-president Niall Fitzgerald said, "The world we operate in is changing. Consumers are demanding more and more from the companies behind the brands, increasingly bringing their views as citizens into their buying decisions. They want the brands they can trust." The result of this new philosophy was expressed in a more friendly corporate graphic style for the logo that signaled to the company internally a new set of values and to consumers that they cared.

The graphic style of the logo is sensorial and decorative, a "postmodern" approach in a world of cold, minimalist visual identities. This emotional design platform has led to brand initiatives with their detergent and beauty business that have inspired the now famous "dirt is good" and "beyond compare" campaigns that are transforming the way people look at these products categories.

As our Brand Focus research shows, people want identities that they can believe in. The goal of this approach is to liberate the brand from its artificial marketing shell. In my work on Coca-Cola's brand identity, I can say that the new visual language we created has inspired new product development and has revealed to the company its brand's vitality and its infinite growth possibilities. If you look at a brand from a strictly functional product-differentiation perspective you will miss the bigger opportunity—the emotional differentiation. One is company-based; the other is people-driven.

EMOTIONAL IDENTITIES REFLECT THE REALITY OF LIFE

Emotional design recognizes the age of the individual and the importance in giving people a way to emotionally interpret brands to fit their own personalities. All brands, like human beings, have the following characteristics in their personalities: some head (the rational side), some heart (the social side), and some gut (the impulsive side), the reptilian part of the personality, according to some psychologists.

This holistic, multifaceted approach is fundamental to a great brand culture. By understanding how people navigate through the world, and through brands, you can create a multidimensional visual expression for your brand. Apple's quality and guarantee is a rational comfort—yet the culture of the company, a heartwarming relationship, and the products and retail stores are truly intuitive and viscerally appealing.

Ideas need to compete with other ideas in order to stimulate and energize consumers. What makes the emotional approach more complex, but also fascinating, is the fact that we want to experience all of those emotional and sensorial possibilities to the fullest. Baruch Spinoza, the famous Dutch philosopher, connected our body and mind as one entity that supports our need to fulfill our lives with joyful sensorial experiences within a free society. They can't be dissociated and this is what is troubling most marketers, who ask, why can't my logical promise work without the sensorial experience?

The challenge becomes even more interesting when the emotional and sensory elements are in conflict, as this offers more adrenaline-fueled situations to experience. A vacation (which is typically supposed to be restful) in the form of a hard jungle trek is for some people more exciting. Buying a leather motorcycle jacket while at Macy's when in reality you are there to buy a business suit is jumping into a world of fantasy and freedom.

This is the theory that I call the good boy/bad boy or good girl/bad girl (Eve/Mary) concept and which I developed in my first book, *Emotional Branding*. The more tension there is in our choices, not knowing how much pleasure we will or should accept, the more unexpected excitement the offer brings. Our need to be secure does not mean that we don't want to take risks; our need to save the world does not mean that we are not irresponsible at times (and perhaps this in fact triggers our need to be good citizens). Our need to be a role model does not mean that we don't sometimes want to be selfish and self-indulgent, and to cross consumer lines.

Competing ideas and the innovation that comes out of them is what excites consumers; the brands that surprise and energize us have come out the clear winners, simply because they make us happy—they let us brandjam with them. Not long ago, Burberry was an old-fashioned "trust" brand from England. It has transformed into a "freedom" brand to attract younger buyers with a new fashion look but without losing the trust and heritage of its history. Young customers admire the heritage but also buy its new style and vitality. There is nothing more exciting than experiencing the dichotomous quirkiness and tension of those rebellious values at play in the classicality of the brand in the most exciting way. The more brands are trusted, the more they can take risks, a notion that is often forgotten by mature "trust" brands.

Competing ideas and the innovation that comes out of them is what excites consumers; the brands that surprise and energize us have come out the clear winners.

Apple, a maverick "freedom" brand, has built a strong following by building "design harmony" with its consumer base. Estée Lauder, once a "freedom" brand, had become a mature, conservative "status" brand. However, their new partnership with famed designer Tom Ford is again the rebellious "freedom" brand it once was. Karl Lagerfeld, a "status" designer, is now making a "status" brand to be sold in lower-priced H&M stores. By rewarding women with his talent he's sending a message that will resonate profoundly on his own brand; it will prepare and motivate young women to appreciate more expensive luxury goods for the future—a huge shift for this industry. The point here is that the delineation between mass, class, price, and exclusive distribution has been blown to pieces; it simply does not make sense from an emotional perspective. People are buying for emotional benefits regardless of the distribution or the price points. Karl Lagerfeld will not go down as a "mass derelict" but instead as a great talent who under-stood the emotions of women who love style . . . particularly if they can afford it.

94

What One Duck Can Mean

If a brand does not deliver on an emotional aspiration, customers will adapt or appropriate brands for their own purposes. I was going through a Brooks Brothers catalog, clearly a "status" conservative brand, and was interested by a photo of an older male model wearing a blue blazer and green pants with little ducks printed all over them. I could not help smile and make fun of that quirky "WASP-y" design. The language was still very traditional, but with, well, let's call it a twist. It was still too conservative for me, however, as I am one of those all-black-wardrobe New York kind of guys. I passed.

Then a week later, as I was flying down to Washington to meet with a client, in front of me was this handsome, athletic blond man wearing the Brooks Brothers duck-print pants but with a cool sports sweater and Adidas shoes. On his shoulder was a high-tech sports bag. Suddenly, the duck pants took on a different connotation: they were cool, not stiff, and humorous in a sexy way. The pants looked completely natural on this man and fashionable. From an emotional design perspective, this man had changed the meaning of the product for me, transforming my brand perception through his own provocative personality. That's my point: we think of our products in narrow-minded ways. Brand meanings can evolve; they can be adapted and reinterpreted to meet individual styles. Brooks Brothers *cool*?

Even a company like Brooks Brothers, which serves a predominantly conservative clientele of a certain age that indulges in the refined humor like duck-print pants, can't think about how some younger segment of the population can get inspired and transform that meaning into a very different message. If Brooks Brothers were to display a young model in one of its store windows or in its catalog wearing a hip, exciting mix of their products, they could attract the ageless "freedom" crowd. It would attract not only a new clientele but would also respond to the aspiring emotional desires of some of its established customers.

Saks Fifth Avenue has moved in that direction, crossing fashion lines by designing an ad campaign under the headline "Saks loves it both ways." The ads show the same clothes worn by two different women, one woman styled more traditionally than the other. The idea is to show the *spirit* of the collection and to transcend its obvious look, feel, and meaning in order to engage "women" regardless of age or taste and invite all to experience the brand. It invites them to come to the store and experiment with clothing in a fun way filled with discovery. Emotionally, it is a powerful idea for a traditional store, as it welcomes younger women to find a way to express their true individuality as well. And, given the double entendre of the tagline from a sexual perspective, it also provokes people to rethink the brand in a humorous way. This is truly an emotional campaign that celebrates freedom and inspiration, discovery and playfulness, transformation and opportunities in an inspired way. Have it both ways segmentation is something brands are not ready for yet, but it works as it explores the sides of us we don't know about yet.

Design, then, can take on a new, more diverse approach that opens up instead of closes down the brand expression. It doesn't change the brand's inner, core personality; on the contrary, it allows it to be more emotive and creative. Design keeps it interesting.

Watch That Attitude

An emotional identity does not stop where a new logo leaves off. It is a culture and a message, an ethos and a commitment always to change, innovate, and surprise. Sometimes product design will change the perception of a brand, sometimes graphic design will be the best ambassador, but the best design has always been a philosophy for sustaining the integrity and dynamism of the brand. An example I want to mention is the GenX brand Google; its second stock issue is a financial project that should raise $4 billion for the company. There is nothing funny about raising money, but Google could not go down that path without sending a message out. So it issued exactly 14,159,265 shares to accomplish its goal. This number is exactly the first eight digits after the decimal point in pi (the ratio of the circumference of a circle to its diameter).[1] Google could not stop signaling its independence from the system, bringing the unexpected and some glamour to the brand. This little detail was covered by most media and reinforces the perception of the Google culture of innovation in a personal, fun way. It connected culturally with like-minded people, even staying hip among the GenY members who thrive in the same innovative spirit.

What this means: *A brand has gravitas but also attitude and emotion. What is important is that it make a stand. A brand should always surprise and evolve, but also be emotionally consistent. That way, it becomes good company, like any of the best friends we have.*

SHIFT 2
Think Brand Iconography

As the broadcast media falters, out-of-media communications will need to have more presence as well as a consistent and memorable message. The management of a new or existing brand iconography becomes a huge play for recognition. Creating an iconic visual identity is critical, as it helps deploy a brand message and releases a "logo" as a real-life evolving message that increases the legitimacy of a brand.

Creating and Building a Visually Compelling Message

From a brand signature perspective, Google has broken a few rules in making their now famous typographic symbol more than a marker. By animating and illustrating their brand typography for different holidays—from the Fourth of July and Martin Luther King, Jr., Day, to Christmas and Mother's Day[1]—Google is showing us that a brand identity does not need to be static or dogmatic, but can also be used as a live expression of an evolving corporate message.

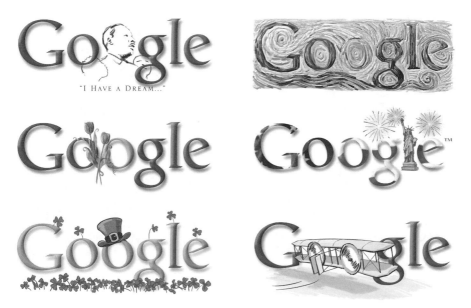

Screenshots on page 99 © Google Inc., and are reproduced with permission.

The image of a brand through its visual expression to the world is one of the most underleveraged ideas and one that connects in a profound way with people.

The challenge is how to deploy a visual language across all forms of visual communication, including ads, print, the Web, and all other out-of-media opportunities that exist to create a dynamic and positive, wel-

comed brand presence in the lives of consumers. Burberry is very focused on that aspect of its brand's impact: it leverages its fashionable tartan outside its stores, in displays, on fragrances, and in ads. The image of a brand through its visual expression to the world is one of the most underleveraged ideas and one that connects in a profound way with people, as it forces brand marketers to discipline and expand the coherent expressions of their brands.

Americana is the historical celebration of U.S. identity around its most recognizable icon, the American flag. It is known worldwide and has a quaint, friendly, and welcoming touch that keeps on reminding people about the best of American values. It is evolutionary, crafted by many, and consistent across the history of the country.

Target Again!

Okay, what else is there to say about Target? I talked about this company extensively in my first book, and Laura Rowley's book *On Target* wrapped up the subject quite nicely. But that brand bunny keeps on going and going down that road of consistent, unique messaging and surprising communications. Not only has Target brought the concept of pop-up stores to a new level by docking its own retail boat in New York Harbor, but it has also drawn the most interesting designers into its stable, such as Michael Graves, Philippe Stark, Isaac Mizrahi, Yves Behar, and now Deborah Adler, who reinvented medication packaging for people's safety. Target continues to motivate, while keeping its business out of the reach of mighty Wal-Mart. Target stands out in the crowd as somewhat of a genius branding soul.

It was Target that bought an entire issue of the *New Yorker* magazine and plastered it with the work of some of the most interesting illustrators, saying in a way that advertising can be fun, inventive, informative, and loveable—just like their brand. In a world where print media is losing its appeal from marketers, Target's initiative is one intuitive idea that can accelerate a more robust relationship between print media and marketers. Target has invented the integrated model of communication, a strategy that is driven by design for emotional experiences, the consistency of a vision in its total form, and the integrity and power of a promise well delivered—it's the model for the future of advertising.

This unique company showed the world brand design's powerful potential as a driver of all forms of communication, particularly in the celebration of one's own visual and sensorial identity. This is what this chapter is all about: the power of brand iconography to create brand iconicity—to have the vision to see, to imagine, and to celebrate with people in mind. "But does it leverage marketing dollars?" was one of the questions I wanted to ask Michael Francis, Target's EVP of marketing.

An Interview with Michael Francis, EVP of Marketing, Target

Marc Gobé: Has the feel of design for Target been one that emerged out of a cultural sensitivity to design, or was it the influence of outside factors such as an advertising agency or new leadership at the company?

Michael Francis: The concept is actually quite organic. Years ago we recognized that we couldn't claim low prices as our only point of differentiation. We needed to define ourselves uniquely. We focused our attention on our product and assortments and constructed our brand promise: "Expect More. Pay Less." The tension between those two promises forced us to think differently about our business and our relationship with the guest. We found ourselves being singled out by the media and other established organizations (The Smithsonian's Cooper-Hewitt, which gave us a National Design Award). We capitalized on this trend, and our agency partners and our internal teams created the communication package.

MG: Has this culture of design allowed Target to save money on broadcast advertising given the vast exposure it has already gotten through PR and its emotional connection with people?

MF: In a word, "yes." "Buzz," or media attention, has had a critical role in defining our brand with consumers. Far from mere fluff, buzz has had an astonishing amplifying effect on our marketing mix. It has helped us to level the playing field with those competitors who may outspend us. In addition, it has added a credibility factor that marketing dollars would have never delivered.

MG: How does the emotional aspect of branding play out in Target's brand strategy?

MF: We are rapid about protecting and nurturing the tone and voice of our marketing. We try to infuse all of our ads with the quirky, optimistic style and a sound that has come to define our work. We remain playful, treat the guests as the sophisticated and worldly people we know them to be. Before it ever became topical, Target was casting our work with a wide variety of diverse models (race, age, physical characteristics, handicaps). We never fell into the trap that has often plagued our industry—the one that mandates "cheap goods equals cheap advertising." We've also strenuously avoided what we call "Jekyll and Hyde" marketing—swooning over a trunk show ad on Sunday but clipping coupons on Monday.

MG: Why, given the success of Target's powerful integrated brand message through design, have there not been more copycats? Why does Target continue to stand alone?

MF: We've never assumed that we stand alone and feel that the time between our execution and competitive imitation has never been tighter. That pressure has ensured that inertia never sets in, we never settle, we never stop challenging, and we never look back.

MG: Who are the main outside agencies that are doing work on the Target brand and which have had the most influence?

MF: Target is blessed with a large in-house organization made up of long tenured and remarkably talented individuals. Much of the work that is seen is a product of their tireless and passionate brand stewardship.

Let's Have a Vodka

When you observe most product categories in a supermarket and look at the growth strategy that has been created for them, it is always along functional lines, not emotional ones. Coca-Cola, for instance, in the past has relied on growth through functional benefits based on flavor enhancement (cherry, lemon, etc.) or dietary concerns by taking away sugar (Coca-Cola Zero or C2), tactical approaches that are mostly distribution driven but not disruptive enough for people to reconsider the brand.

Let's take the vodka category. You may remember, a couple decades ago, the Stolichnaya and Smirnoff dominated the vodka market. Both being classic and authentic, they were trust brands. The packaging communicated authenticity and the power of the product's origin: vodka is Russian; the labels depicted shields, crowns, graphic icons, and symbols of the Czarist era. They were dominant vodka brands that traded mostly on images of authenticity, tradition, and elitism. Most liquors actually seem to trip over each other in order to communicate the same message of authenticity and qualified origins to win consumers' endorsement. From one liquor to another, the same message, the same emotion, the same design. Tradition without fizz.

Then Absolut Vodka was launched. In the word *Absolut* there is a statement and an emotion, an arrogance that speaks of unbridled youthful confidence, especially when associated with a branding design that broke all category codes. Absolut is a freedom brand. Instead of competing around the same old message of tradition and origin and understanding the emotional possibilities of a brand's experience, Absolut gives people permission to reconsider the category in a positive light. You could stand out and be rebellious, it says. The brand, which transformed its entire category, could transform you as well. We do not know yet just how far design can lead a brand toward success.

The brand, which transformed its entire category, could transform you as well.

An emotional strategy is best expressed by a design that connects with people in an immediate and provocative way. Design does that; it is the best way to signal a message. The design, then, becomes the center of the communication; it brings gravitas to a new idea. The Absolut bottle design influences the Absolut advertising campaign, as well as the attitude of the brand in ways that attract attention and trial. For example, if we compare vodka sales to gin sales over a period of twelve years, 1990 to 2002 (a time when cocktails became popular again, and, to be fair, we need to recognize that vodka is very neutral in taste compared to the more recognizable flavor of gin), the number of cases of gin sold dropped from 11 million to 9.7 million (ouch!), while the vodka franchise rose from 22 million to 36 million!

Absolut, which comes from Sweden (not Russia), packaged itself around a new design and not only changed the way people looked at the liquor category, but changed an industry as well. But Absolut did not cannibalize the category: *it inspired the category as a whole to be successful.* Today, if you go into any liquor store you'll see the dominance of vodka over any other type of liquor. In fact, I counted sixty-five different brands of vodka at a large New York liquor distributor, exactly the same number as imported whiskey brands, while there were only twenty-six brands of gin. Just one design changed perceptions, connected a brand emotionally with a new audience, and transformed a business.

Curious as I am, I wanted to find out how the category had expanded beyond Absolut and if the new products positioned themselves to copy Absolut or to create new brand niches for themselves. Expansion through flavors clearly brought some energy to the experience, but it was done best when expressed in an emotional way. Smirnoff, for instance, launched flavors under the brand "Smirnoff Twist" and gave a bite to the concept by packaging it in a twisted bottle. This move led to a 64-percent increase in sales from 1999 to 2002. The Smirnoff brand is now the category leader with 35 percent of all vodka sales. Could you imagine the impact if Coca-Cola or Pepsi changed the shape of their packaging when launching new flavors?

What is most intriguing is that in this vodka market you will find a product segmentation that matches the corporate emotional segmentation I describe in Shift 1. Absolut has kept its *freedom* brand quality, and Smirnoff, with its foray into the flavor business, has become a fun *harmony* brand. Ketel One, the Dutch brand, with its authentic label and Gothic graphics, handmade promise, and traditional recipes, fits nicely as a *trust* brand. Its sales have reached a 57-percent increase from 2000 to 2003. Grey Goose, with its beautiful graphics and connection to French origins, has taken over the *status* niche and has succeeded as the first real premium brand in this category, with a 30-percent price difference. It sold 1.4 million cases in 2003, more than five times its volume in 2000. The company has been acquired by Bacardi for almost $2 billion. Nuage, with its promise of purity and naturalness, is positioned as the perfect *citizen* brand, completing the emotional spectrum.

	CITIZENSHIP	FREEDOM	STATUS	HARMONY	TRUST
EMOTIONAL DRIVER	CITIZENSHIP	FREEDOM	STATUS	HARMONY	TRUST
CONSUMER ASPIRATION	"love of the world"	"love of thrill"	"love of class"	"love of tribe"	"love of ethics"
EMOTIONAL PROMISE	ENGAGEMENT	ESCAPE	GLAMOUR	CONVIVIALITY	SECURITY
CONSUMER MOTIVATION	doing good sustainability justice equality humanity	breaking out stimulation survival risk change	shine recognition predictability craft pleasure	sharing joy connection celebration renewal family	stewardship knowledge solutions heritage support

106

More brands are piling up trying to share in the growth of the vodka business, which has been spurred by Americans' return to the cocktail as the bar drink of choice. But each one of those brands fights for their own niche: Ciroc works well as a status brand to challenge Grey Goose, and Frank Ghery's Wyborowa trumps Absolut from a design perspective as a freedom brand. All are positioned emotionally, including the Colorado-born Pure Pleasure, a vodka that claims to use only pure mountain spring water from snow that melted thousands of years ago, which appeals to the naturalist side and works as the ultimate citizen brand.

Voluntarily or involuntarily, you can find a vodka that matches any of your emotional needs. In a business where taste is irrelevant and where one product cannot realistically compare itself to another, the emotional positioning is all the brand has to stand out in the marketplace. When there is little in terms of taste differentiation, brands must revolutionize their presence in order to convince consumers that they can enjoy a product that they might think of as generic. Now there are dozens of different vodka brands to choose from; you can even offer one with a sexier bottle design as a gift. Instead of caving into the monopoly of one brand style, the vodka category has expanded along emotional promises that allow every brand the opportunity to succeed by connecting with people's various desires.

One of the puzzles I have tried to solve is why, given its success, Absolut has veered toward a more functional, flavor-driven marketing strategy rather than occupying the emotional territories that were left open for other competitors to take. It let Grey Goose, for instance, occupy the premium position, which was a huge opportunity for Absolut. Still, the Absolut model fills pages of marketing analysis and will be the topic of business-strategy conversations in the future—not bad for a brand that was flatly rejected by research in the first place!

The Bahamas, Islands of Many Surprises

In a conversation with Joe Duffy, the president of Duffy & Partners, a leading American design firm, it did not surprise me to discover that this very talented designer had already made the jump into exploring the idea of "design as advertising." While riding the subway to work on a cold New York day, I was compelled by the vitality of the Bahamas print ad campaign. If you had asked me to tell you about any commercials advertising the Bahamas, I couldn't remember even one; and more importantly, if you had asked me to describe any print campaign I've seen in my years riding the subway, I probably couldn't mention one either. But this campaign took me out of my daily routine of reading the piles of newspaper and magazines that I carry and made me dream; it made me happy. The whole subway car felt like it was filled with sunshine.

I knew Joe Duffy had created the logo, but I was curious to see how he pulled together such an integrated iconic program. The Bahamas identity was commissioned through Fallon worldwide ad agency, which had gotten the project from the Bahamas visitor's bureau. Joe Duffy was able to convince the agency that this was a design-lead project and that design could add new dimensions to the power of the message. "Let me do a design campaign," Duffy said to Pat Fallon, the eponymous leader of the company, "before you do an advertising campaign." His wish was granted and evolved to be one of the most defining graphic design branding programs as advertising.

The Bahamas are a series of islands with different personalities, offering quite a variety of lifestyles. You can, for instance, chill out or indulge in the gaming and party frenzy at famed Atlantis. The diversity of these islands extends people's choices and ability to craft a personalized vacation, making the Bahamas' multifaceted offering that much more compelling.

But how do you communicate that feeling through a unique and proprietary language that will make the destination stand out among others? "Brand design gives people a feeling of what an experience is compared to listening to what the brand wants you to hear through a tactical thirty-second commercial," says Duffy. "We needed to paint the inside of the brand: its soul and emotions." If brand design is about painting and art, as Joe Duffy loves to explain while talking about his work in a metaphoric fashion, then we might be seeing the birth of the impressionist movement of branding.

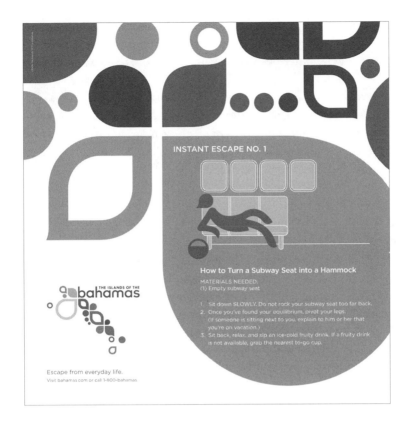

The Bahamas logo itself is an abstract expression of all the islands that form the Bahamas. It is expressed in a variety of colors so as to show diversity, the many choices and opportunities the islands have to offer. On the Web site, you can click on each island and discover the variety of choices to seek and experience. The logo is the message. "It is also, when you squint your eyes, a palette of textures and emotions that become a filter for verbal and visual decision," according to Duffy. Here, the logo is much more than just a signature at the bottom of the page; it is the essence of the brand, both its reality and dreams formalized. It has the vitality and imagination that lays the ground for a unique and robust message; it is the gate to new worlds and, in this case, the gate to our imagination and feelings.

"The logo is a true palette with which to paint a picture of the brand," concludes Duffy. And indeed, the agency has not lost the message. The print campaign is visually compelling and refreshing as it offers a unique graphic vocabulary inspired by the powerful logo style. It delivers a consistent message of fun and beauty. You see this brand and want to live in this brand, it touches you like no other destinations do.

What this means: identities become iconic through the deployment of a visual language that brings out the feelings brands want to convey and the feelings people are expecting across a variety of media and brand experiences. An iconic brand design campaign keeps on refreshing itself and, most importantly, stands out with a message that connects to our hopes.

"Dirt Is Good": Repurposing the Visual Language of Dirt

Laundry detergents have always been about fighting dirt and celebrating "whiter!" That is what Procter & Gamble had us believe very successfully for the longest time. For competitors such as Unilever, playing on the same product-focused approach meant very little hope to differentiate their brands from a formidable competitor. An alternative needed to be found that would help preserve Unilever's brand franchise. The only way a brand can compete in this category is to reframe the offering by shifting the product's fundamental benefit proposition to a new emotional identity.

The only way a brand can compete in this category is to reframe the offering by shifting the product's fundamental benefit proposition to a new emotional identity.

It starts with the brand itself. How do you bring to life a brand vocabulary that will support a good TV campaign but also do much more in changing people's perception of the brand itself at the retail level?

When Lowe, the advertising agency for Unilever at the time, proposed as an alternative to Procter & Gamble's dominance a more emotional approach that would resonate with consumers—the celebration of dirt as a positive way to communicate the brand message—the agency was breaking into interesting new grounds. By doing so they were in fact psychologically shifting the perception of this product category from a "head," or rational, perspective to a more emotional one by opening the doors for the brand to resonate in people's hearts, in their environments, and in their lives.

If you take most detergent brands, they all focus on good behavior and "cleanliness," which is the benefit of the product and the promise of most ad campaigns that claim "fighting dirt" as their strategic platform. Parents hate to see their kids dirty, feel the grunt of cleaning those clothes, and as a result this reinforces the sense that the parent-child relationship is a negative one. This does not help build harmony in the family and therefore love for the brand.

But is dirt really bad? It is my impression that, from a kid's perspective, or from my own past experiences, dirt might be a lot of fun after all. From an athlete's perspective, sweat is good and healthy. From a parent's perspective, seeing a child enjoy him/herself competing in a football, baseball, or rugby game is associated with stronger psychological and physical balance, since children tend to experience and discover life freely with all their senses. The will to win seen in a lot of sporting events is associated with a full engagement with life, which isn't always pretty, such as when one lunges for home plate, head first into the dirt. But it is always exciting.

There is a different way to look at dirt and mud: what about a mud bath? Or mud you trek through when hiking, mud you master when charging up- and downhill on a mountain bike? What about food fights, or food spilled on your ties, shirts, or dresses as a sign of enjoying good company, a relaxed atmosphere, freedom? Dirt from an emotional perspective is an object of fun and proof that we are enjoying our lives. Dirt becomes a freedom statement and an escape from the rigors of societal rules, a unique moment in our disciplined daily life. Dirt then is about joy, not crisis; positive emotional relationships, not chores!

Loving dirt is an emotionally transforming idea for a detergent brand. It speaks in a personal way to the challenges parents face, a challenge that not only includes "having to clean" but also the quality of the parent-child relationship as a whole and its impact on a child's life. From the parent's perspective, the celebration of dirt takes the pressure and emotional drama out of the equation. Detergent becomes something that is aspired toward and a tool for well-being, a powerful ally that takes anxiety out of our chores. Unilever brought the idea of joy into the brand relationship by building on this strategy. Its message is now about more fun, more dirt, more sweat. Live life, feel better; don't fight the dirt, embrace it. The detergent brands are here to take that "dirty" worry away; the brand is not an obstacle between you and fun, it is here to help you have *more* fun! This is the potential of an emotional shift. In this case, it was a great way to repurpose a category that had fallen into the abyss of commodity and price wars. Unilever had become a relationship-building brand.

A TRUE BRAND DISCOURSE NEEDS TO LEVERAGE A DESIGN PERSPECTIVE: VISUALIZING AN EMOTION

A powerful idea like this needed to be leveraged and connected to all communications material that inspired people to buy Unilever products. That powerful message needed to be expressed further in the packaging, the store environment, and the lifestyle of consumers.

That was the feeling of Unilever, and on that basis the company asked Desgrippes Gobé to find a way to connect the new message in a more intimate and long-lasting fashion. Brands need myths and myths need symbols, just as Nike is the expression of a brand attitude and the Apple logo a beacon of innovation. Those symbols have rich meanings that go beyond the product category to reassure, solidify, and continue to convey that the brand promise is still alive.

But could a symbol express an "advertising idea"? Products with an iconic and unusual shape such as Absolut Vodka or the Mini, for instance, have become ambassadors of a brand promise, but can a graphic symbol express an emotion and continue the dialogue with consumers after the TV is turned off? This was the fundamental question Desgrippes Gobé faced.

More importantly, the agency felt that this was a new way to approach branding from a more experiential perspective—from product to experience (the second commandment of emotional branding). Our belief was that commercials always fell short of carrying their message into consumers' lifestyles through the experience of the product. That gap needed to be closed and the bond established. Great commercials that have resonated with people have failed to create the expected sales results because the experience people have had with the product or the environment of the product was either unchanged, undifferentiated, or disconnected from an optimal message.

We felt that a symbol would carry the power of an idea further into the after-screen TV life to continue to resonate in people's experience with the product. Symbols are memorable and powerful enablers of the continued transmission of a message if the message indeed is profound, transformative, and above all relevant.

SPLAT! WAS BORN

Splat! is what Desgrippes Gobé called the organic star-shaped "dirt" graphic that now adorns most of the packaging expressions of Unilever detergents worldwide, including Omo, Skip, and Rinso. It brings beauty to the feared "dirty spot" and conveys a spirit of freedom and liberation for consumers.

Not unlike the dynamic ribbon or the Nike swoosh, the newcomer Splat! will also become a known identity for people who are looking for optimism in their lives. The symbol will sign all events and brand programs and bring parents and children closer to their detergents.

Unilever's detergent campaign was test marketed in Brazil with commercials that depict Neil Armstrong on the moon, Pelé playing soccer and falling in the mud, and century-old flying machines fumbling to the ground in a cloud of

dust. The Splat! logo made the cover of *Strategies*, a major advertising trade magazine in France, where it also received the coveted Grand Prix du Design for 2005.

Coca-Cola's Emotional Iconography

Coca-Cola's iconographic elements are the type of powerful brand assets that help build powerful emotional connections with people, if managed effectively. Clarifying the meaning of these brand assets helps to build people's positive perception of the brand and its promise. They are powerful tools when integrated into all forms of communication in a dynamic way. Based on Coca-Cola's packaging brief, we knew that we needed to communicate the key values of youthful spirit, energy, refreshment, and optimism, but we also knew that fundamentally the graphic expression would need to evolve to rely more on the emotional aspect of the brand.

Coca-Cola's iconic symbology needed to evolve and change to inspire consumers, including the famous contour bottle. How would you feel if you were still offered to drive the same Ford Mustang half a century later? Confusing memorabilia with renewed consumer experiences can lead to a message that stops engaging people emotionally. In the case of Coke, it does not mean discarding the old but constantly bringing in the new. The Mini and the Beetle have evolved new models, and Chanel 5 is not the only offering in Chanel's fragrance proposition; it is one of a multi-offering that connects with different groups of customers.

As we were designing the new visual language for Coca-Cola, we knew that we first had to make sense of the Coca-Cola iconography and its emotional meaning. Until we started this project, the visual iconography had been the same for decades, and a ubiquitous approach to sameness for the brand had dampened all the vitality such a brand can muster. All over the world the brand's iconic visual vocabulary was similar, dogmatic, and limited in its emotional expression. The example set by Target and the work we had done in the fashion industry were, for me, a new way to look at brand building, and we proposed what has become the first truly emotional interpretation and expression of the most recognized brand in the world.

Before   After

The new visual approach led to the creation of a better balance between the functional and the emotional. Our goal was to probe deeply into those visual assets to understand what each design communicated so that we could celebrate the unspoken brand promises with a new emotional language. On that basis, a clear graphic language could then be deployed not only in packaging but in presence graphics, in advertising, and in entertainment venues such as sports and on the Internet.

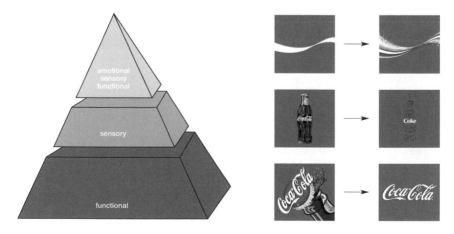

This led to three levels of consumer engagement, which we qualified as: Functional, Sensory, and Emotional. Functional was mainly supported by the Coca-Cola script and the red color. Sensory was associated with the contour bottle, and Emotional became the foundation for a new visual language and the basis for new packaging that centered around the dynamic ribbon.

WHAT EMOTIONS DOES MY ICONOGRAPHY ELICIT?

Coca-Cola has five major icons that have been haphazardly managed throughout the history of the brand, each with a different level of meaning and emotional connection with people. Our first step was to clarify the meaning of the brand and its communication goals. We asked the question: which of those visual assets needs to be brought forward to support the brand's growth and future, and how do we assign a role for each of those visual assets?

1. **The contour bottle:** The most mythic and recognizable of product icons, even more powerful than the Perrier bottle and Absolut vodka bottle.

2. **The dynamic ribbon:** The more modern visual icon, which offered a new global visual language and opportunity for the brand.

3. **The Coca-Cola script:** The most recognizable typography in the world and a signature of the brand's past and history.

4. **The red disk:** Mostly used as background for the contour bottle or script and mainly for retail expressions.

5. **The color red:** Particular to the context of the Coke can identity and promotional language.

All of these are valuable brand assets that articulate its vast iconography and its brand essence. The brand meaning and perception happens most often around people's experience with those icons, and their interpretation and expression is key for reinforcing a change in perception. As the brand strategically moved from a strictly sensorial and functional approach, as expressed in the "sensation" cans introduced in 2000 to be more emotional, it was time to update the brand's visual expression to champion emotional values the world could get excited about.

Desgrippes Gobé's objective was to communicate the key values and equities of the brand around a new contemporary authenticity. This gave us full liberty to proceed on a more updated visual program, and the team's endorsement of "emotional branding" as a strategy gave us the go-ahead to dissect and segment the brand's iconic values around a new emotional architecture. In play was a desire to update and contemporize the icons if necessary, to create new refreshment imagery and graphics that would invite young people into the brand.

With the help of the research discoveries made by Censydiam and our own observations, we were able to connect the icons with fundamental human motivations and various life experiences. This research led to the conclusion that some visual assets needed to be placed in order of importance and consumer connection to engage people in a new way. It led to the need to bring more innovation to the brand and connect it to the "gut" values of innovation, imagination, and visceral interaction.

Desgrippes Gobé acted upon these key steps in the activation of new emotional iconography for the Coca-Cola brand:

1. The return of the dynamic ribbon as an international emblem of the brand was the basis for the new visual architecture. The dynamic ribbon now signs all expressions of the brand manifestation and has the potential to become iconic like the Nike swoosh and Coke's most important international visual asset.

2. The introduction of the dynamic ribbon associated with the prominent role of refreshing bubbles added an element of thirst. This graphic association activates the sensory element of the brand experience.

3. The color yellow as a third color to be integrated into the red background provided another opportunity to create an optimistic and dynamic presence for the brand at the gut level. It also connected the brand to culture.

THE ARTICULATION OF A PRESENCE PROGRAM THROUGH HEAD, HEART, AND GUT

To connect the emotional brand meaning throughout all brand-presence materials and deploy the new graphics, we needed to identify and qualify different types of usage for the brand and the environments where it would resonate with people. The three most important emotional connections with consumers—head, heart, and gut—were the basis for an approach to activate and articulate for the first time a comprehensive visual program for Coca-Cola and its visionary progress.

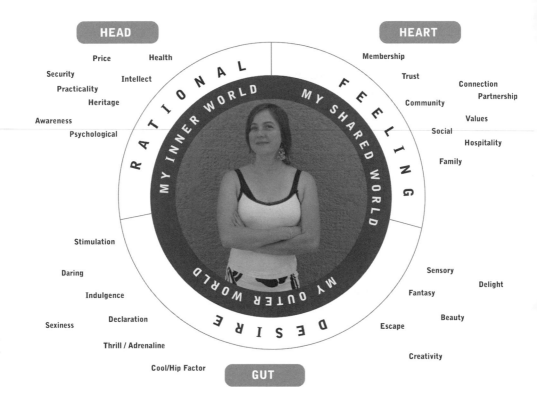

HEAD GRAPHICS need to make a rational connection and are used in literal communication, brand identity, corporate branding, and presentation templates. These are the graphics that need to be visible and recognizable. The red color and the Coca-Cola script are the most valuable assets in making that impact and consistency.

HEART GRAPHICS are created to be less about "impact" and more about "contact." They make a connection that is more sensorial and socially connected. These graphics are created to live in social areas, family outings, or sports events. They celebrate the product. The contour bottle is the ultimate statement of the brand experience, the best symbol of the brand's refreshing power and shared good times. When deployed in "play" areas such as the beach, popcorn bags at the movies, in transportation, at the airport, or in supermarket promotions, the contour bottle becomes the basis for the celebration of physical and spiritual well-being. The contour bottle celebrates the brand in a group or family context, in shared moments that are memorable and relaxing.

From a social and sustainability perspective, the red disk is also an interesting and underleveraged icon that could represent the world of Coca-Cola, given its round shape, and its impact on society. (We did not develop this idea in the program, but it has been a part of our thinking for the project.)

GUT GRAPHICS are created to emotionalize the brand and connect it with youth and the vitality of their lifestyle. You find great gut graphics in sports and music; those graphics live a different life, and they bridge the gap between our reality and a higher perception of life. Gut graphics are about bold statements and badge status; they are amazing, daring, and energizing; they are on painted walls, in nightclubs, on clothing, in radical posters, and in new product developments. They rock; they pop up; they create a buzz and get talked about. Nike and Adidas are two of the most powerful creators of gut graphics in marketing today, and our belief is that the dynamic ribbon could make it the third one.

Looking at the brand from a gut perspective led to innovations such as these new "slim cans."

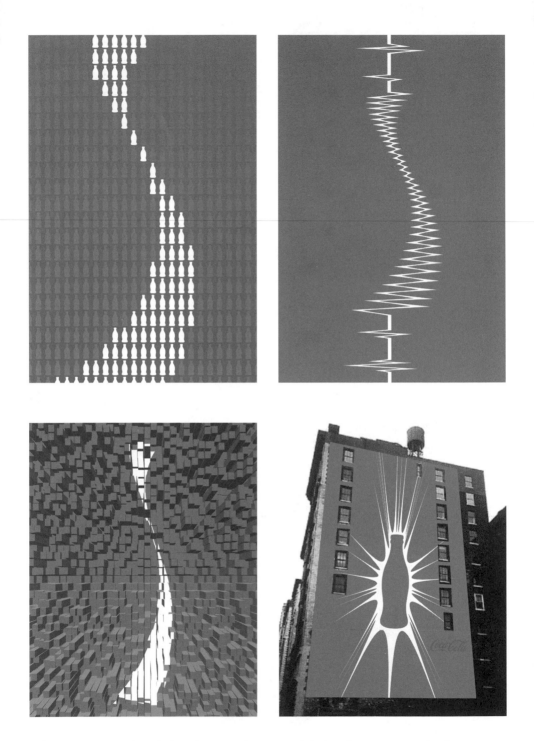

Energizing the Coke brand iconography to expand the brand's message emotionally.

These new visual assets were captured in a brand video as part of an overall communications program that would clarify and celebrate those core emotional and sensory opportunities. The video was designed to help the Coca-Cola organization believe in the enormous emotional power of the brand and give them liberty to imagine what it could be in their different markets. Our belief was that the lack of integration and understanding of those visual assets diluted the brand's overall impact. By using those iconic assets, a brand's connection to people can be made more powerfully, and Diet Coke was the first to leverage this new idea in recent commercials to great success.

Diet Coke understood the power of those visual connections and created an ad campaign that celebrates people's devotion to the brand. Making the connection between the advertising promise and the packaging's graphic language brought greater consistency, dynamism, and emotional impact to the TV commercials. Created by Foote Cone Belding, New York, the commercials feature actors Kate Beckinsale and Adrien Brody interacting with bubbles flowing from a Diet Coke can in an effervescent way.

Providing emotional definitions for Coca-Cola's iconic portfolio was a new approach that not only convinced management that the brand possessed a rich, dynamic, and underdeveloped emotional life, but also gave the organization the liberty to innovate and break the status quo for communications purposes. It opened the road to a unique and relevant visual language that would be felt by many.

The key is to build the type of unique visual iconography that will help differentiate your brand emotionally and expand, energize, and empower the advertising message in ways that are not yet used so that the brand is always welcomed and admired. Flexible, fun, and interactive, an iconic expression of a brand is brandjamming at its best, a powerful way to leverage those visual assets to build a brand that is full of sensations.

The War of the Icons

The iconic power and value of a brand's visual asset is best expressed in sports brands. We all know there is a logo war out there between brands such as

Nike, Puma, and Adidas, the stakes being so high in winning the hearts of people with a symbol. We all know about the Nike swoosh, the Puma visual, and the Adidas stripes: they are ubiquitous, recognizable, savvy, and have adorned the wardrobes of most sports celebrities we are in awe of.

The recognition of these icons has been the result of billions of dollars spent on advertising, sports events, athlete endorsements, and retail presences. So why is it so important that my logo not only be recognized but also desired; why is it that those logos are so special we don't mind carrying them around on our bags, T-shirts, or shoes?

More than anything else, a visual expression of an idea when emotionally connected becomes the manifestation of our most profound emotions and feelings. This is why we cry when our national flag is raised after one of our own athletes has won an Olympic medal. The flag is more than just a piece of cloth with some graphics on it; it is the visual expression of who we are, who we want to become, and what we believe in. And the ownership of this belief is at the core of the marketing wars that make brands spend millions to protect their visual franchise. The emotional perception of those visual icons can impact the success or failure of a business, or at least have a huge impact on their sales.

I have always believed that among all sports icons the most powerful and smartest is Adidas. The reason for this, I think, is that those three stripes are powerfully adaptable to any scale of fashion items in a way that others are not. Let's face it, the Nike swoosh has its limitations outside of its signature statement, and Puma also. Adidas's dynamic three stripes adorn their clothing in ways that make them more stylish and more visible from a marketing perspective. Most importantly, they make the person feel more athletic wearing them.

The debate has now taken on biblical proportions and finally has come to its logical conclusion—the courts!—though in an unsportsmanlike fashion: the courts of law. Both Nike and Puma, the leading sports brands in the world, have admitted the fact that those Adidas stripes are superior to their iconic portfolio and have lobbied the International Tennis Federation to ban the famous stripes on all players' clothing in all four grand slam events.[2] Athletes have always been authorized to wear their sponsors' logos on their clothes, but both Nike and Puma feel that the three-stripes graphic included in the styling of the products the athletes wear gives an unfair visual advantage to Adidas. In return, Adidas is fighting back and is seeking an injunction to stop this ban and retain the right to express its visual style in a way that pleases Adidas. The war of the swoosh versus the stripes has begun, and we will not see the end of it anytime soon.

Air France's Visual Touch

An airplane could be a store, a restaurant, a movie theatre, a lounge, or a hotel. What does a great advertising campaign mean if the inside of that plane is not right, the service bad, the lounges dirty, the movies uninteresting, and the food horrible? How can you make people dream if you are not a dreamer yourself? When approached to create a new emotional identity for Air France, Desgrippes Gobé was asked to create a visual and sensory vocabulary that conveyed the look and feel of the brand at all points of contact with the consumer. This included not only the graphics style but also the design of the passenger lounges, the styling of the cabins and the seats, and the design of the restaurant accessories and all printed material, including menus and informational brochures.

The idea was to create an emotional experience through design that would serve as the inspiration for a memorable Air France experience. I personally was not involved in the project—it fell under our Paris office's responsibilities—but as I explain in my second book, *Citizen Brand*, I followed the creative process with great interest. Born on a farm in western France, I remember vividly watching the Paris–New York supersonic Concorde as a child. The symbolic white trail of smoke left on a blue sky represented for me all of my aspirations. I dreamed of being on that plane one day, or to be where it was headed in the future. So when our creative director used the symbol of the white trail of smoke as the basis for the Air France project's creative inspiration, I could not help but be enamored with the work. Both the creative team in Paris and I shared the same dream; we wanted to attach the same story to the brand in order to inspire people.

Air France is one of the most successful airlines in the world, and I can only feel pride in knowing that our story has been part of a company message that has reached people positively. Later, when Desgrippes Gobé was asked to style the Air France first-class and business-class cabins, we made comfort a priority for the brand image in selecting material and colors that would be elegant and soothing. This was revealed to Air France travelers through our design of the red passenger pillows, which incorporated embroidery and the Air France insignia. The pillow, a physical, sensorial object, acted as a symbol of the "sweet dreams" the airline would provide for its customers. The new identity of Air France was fashioned from a people perspective, an emotional perspective, which led to a warm and elegant expression of the culture and charm of France.

Urban Art as an Emotional Message

How more emotive could the work of Christo and Jeanne Claude be? They create art on a grand scale that only stays up for a few weeks but lives in our hearts and minds through photography, films, and books. Technological progress has given creators a new medium—earth! Art today does not have to be hung in a museum forever but lives among us for everyone to enjoy before disappearing forever, saved only by our technology-made memories. Christo is a designer, an entrepreneur, and a capitalist; none of his art would be possible if not planned to finance itself. In an age of consumerism and entertainment, beauty needs to participate in the joy of life. The elitist approach to art that resides only in the dining room of the ultra rich is contrary to what Christo is imagining. His work is for the many to see in the greater living room of our coasts, bridges, public buildings, and parks. The tour de force is to convince everyone on the validity of the project and sell a vision before it could be realized, a democratic process that is not unlike the process of branding. The work is created in order to be shared by all. His work is inspiring as it brings beauty for the public to experience; it is a message of freedom and vitality, reminding us that life is beautiful and precious.

With *The Gates* (planned in 1983 and finally brought to life twenty-two years later in 2005) erected in Central Park, Christo challenged the world to see life differently, to use our imagination and interpret reality through a different visual vocabulary. It is a provocation and a dare, a flash of color that entered the lives of New Yorkers for just a short moment but like lightning highlighted the power of our combined imagination if we choose to exercise it. Design is about that dare, that teasing, that motivation to discover feelings that bring the good out from within us. What Christo resurrected is our craving for newness and beauty, our craving for the surprising and the pushing of human limits that seems always to be our biggest hurdle and frustration. By showing a flash of genius, we all feel genius, we all feel blessed and awakened to a greater reality. Christo and Jeanne Claude bring out in their work our emotive aspirations.

This work will do more for the notoriety of New York and tourism than any advertising campaign could ever dream of achieving at no cost to the city. With Christo's help, New York showed the world that optimism and innovation is more than ever part of New Yorkers' passion for art. And as usual they are not shy to flaunt it.

Cirque du Soleil

Anyone who has seen Cirque du Soleil's famous blue and yellow striped "tent," their logo, and their show knows instantly what he will find and the type of experience he will have. Between the identity, the look and feel of the brand, and the style of the performances, there is a cohesive tone and feeling that is unique to them and highly recognizable. Their shows are about pushing the limits not only of human performances but also the limits of our imagination. "Imagination is more important than knowledge" is the quote from Albert Einstein that Guy Laliberte, the founder and CEO of Cirque du Soleil, likes to use when speaking about his show, and there might be something to learn here for brands as well. Its brochure reads, "Entertainment is ephemeral as it lives only in the imagination of the spectators." This inspires Cirque du Soleil to always invent and inspire its public.

From a branding perspective it seems that the philosophy of this entertainment business reflects exactly who they are and what they do. Their unique logo representing a smiling sun designed with the graphic attitude you find in the clothing of Italian clowns sets the tone for the unexpected "tent" that was the earlier venue before their permanent move to Las Vegas. "SPECTACULERA"—the naming itself is a unique language that fits the imaginative universe of the brand and is consistent with the promise.

From then on everything is an unparalleled, magical experience: clowns mock you when you enter the arena, the décor transports you to a different place, and the mesmerizing show itself is a pure jump into the world of fantasy as you never have experienced before.

The brand is a promise; it is designed as a promise and feel all the way to the end. The powerful culture of Cirque du Soleil is perfectly integrated with its product and passion, one vision perfectly articulated and executed. No wonder Cirque du Soleil prides itself on its humble street origins and commitment to donating 1 percent of its revenue to programs that support corporate citizenship for young people. This attitude helps them connect with the public they are entertaining but also creates loyalty with their artists. Internally, they have created a grant that supports the emergence of new ideas to help employees participate in the creative content of the programming. Is this brandjamming, or what?

Cirque du Soleil's unique and consistent brand iconography.

Typography, or the Language of Iconicity

My wife and I always love to go with some friends to see Handel's *Messiah* performed at St. John the Divine, the famous cathedral in New York City. It is impossible not to be transported by the magnitude of this piece, the sound of the chorus, the instruments, the Gothic environment. This musical masterpiece is unique in its beauty and power. For me it is an exquisite experience of beauty and inspiration.

During what is a riveting two-and-a-half-hour nonstop concert, I have the tendency to let my mind wander and let my subconscious bring visual expressions of what I feel in those particular moments. It is dreaming and plunging at the same time into a new reality created by the emotional content of the concert. Music always helps transport me into a creative visual self-discovery.

What was new for me was the experience on one particular night: Gothic typography! Gothic typographic characters, meaning the alphabet, kept flashing through my mind. I must have been influenced by the cathedral's Gothic beauty. One character in particular kept flashing before my eyes: the Gothic letter *T*.

I am not superstitious and do not believe that I have any special connection with heaven, so I discarded any signs that would otherwise be of a religious significance or calling and did not draw any conclusions. I thought of the typography that elegantly crowns the front page of the *New York Times*. One letter, a gothic one I thought, one powerful letter could define by itself such a compelling message and define style and beauty with authority. The curvy Gothic type, with its thick and thin nuances and powerful structure, has always seemed to me to be about life, authority, beauty, discipline, and imagination.

And then I realized that the *T* I was thinking of was the title of the *New York Times Style* magazine. Of course, *that T*, in the top left corner of the front page, stood alone in its pure magnificence, with such authority and confidence. That letter was an ultimate statement of style in a language that seemed to define who it was as a brand, in a language that defined its authority. Not unlike Coca-Cola, the typographic style of the *New York Times* is certainly one of the most recognizable in the world, but I could only think that this "established" typeface could also be cool and lose its seriousness without losing its authority while on the front page of an artistic lifestyle supplement. What a way to extend a product and make it stand out.

The music was inspiring, the thought engaging, so I started to write on the back of my program, trying to put my thoughts together and jot down my inspiration. The mezzo-soprano was just then singing, "Then shall the eyes of the blind be opened, and the ears of the deaf be unstopped. Then shall the lame man leap as a hart, and the tongue of the dumb shall sing."

The fact that my mind was thinking Gothic that night is an example of the mysterious ways creativity intuitively connects thoughts through visualization. That fiery, authoritative style of characters, the official typography of the church and the one that decorated ancient manuscripts before printing was even invented, intrigued me. Often found on the facades of government buildings, the Gothic typeface expresses authority. The character, which has a Germanic heritage, was used during the Second World War on most German army signage as the writing of fear and dominance. Gothic type illustrates all those medieval stories we were told when we were children. But now it is also a favorite of the hip-hop scene. Gothic is hip and the new cool type gracing the front of T-shirts, music albums, and even Reebok's advertising. It seems to define that scene, the power, the badness all in one message. The success of Kettel One vodka might have something to do with the typography of its label and advertising.

The type clearly has reached celebrity status, and inspires respect. The emotion of younger generations seeking relief from the fake to the authentic and to heritage is clearly projected by this type. How much meaning a type can convey is sometimes an obvious but underestimated visual vocabulary that can define a brand's culture and character. Another interesting observation is to see how graphics and their emotional content can be appropriated by different groups and given new meanings. Most importantly, the Gothic type is "iconic" and a brand in itself, lending its own power of iconicity to any brand that dares to use it.

Iconicity indeed is a trait of the *New York Times* and only they could have pulled this off with such smartness and panache. That letter alone standing there, noble, beautiful, elegant, majestic, the quintessential essence of the paper, crystallizes in one mark the expression of both leisure and fashion. Both an iconic typeface and an iconic paper blend their messages in the most provocative and modern way by reinterpreting the old in the new.

A typeface is ownable and should be proprietary. (Now I am writing furiously, and this is the object of scorn by some concert attendees.) Designers create typographic alphabets that are the unique signature of a brand and for only those brands to use. It is an amazing way to reinforce a brand image and message when used. The writing style of a company can be differentiated, recognizable, memorable, and a statement about who the company is.

"Let's break their bonds asunder, and cast away their yokes from us!" continues the chorus.

It reminds me of when I spent four years in design school in Paris in a very strict and academic environment where everything had to be rationalized to justify the creative process—which was a surprise for me, who thought that I would have a great time designing posters and advertising commercials. The training was rigorous, with the first year dedicated to copying and then inventing a type style. We did not have any computers, and we had to do everything by hand with compasses, rapidographs, and antiquated tools. If you messed up one serif on one letter of the alphabet, you had to start all over again—which I did over and over again, spending nights crying and trying to achieve perfection, until I realized that a typeface is not about technicality or precision, but emotions. If you befriended the type, it would be easier to create beauty with it without making any mistakes. Breaking through the obvious to find the core personality and essence of the type made the project so much more pleasurable, and so I learned how to respect it and love it.

By understanding a typeface's unique personality, its guts, by building its powerful meaning, you get closer to the reality of human life and can reveal a brand's true beauty and style. A magical moment happens when a new typeface comes to life. But the best moment is to experience the harmony created by the different letters of an alphabet when joined to form words—it is a great feeling and aesthetic pleasure.

At this point I was looking at the musicians playing in the concert and suddenly connected typography to notes of music. Not unlike a musician, who understands how all individual aspects of the music—notes, rhythm, harmony—come together to create the total musical piece, the typographic designer understands how all the aspects of type design come together to form a complete and harmonious family of characters. It all comes together, giving shape to words, the merger of the invisible with the expression of the meaning. It is a work of craftsmanship unique in the feeling and accomplishment it provides.

Why would we have to do this? I asked my professor once, knowing that in a professional environment we would never have the time to do type by hand, and that prefab characters were available commercially. For respect, was his answer. You know now how to appreciate the power of typography. His most famous project was always to ask us to design the cover of a matchbook to see if we could create beauty in such a mundane, tiny space—"with no more than three letters please!"—something that would be seen and recognized by everyone in a café.

Beauty is not a question of size, but personality and resolve. In a visual world where we are always faced by new messages, how does one stand out, how do you fill the gap between people with an identity that has cultural relevance, that is iconic in its expression? Iconic brands need to build a graphic language that will be music to our eyes. They need to build a language that communicates that feeling one letter at a time.

What this means: *First, the financial assets of a company are rooted very deeply in its visual assets. Far too little investment is directed to protect or explore the emotional power of those visual assets as the best means of connection with people's lives. "Visual management" should be a priority, on par with if not more than advertising, because an ad or a commercial will be more effective if supported by a recognizable and meaningful graphic language. Without that, a commercial will feel mostly emotionless.*

SHIFT 3

Think Advertising as Experiences

Advertising is still very much alive and among the best media for building brands. The word *among*, however, signals a shift in the one-time dominance of television commercials and emphasizes the medium's relative impact in a vastly *diverse* consumer market and media world.

Historically, advertising has been one of the most significant factors in a brand's success in democratic countries and the first communication tool to leverage the new power of radio and television to promote corporations and their products. In fact, advertising benefited greatly from the robust postwar growth of the world economy but has also been one of its most powerful actors, energizing people's appetite for a vast array of new product offerings. Advertising helped build entire new businesses, such as Frank Perdue's family farm, which has become a giant chicken processor employing 20,000 people and with sales close to $3 billion.[1]

American advertising then was revered all over the world: a dynamic, thirty-second commercial was like an Academy Award–winning feature and ad people were like celebrities. Fifteen-percent commission on media buying was the norm and provided rewarding revenue streams and compensation to all. Advertising attracted some of the most brilliant creative people into its midst. But most importantly, *it worked!* It reflected the dominant "modern" approach to marketing at a time when factories were the heroes and advertising worked as a welcomed "push" message that brought constant discovery through, at that time, a new and magical platform: television. It addressed a fairly homogeneous consumer field looking for a continuous flow of new product choices, with the wallets that measured up to those new offerings. Unbridled innovation was the norm; it was the birth of what is now known as the "consumer" or "market" economy.

From "advertising" to "consumer democracy"

Advertising was a growth business that attracted financial investors who, through acquisitions and mergers, built mega communications empires to serve the marketing needs of multinational corporations. The model was exponential, as more people across the globe bought televisions and radio sets. Mega-brand strategies were the rave—the same product for everyone everywhere and the whole world endorsing the same values and beliefs as defined by the brands. Brands were teaching the world to sing in harmony . . . "our" harmony!

Freedom of Choice

The twenty-first century has brought a new set of challenges for marketers and the traditional advertising model. The world has shifted away from a business, consumer, and media perspective. Globalization, price competition, falling profits, a more fragmented audience and media vehicles, a glut of new products, a more diverse distribution offering, and the short lifespan of innovation has forced corporations to limit their growth expectations and fight on price and promotions for products or services in order to convince a new consumer reality. The consumer democracy based on "freedom of choice" reflects people's empowerment and desires. The tables have turned: people are empowered in their choices. Manufacturers under pressure and frustrated by their loss of control over the multiple new elusive target audiences have erroneously continued to try reaching people with the same communication tools by spending more in channels that were already screaming of overload.

The twenty-first century has brought a new set of challenges for marketers and the traditional advertising model.

Advertising Is No Longer in Step with Consumers

TV, radio, print ads, and billboards that used to be the lead placement for advertisers have been challenged by cable television, the Web, entertainment branding, retail innovation, podcasts, and blogs. Most importantly, the convergence of all those media around an interactive information-sharing process that drives people to move from one medium to the other is the most fundamental change in recent years. Through text messaging, for instance, my daughter was able to move about forty people one New Year's Eve from one bar to another in a matter of minutes.

At the brand level, this is also how decisions are being made—swift and irrevocable; final decisions whether to buy or not, shop or not, will be made using new connections that bypass traditional mass media, leaving broadcast and print advertising as we know it transformed into something new and most likely interactive.

"Mobile" devices that reflect society's mobile lifestyle are becoming the main source of information. Cell phones now are bringing commercial-free content to viewers where they want it when they want it. From the iPod, the iPod Nano, GPS, handheld electronic devices that help you bet online while watching a sports game, the billboard you can connect with electronically, the cup of coffee you carry around that has "Inkbyte" messaging you can interface with, to the electronic armbands you listen to while running—we are living an active life of connective mobility. We are constantly connected to each other. Most importantly we are in control of the communications we want to interface with.

This is the opposite of today's advertising model that relies only on "fixed" media to offer messages that you can't avoid. In a postmodern world where everything is experiential and in motion, we can see the limitations traditional advertising is facing and the great divide that separates the push, one-claim advertising world from the reality of today's market. The fact that people are spending more of their time on the Web—some 32 percent according to industry information—is slowly but surely being understood by marketers who have an influence on the media landscape. The impressive success of Web sites such as YouTube, MySpace or JibJab is showing an open and interactive model of communication that reflects a new generation of viewers. On Adage.com, a survey conducted quarterly by TNS Media Intelligence on Fortune 500 CMOs revealed that more of the companies' ad dollars will be diverted toward online spending, projecting to be $16.6 billion or an increase of 32 percent over the year before.[2] More and more, it's becoming harder to understand why so little money—only 5 percent of the total advertising budget—is spent online.

The fact that people are spending more of their time on the Web—some 32 percent according to industry information—is slowly but surely being understood by marketers who have an influence on the media landscape.

NOT ONLY IS BROADCAST-BASED ADVERTISING OUT OF STEP, IT IS ALSO OUT OF TOUCH

There is a media revolution going on that will have massive effects on the way advertising communications are made. Although, as of this writing, television and print still reign as the main advertising media, the major network companies are seeing consumer changes in their consumption of information and are moving fast to create experiences through venues outside of traditional broadcast stations, on alternative platforms such as Google Video and YouTube.[3] NBC universal and CBS broadcasting are choosing to make top shows available via video on-demand services. "We have great content, what we need are new revenue streams," says CBS CEO Leslie Moonves.[4]

What broadcast stations are trying to understand is the new way people are paying for content. If people can download 90-cent songs, why couldn't they download TV programs for a fee? Apple is training a new generation to pay for self-selected music—why not great sitcoms? It's in the works. ABC struck a deal in 2005 to have episodes of its hit *Desperate Housewives* available for download on Apple video iPods for $1.99 each. Broadcast TV stations might soon be a different animal altogether as podcasts of all kinds become more relevant, received anytime, anywhere on individual mobile screens.

THE GREAT DIVIDE

The lack of comprehension of the new media and the migration of people toward this media does not help solve a lack of understanding between the branding world looking to forcefully control the minds of people and the consumer world looking for innovation and new experiences in an open forum. The media proliferation that offers more options for people to get content, the counterintuitive tactics of media organizations, and a poor understanding of the relationships people want to have with brands is building a divide between brands and people. "Audiences are splintering off in dozens of directions, watching TV shows on iPods, watching movies on videogame players, and listening to radio on the Internet," say Brian Steinberg and Suzanne Vranica[5] in The Wall Street Journal.

The gap is so large and the misunderstanding so great that instead of focusing on the product experience and refreshing ideas, marketers continue to push undifferentiated or unappealing offerings supported by massive media investment. Tons of media glut is being served to unwilling buyers by media con-

glomerates with no interest in how people will live with the magnitude of information. It is almost as if they think yelling louder will get through and create an emotional bond with a brand.

Worse, the focus on advertising tonnage through expensive traditional broadcast media to promote products that are not relevant or stimulating enough frustrates consumers. The false belief that this approach will create sales and success for any product, particularly those people don't care about, is clouding the most important focus that marketers should be concerned with: the importance of great product ideas that sell themselves. There are so many hyped-up and undelivered promises created at huge expense to companies that consumers are losing their belief and confidence in any promises that the world of advertising makes. The focus is so much on TV that other more potent opportunities are left behind. When Jim Stengel, head of marketing for Procter & Gamble, is quoted as saying that television commercials are losing their punch and that thirty-second commercials have eroded the ability of advertisers to reach consumers, you know something has changed.[6]

Valerie Seckler, in a *Women's Wear Daily* article, brings forward the nascent idea that commercials are often better than the products they promote and that the established idea that great advertising automatically leads to increased sales is not a reality today. In this article an executive for Levi's admitted that her purchase measures were flat even though the brands attracted strong response from their ads.[7] This gives a bad name to branding in general, as expressed by Roy Disney to the board of directors of the Walt Disney Company in venting his frustration: "Branding is what you do to cows. Branding is what you do when there is nothing original about your product."[8]

From a financial perspective, it is worth looking at the advertising model to figure out why so many billions can't buy success. Is it the lack of creativity in commercials, as some claim, or a lack of interest in a product? Why are so many manufacturers, such as the American auto industry, for instance, not getting leverage off their billion-dollar ad budgets, when Toyota seems to do fine? Is the public turned off by the sheer glut of advertising, or is it upset by the low-quality offerings manufacturers keep pushing?

It might be time to reconsider the strategy of believing that "dumping" ads on top of the advertising glut will resolve a brand's poor performance. Even Coca-Cola recognizes that problem when it comes to understanding the new mood prevailing among its customers and its relationship with advertising. As Katie Bayne, a senior vice president at Coca-Cola North America, says, "We're not just going to shove commercials at people, because they will go away."[9]

In going over the Nielsen monitor and other industry sources, you get a rough idea of the kind of money brands are spending. What struck me is that the more your brand is innovative, designed, esteemed, and trusted, the less you have to spend on advertising! Spending more on advertising, to paraphrase Katie Bayne, seems to be the realm of brands that have a tough time competing. Target, for instance, spends on average $602 million a year and Sears, $770 million. This is nearly the same amount, and yet look how much more notoriety Target gets. Why does Apple spend $155 million while Microsoft spends $463 million? Why does Red Bull spend only $51 million, versus Coca-Cola's $426 million? Red Bull is a much smaller brand than Coca-Cola, yet is as well known worldwide. What about Ikea's $25 million versus Kohl's $166 million? Starbucks' $36 million versus McDonald's $742 million? What is it that Armani with $15 million, Tommy Hilfiger with $21 million, and Ralph Lauren with $37 million do to create such notoriety for their brands, while others spend far more without getting the same great results?[10]

Does spending more money in traditional media buy results?

Source: TNS Media Intelligence, copyright 2006.
Figures rounded to the nearest million; includes TV, radio, print, outdoor and internet (display only).
*Includes Sears and Kmart.

The debate has become so hot in branding circles that a new villain had to be recognized as the source of the problem. And guess what? The thirty-second TV commercial got the honor! Not the media glut and the lack of product innovation, not the lack of courage by some marketers to innovate, not the lack of trust brands created when they failed to deliver on a promise . . . no, no, no! It is the TV commercial and its perceived lack of creativity. Is it the advertising commercials that are losing their punch or the product offering that has no punch at all?

Rather than calling for the death of the thirty-second spot, media creators should be resurrecting it. The thirty-second commercial needs to regain its former gloss as one of the messengers of great promises. Good TV spots that promote the great products people want to find out about will always be welcomed in people's lives. If great commercials can migrate to different venues, they can become cultural markers like other communication tools. They can help to celebrate great products, though not without the passion of every marketer to make products that people really want.

"The whole model needs to go to rehab, there is an addiction on the part of powerful media conglomerates to wanting to beat consumers over the head. Clutter on TV is the number-one complaint by viewers," says Joe Plummer, a former ad executive and the chief research officer at ARF. "The problem is not only the clutter of ads but the clutter of products that do not add value to people's lives. And it is not just because the company has the cash that those bad ideas need to make their way into our living rooms."[11]

In the twenty-first century it is finally time to recognize that there are other forms of more intuitive nontraditional media. The relevance and power of programs such as cause marketing, reputation-building on the Web, and experiences through retail expressions, design strategies, and packaging have as much, if not a greater, impact on people. Those initiatives, until recently considered marginal or add-ons, are actually the *real thing* in terms of creating a lasting impact in an emotional economy. This is where some of the advertising broadcast money now has to be spent, to connect with people's lifestyle realities.

TV Does Not Know Who You Are—the Internet Does

What's more, broadcast advertising can be unwelcome, especially to those people who are not in an ad's target group. TV-only advertising is increasingly becoming nothing but an overwhelming "push" medium that misses on the opportunity to customize its message.

"Content is no longer pushed at consumers, it is pulled by them," says Sir Howard Stringer, Sony's chairman and chief executive, as he revealed Sony's new focuses: high-definition video; audio technology; digital cinema; video gaming; and e-entertainment. In his presentation, according to the article, Stringer said he believes that this reflects consumers' desires for more choice and convenience in how they access entertainment.[12] I believe this is exactly applicable to advertising: people want more choices in how they access their brands' communications.

People want more choices in how they access their brands' communications.

The Internet, on the other hand, knows you personally. Amazon knows your choices, AOL knows the content and functions you need. Google knows how to find what you need—to the point that the government is all over those media trying to find more information about who you are and what you do. The

Yahoo!s and Googles of the world are becoming legitimate power brokers and seek to build on digital television the same presence they have online, as if the future of television will be virtually subsumed by the Internet. From a creative perspective, I am looking forward to the birth of "video ads," the new form of cool and connected advertising commercials not unlike music videos people download and pay for. Just as video clips are commercials for bands, video ads will act as cool commercials for brands. Would that mean that Pampers will have to "rock" or Campbell's Soup to jazz? Unlikely, but many brands have the capacity to thrive in this way as the opportunities become available. Music could also be a new vehicle to reach consumers and create new revenue streams. Grey Worldwide, a global agency and part of the WWP group, wants to make "hit records" of the songs it uses in commercials, creating revenue for the agency from those sales.

Against the Tide

As companies change their approach, more robust technological players will taken on the responsibilities (outside of creating content) once handled by ad agencies. This evolution will provide for more flexible and intuitive interaction with people.

Digital is the beginning of a challenge for the media-buying industry as major players like Google will be brokering and distributing most media buying and content across multimedia platforms. What Google will bring is the customization and distribution of digital messages based on its rich understanding of the consumer's interface with digital media, and the flexibility to migrate people across different digital "touch points."

For instance, a commercial spot on Google could be changed at the last minute based on a specific current event or a new direction in consumer preference, giving extreme flexibility to marketers. Google is seeking the partnership of advertising agencies for content but soon will be able to reach people through its own rich connection with various digital media, including radio and television.

ADVERTISING MUST TAKE PART IN BRANDJAMMING

A postmodern society is challenging the advertising business by redefining the notion of brand control; it wants to liberate itself from the dogmatism of traditional branding. It is throwing the entire industry into a state of shock and doubt, even though the advertising world doesn't fully realize this yet. The old modernist "push" model of advertising goes against the reality of an empow- ered, marketing-savvy consumer who prefers to choose "on demand," having the freedom to access information at will. Consumers in the twenty-first cen- tury are in charge of their lives, and they want control over how they will interface with the brand's communication. The message itself will have to adapt to reach people in a more participatory fashion, inviting people to engage in a more direct and richer shopping experience.

A case in point is the success of shopping networks such as QVC in reaching women. Those shopping networks are the little-known secret in building brands. I have a friend who has built a career on QVC and would not have been able to launch her brand in the complicated and expensive maze of tra- ditional distribution. She is not the only one. In a *Wall Street Journal* article, the writer explains how a retailer "vaulted her luxury cosmetics line through QVC onto the national stage and boosted her sales by 33 percent—all without spending a dime on advertising."[13]

If we add the fact that because of this exposure she has also been contacted by venture capitalists and her Web site has registered a 16-percent rise in sales (according to the article), we see how this is certainly a valid way to build brands. Leslie Blodgett, president and CEO of Bare Escentuals, explained in a profile article how she was able to build her business from $6 million to $150 million by leveraging QVC. "The old style of connecting with people is coming back," she says as an entrepreneur and now best-selling vendor in this format.[14]

Shopping networks in reality are ongoing commercials, with instant sales attached to them. They are woman-friendly in terms of their presentation, and I have not yet found a "Crazy Eddie" (the 1980s' infamous screaming spokesperson for a now-defunct electronics store) style of presentation in this network. For packaged goods companies such as a cosmetics company, design is critical as it is the message and the appeal, the product dress, that is key and the center of attention. Plus, there is so much sincerity that comes through these women selling their wares; they clearly love their stuff.

Those real-life "commercials" don't have to worry about TiVo, but they sure are bringing a free and willing audience to their brands. The technique is being "poo-pooed" by the industry as a low-brow type of communication, but it works. Bath & Body Works has added infomercials to promote its Patricia Wexler MD dermatology skin care collection with Christie Brinkley as the spokesperson. Camille McDonald, a marketing executive at BBW, is quoted as saying, "Infomercials are a viable retail channel for any brand that has a multi-dimensional, highly differentiated story to tell."[15] This is what branding is all about. A captive audience on TV waiting to be sold, what else do you need? Direct selling is in a subliminal way an example of the relationship people want to have with a brand: respectful, trustworthy, engaging, and low key.

One Hot Ticket

Companies today will need to recapture lost audiences by using their imagination to reach people through cross-media outreach. "No More Same-Old," reads a headline in the *New York Times*, and "GM Signals a New Marketing Era" in *Ad Age*, flagging "the brand's continued step away from traditional network TV advertising."[16] Panasonic, meanwhile, has dropped its otherwise successful traditional ad agency in 2005 to "find one that is more holistic, capable to handle new approaches such as events, internet promotion, and other activities beyond traditional marketing."[17]

When Stuart Elliott, the *New York Times* journalist covering advertising, returned from the 2005 meeting of the American Association of Advertising Agencies, he did not exactly bring back breaking news. Elliott observed major heads in American advertising lamenting the fact that consumers are "ignoring messages with increasing frequency," claims that clients seek "the power of the big idea," and assertions that "the challenge for our industry is to make advertising a business of ideas instead of a business of ads and their distribution."[18]

> **More than $90 billion is spent by the top one hundred advertisers every year, $6.7 billion in research and $52 billion in media, but if you go to any supermarket or car showroom to see the result of that investment, there is certainly cause for concern!**

If the advertising business is frustrated with itself, it is easy to understand why marketers are frustrated with the agencies they hire. More than $90 billion is spent by the top one hundred advertisers every year, $6.7 billion in research and $52 billion in media, but if you go to any supermarket or car showroom to see the result of that investment, there is certainly cause for concern![19] Anyone can see in a supermarket or other retail environment the weakness of brands on the shelves, the parity and commodity feel of most offerings, and how many products are sold only on promotion, if they are ever sold at all. There is a lot of money spent to support the same old tired products when the best "news" is the products themselves, their design innovation, and their potentially imaginative message.

"What is the future of branding, Madame Irma?"

"Your product will not evolve. You will not create waves. You will not take risks. You will spend $95 billion a year on research and advertising."

The Super Bowl ads, which are the most expensive in the world, provide another example of mismatched advertising. Why during most Super Bowl broadcasts, which admittedly are and always have been mostly for a testosterone-driven, beer-infused male audience (does anyone ever see the second half sober?), would both beer and soft drink marketers promote their sissy "diet" drinks?

The 2006 Super Bowl was no exception, demonstrating how so much spectacular creative talent is spent around really uninspired products. In my opinion, the only good commercial during the 2006 Super Bowl happened at half time. This ad was about a brand that didn't have to pay a cent—the Rolling Stones! In a stunning presentation of its brand identity, the famous lips-and-tongue logo in three dimensions and the band's energy continued to promote the brand's attributes. Most newspapers around the nation covered the Rolling Stones with full-page free coverage; *USA Today* titled one of its sports pages "One Hot Ticket" when talking about the band's performance. I don't know how many CDs were purchased or how many instant downloads occurred after the show, but I'm sure that sales results of the beer and soft drink commercials paled in comparison. If a brand does not fit culturally with people through a stimulating, energized environment where everyone can experience it and "rock" with it, the investment won't go far.

Brands like Wal-Mart, for the first time in their existence, decided to make a huge commitment to advertise on television with "lifestyle spots" instead of the promotional ads of the past—without any results (only 2 percent of comp store sales for Christmas 2005 versus a 4.7-percent increase enjoyed by another "hot ticket" competitor, Target). This articulates the main message of this chapter. Spending money on advertising that promotes low prices is not worth it, because people no longer get excited about low prices. Price as a concept has its limitations in an emotional economy, since there will always be someone somewhere with a better offer. Target, with a more intuitive and emotional brand-image campaign that supports the company's belief in design, has achieved success because its brand matters emotionally. This is why the *emotional brands that people desire* are the most important element of the marketing mix today.

The biggest opportunity is to get consumers to migrate across those different experiences in an intuitive fashion, to guide them in a nondirective way in discovering more about the brand.

Advertisers need to get in touch with the consumer in this new media world, and the challenges are even greater going forward. Even the best examples of cross-media experiences—such as Victoria's Secret inviting the millions of viewers to watch an online lingerie fashion show during Super Bowl half time—fail to inspire! The biggest opportunity is to get consumers to migrate across those different experiences in an intuitive fashion, to guide them in a nondirective way in discovering more about the brand.

Businesses must return to using the advertising industry in the way it was originally meant to be used: as a creator of content, and a provider of ideas and brand-building initiatives around a new set of media tools. In a less structured future and changing emotional realities, branding communication needs to rely more on intuition and creative flexibility, which is exactly what the communication business is all about.

Don't Just Shoot the Messenger: Fix the Product

Even though the advertising model as we know it is undergoing a huge revolution, it is not the creative talent who is to blame. Corporations with a short-term focus on immediate results, narrow approaches to consumer relationships via traditional push advertising, poor product and service performance, and fear of the creative process are at the core of the problem. The obsessive reliance on consumer research has taken the life out of most creative ideas. When you compare the creative potential with the type of work that finally ends up in the marketplace, you know that people are not doing their jobs; someone is not taking the necessary risks to bring new ideas to the market. (See Shift 5: "Think Design Research.")

To make matters worse, it is common knowledge that advertising nowadays is less targeted to consumers. Rather, it is directed toward Wall Street analysts who study traditional media ideas for signs of how a brand will perform in the future. If you pass the mustard with the analysts and get lucky with a good rating in Bob Garfield's *Ad Age* column, you could have a huge impact on the company stock—hopefully buying along the way some time for the company to fix deeper brand issues, maybe even after you have gone to another job!

Sometimes advertising is seen as hope in a bottle when it is too late for the investment to work. When Dell not only missed the growth of laptop demand due to wireless technology but also failed to pay attention to customer experience, the company decided to invest a whopping $150 million in advertising to improve its image. To change people's minds in a case like this will require a lot more money to fix the problem, and advertising alone won't do it, no matter what the amount. Is this another case of "overhyping?"

Has the Communication Business Lost Its Soul?

Some brands are not marketable, and no amount of advertising money will change that. When you add the massive glut of commodity products and the relentless dumping of advertising tonnage, you must be prepared to get a pretty nasty rebuttal from people.

In a *USA Today* article, Gary Levin explained, among other things, that people are complaining about the higher dose of commercials in shows. This results in a worsening of ad recall, the heightened interest in Tivo, and a plain bored reaction to anything that smells of advertising.[20]

There is a negative reaction to the obsessive and counterintuitive marketing techniques of some brands. For instance, those failed "buzz marketing" tactics that enlist people to coax their friends to use a particular product, without telling them that they are paid to do so. Short-lived games such as "bud pong," a national promotion based on a new drinking game supposed to be played with water (while promoted by Budweiser!), was an embarrassment and had to be stopped, as people were actually playing it with . . . you guessed it, beer.

The trend to "do whatever it takes" to reach out to consumers is so out of control that in China (a country that, like most economically emerging countries, enjoys ads), commercials by Grey for Procter & Gamble's Pantene were so over the top in their promises that the Chinese government had to come in and ask for "proof" of some of the brand's claims, such as "Pantene makes your hair ten times stronger."[21]

The worst part is the comment made by a Chinese consumer after the incident: "I will never believe in ads again." She is not the only one. Consumers are so fed up that *Ad Age*, the leading U.S. trade advertising magazine, published a survey in 2004 expressing people's frustration with advertising today. One young viewer of commercials is quoted as saying, "[Advertising] is about lying and selling shit; why don't they just say that their product is shit from the start?"[22] Not withstanding the legality of such marketing practices, it shows that brands themselves continue to influence the types of techniques that taint people's acceptance of brands and that could have long-term impact on brand reputation.

It is no wonder that brands themselves are under attack. For every McDonald's commercial, we also see a *Super Size Me* film. For every Oreo commercial, we see blogs talking about processed food and kids' health. Thomas Friedman, the *New York Times* columnist and author, blasted General Motors for being unpatriotic by offering future customers unlimited gasoline at $1.99 a gallon for one year.[23] Blogs also are the place to be for both marketers frustrated by their lack of broadcast impact, and their opponents. The challenge for brands to play on the blog scene is also quite dangerous, as Coca-Cola has found out with Cola-Cola Zero.

For the launch of Coca-Cola Zero, Coca-Cola created its own fake blog as a clandestine element of the campaign. Once found out, the backlash was not pretty from the blogging community, which felt the intrusion was dishonest. One blog talked of suicide for the brand, and other comments used words such as "lies," "fake," and "misleading." Coca-Cola knows instinctively that its brands need to be in front of people where they are during the day, and blogs are that place, a consumer-controlled space, but clearly the approach the company took was not the right one.

Why risk it all? What is not taken into consideration is the unwanted intrusion factor. If a product is great and aspiring, people will gravitate naturally to it and the communication will fall into place. If the product is not innovative enough or perceived as manipulative, the market will send you signals that you need to go back to the drawing board. But that's not the only thing you will need to do. The consumer democracy works here also. You just have to learn how to play the game.

Businesses often can't see the impact their brands have on people and seem to be oblivious to how uninteresting messages can just spoil people's private time. If the "tastes **There may be a credibility crisis in advertising, but there is an even greater credibility crisis when marketers are not realistic about their products' potential.** good, less filling" debate bores people, just drop it! There may be a credibility crisis in advertising, but there is an even greater credibility crisis when marketers are not realistic about their products' potential and the promise they can deliver.

It does not mean that the advertising business does not have standards; everybody agrees by now that the entire branding industry has standards—they are just very low! There is a lack of realism from some marketers regarding their brand's quality, and the advertising industry will not stand up for consumers when it could mean losing an account. Why should they? Their actions go unpunished, as businesses continue to hire ad agencies that perpetuate an obsolete model.

One of the reasons movies were not as successful in 2005 as the entertainment industry expected, was because, as one marketing professional explained, "movie goers may have suffered ad fatigue" and there has been "over-hyping of movies that simply didn't deliver what they promised."[24] Using screen-based media in retail stores is also just adding to the media glut. Wal-Mart, for example, is already selling its own store space to advertisers. This means that consumers will be forced to watch the commercials they thought they had avoided with Tivo while they shop.

As a metaphor, I visualize a camel in the desert on the verge of collapsing from thirst and being beaten to death for not performing, when just a bit of refreshing water would do. The continued lack of flexibility and agility on the part of marketers and agencies alike will lead to the disappearance of the larger agency model as we know it. As the consumer looks elsewhere for information, the media will change hands and a new breed of creatives will emerge to respond more efficiently to the needs of reawakening brand managers. The new model will center around the creative process and content in multimedia shops that integrate all aspects of the "new world" communications paradigm.

Where Have All the Creatives Gone?

The best creatives have launched their own shops and are thriving on risk, passion, the love of the work, and the option to say "no." If you are working on a $500 million-dollar global account in a large agency, you most likely will limit the risks and never present a jazzed-up, Target-like visual campaign, even if it is in the best interest of the brand. Smaller ad agencies *will* do this because they rely on serious creativity to survive. The best ideas seem to come out of these smaller communications firms, those that embrace risk.

We can see a preference for smaller more nimble and provocative advertising firms. Bartle Bogle Hegarty, the British creative hotshop, landed most of the Unilever detergent business from Lowe Worldwide (of Interpublic group) and JWT (of the WPP group), two of the biggest advertising conglomerates in the world. According to an article by Stuart Elliott in the *New York Times*, "Lowe would keep some of its duties for the OMO brand, but will work with campaigns created by Bartle Bogle Hegarty," sealing the fate of the bigger models of having to give out their lead roles in the creative process too.[25] Sir Martin Sorrell, the chairman of a large advertising conglomerate, has even been quoted as saying that some of the best ideas in his group these days have come from its smaller business units, such as branding agencies.[26] Crispin Porter & Boguski (CPB) won the very desirable BMW Mini USA account. When managing this account, they showed a Mini on top of an SUV driving around major cities in America.

Coca-Cola and Nike work with Wieden & Kennedy; Volkswagen and Burger King with CPB. In an interview for the magazine *Creativity* after winning the coveted 2005 Agency of the Year award, Chuck Porter of CPB expresses this idea best, "The reason why we're able to get the stuff produced that we get produced is that we really try to function without fear." What is unsaid is that all the up-and-coming agencies are leveraging new ideas about entertaining people in their neighborhood and on the Web. CPB is famous for leading the trend in this area. CPB's now-famous "Subservient Chicken" for Burger King is a way of using the Web to attract millions to a brand.

> **"The reason why we're able to get the stuff produced that we get produced is that we really try to function without fear."**

The Subservient Chicken

The best recent commercials haven't just entertained during commercial breaks: they've become top content on the Internet. For an example, I suggest getting online and Googling Burger King's promotion, "the subservient chicken." This campaign is so popular that users return to watch it *again and again*. The commercial *is* the entertainment content.

When visitors log onto the subservient chicken Web page, they are con-fronted with a low-budget Webcam video of a man dressed as a chicken standing in a shabby living room. Visitors are invited to instruct the chicken via text mes-sage to do whatever they imagine. The chicken is presented as a real, servile, living person. Sure enough, the chicken responds to commands as varied as "do push ups," "read a book," "go to hell" (he doesn't like this last one), "show your muscles," and so on. Of course, it is, in fact, a pre-recorded video of a guy in a chicken suit doing a few thousand commands. His vocabulary is mind-bogglingly large, and most visitors will spend ten to twenty minutes through various com-mands trying to determine how low the chicken will sink. Others just want to test whether it is a real live man (though the chicken's command of profanities is wide enough that sometimes he does seem uncannily human).

Most importantly, the site is not simply frivolous: it builds upon the existing Burger King "have it your way" campaign in a way that is amusing. The individual message is carried out by a combination of traditional and new media that guides people to new destinations and connects them to more exciting discoveries.

www.subservientchicken.com

The Brand Message Is Up for Grabs

Frustrated by the lack of innovation that comes from the advertising world, brand activists are taking the brand message into their own hands. Even at the most innovative firm, their work is cut out for them. Beyond the inherent frustration marketers have had with bigger organizations, they will constantly have to champion new ways of connecting with their audience. Organizations strong in design will have to step back and consider the relevance their work has in terms of connecting with people's sensory needs. Even some of the most so-called creative shops are way behind the curve in understanding the eclectic way people want to live "in the life of their brands."

As the advertising business slowly emerges out of a dogmatic approach to brand building, it is being bypassed by other visionaries that have taken total control over their own communications. While at Gucci, Tom Ford was directing advertising and now directs the brand building effort he is responsible for at Estée Lauder. In a refreshing way, *WWD* quoted John Demsey, president of Estée Lauder, saying, "Tom was the ultimate band leader, and we were his orchestra."[27] Not a bad metaphor for the relationship between a creative and his client—it might even provide some answers to many of the problems I talk about in this book! Karl Lagerfeld, himself his own design business, is also the creative director for Chanel advertising—he even shoots the advertising himself. Ed Razeck, chief marketing officer of The Limited, is likewise in control of managing the advertising for Victoria's Secret in-house.

One of the most powerful brand ideas of all time was "Project Red," the brainchild of none other than Bono and Bobby Shriver. This vision connected brands such as the Gap, Converse, Motorola, and Apple to fight AIDS with the support of their consumers. This effort is "brandjamming" at its best: businesses showing their human side in partnership with people to fight one of the world's most deadly illnesses.

Entering the fray are consumers or would-be creative aficionados who are using the Web to reach others with what they feel are either the missed opportunities or the better commercials. This trend that could go as far as "spoofing" existing advertising commercials and making them suddenly very popular, as a joke! For example, on the sixteenth green of the Masters, everyone watched, in slow motion, as the Nike logo on Tiger Woods' ball, blown up

Entering the fray are consumers or would-be creative aficionados who are using the Web to reach others with what they feel are either the missed opportunities or the better commercials.

full-screen, dropped into the hole. Joseph Jaffe, an advertising iconoclast and self-proclaimed "New Marketer," began to advertise this historical, branded moment on his site ahead of everyone else. Before Nike's agency could even leverage this opportunity (it did later), Jaffe had already two ads up on his blog (*www. Jaffejuice.com*) for the world to see.

Coca-Cola and Apple have had their share of "unauthorized" ads on the Web. Harry Webster reported on a Web site (*www.MadisonAveNew.com*) that takes a shot at what he thinks is better communication. His belief is that Madison Avenue has lost its touch and that it is up to the people now to take up the cause of the brand.[28] Welcome to the postmodern consumer democracy.

Designers are doing the same. Ora Ito, a twenty-eight-year-old French designer, built his reputation and early fame by doing "faux design" for brands such as Vuitton, Apple, Levi's Strauss, and Adidas, among others, and managed to get published in two hip French magazines, *Crash* and *Jalouse*. According to a *Business Week* article, covering what it titled "design enfant terribles," such a bold move landed the designer major assignments for Heineken, Toyota, and Artemide. After the publication of an article on "made-up" designs, Ora's Web site got 200,000 visitors a day and Vuitton could not keep up with demands for the "faux bag" he had just designed that didn't even exist.[29]

In a consumer democracy, the creative process is unstoppable and people are ahead of the communication professionals as far as their relationship with brands is concerned.

In a consumer democracy, the creative process is unstoppable and people are ahead of the communication professionals as far as their relationship with brands is concerned. This is refreshing to me as it shows that people care and are excited about those brands they love. But it also means that people are unsatisfied; it shows that they love brand communication but not the kind they're being served. Consumers are frustrated and make no bones about showing us what they mean.

If the unauthorized communications people see most have better exposure, it is time to stop and think: is advertising about intelligent design as most professionals believe or about evolution as most consumers are expecting?

Branding Is More Than a Commercial

There is a lack of understanding today when it comes to the changing consumer, as well as a lack of understanding of the power of design or other modes of communication that connect with people on a sensory and emotional level. This will change as in an emotional economy the advertising dollar is spread more evenly over a new diverse form of integrated connections. "There is a disconnect between creative thinking and communications channel management at the moment," says Alan Rutherford, Unilever's global media director, emphasizing that Unilever's advertising budget accounts now for 65 percent of the company's global budget, down from about 85 percent in 2000.[30] Unilever's launch of the "Small Bottle, Mighty Convenient" concept for its All concentrated laundry detergent is a good example of making use of integrated connections. The company positioned a bus covered with clothing in key traffic spots in New York City. If you can spot the bus, you can enter a contest by cell phone or by visiting *www.spotthebus.com* for a $5,000 shopping spree.

Brands need to be close to people, genuinely ready to inspire them. Advertising works when it creates an integrated awareness for a new idea that is truly differentiated and novel, the type of product idea that makes people want to try it. The *idea* is key: there is no brand without a powerful idea, and there is no communication without an idea that can be leveraged across all the new medias we are experiencing in this age.

Apple Computer, for example, has the best commercials because they have the best products. It also has the most invested connection with its customers, through products designed to inspire, and through its retail environments that have become a top destination for shoppers. The brand never stays in the same place, and the brand communication enhances its promise. A year after the iPod, you get the Nano. A writer in the *Wall Street Journal* commented, when speaking about the iPod Nano, "The product performs as advertised or better."[31] *Better* than advertised? Wow—that's a far cry from the testimonies we've heard from consumers so far in this chapter! The benchmark exists for everyone to follow . . . so what are we waiting for?

Danacol's cholesterol-lowering yogurt from Danone.

If a product has no perceived benefit or attribute and can't sustain its growth by fighting over price points, only an emotional design-driven approach will lift that brand into consumer preference. For example, Danacol, a yogurt sold in Spain that helps lower your cholesterol, set up "health booths" in airports in Spain where travelers could have a blood test taken to inform them of their cholesterol level. The brand felt that it stood for something important and made its commitment to this apparent. Absolut Vodka has sent an original message to the world about its brand, and about the category in general. Linking the brand to programs that reinforce Absolut's commitment to innovative fashion and product design has changed perceptions and helped it build bold and memorable statements that boost sales.

Even with a good understanding of the people you want to connect with and a breakthrough new idea, the perceived difference will eventually be less visible and eroded away by competition. Therefore, the important element of brand building is to attach an innovation or a product benefit to a higher emotional message in order to keep people's loyalty and trust. This emotional message is best expressed through innovative design approaches that build on trust and loyalty. Branding is more than advertising: it is an adventure continuously filled with new discoveries. Many questions are yet to be answered, but what most advertisers are exploring is the idea that the media is not a mosaic of different vehicles but an integrated system that touches people at different times differently throughout their lives.

Branding is more than advertising: it is an adventure continuously filled with new discoveries.

Understanding that some media might be ad-free for a long period of time is also a notion that the communication world needs to integrate into its thinking. People now have an intimate connection with their portable electronic devices, from cell phones to PDAs. Confronted with the generic, inflexible TV set, new portable technology is a medium that is too intimate to violate with unwelcome commercial content—unless it does not *feel* like commercial content. And this is the challenge posed to us by consumers: can you create the communications that we want for the intimate products that are a huge part of our identity without violating our personal space?

Advertising Today Does Not Have All the Answers and Will Never Have Them
By now everyone knows that the "whole egg" idea of a mega-agency offering all types of brand services hampers the creative process. What is this idea of 360 degrees anyway? "What kind of consumer wants to be surrounded?" an advertising executive friend of mine asked me. The response by large ad agencies to this—along with listening to their smaller business units—includes reinventing themselves around brand specialties. I met the president of a leading ad agency in Paris who explained to me how she reinvented her persona as an architect. "I had a minor in architecture while in business school," she said. As an advertiser, she can use her training in architecture now more than ever.

Gallo's foray into the "fashion" crowd with a new wine was quite remarkable as it took a different road in connecting with potential consumers—the fashion road. By establishing a fashion foundation that gives grants to promising fashion designers, the new fashionista-looking black bottle branded with an Italian name made inroads onto not only the fashion runways but also the media establishment, where it was featured on CNN and in newspapers like the *Wall Street Journal* and *Washington Post.* "In total Gallo awarded $600,000 to 27 designers, or about $150,000 a year less than the cost of producing the average 30-second commercial," mentioned the *Wall Street Journal.*[32] In fact, the Gallo wine is nondescript, and the Italian name "Ecco Domani" is not particularly original. The success of this product has more to do with the fact that it had an emotional impact because it was in the right place with the right people around the right cause.

Ann Moore, chairman and CEO of Time, Inc., says that the changing advertising landscape, the emerging of new technologies, and a splintered audience is refocusing the business around content. "We will become a provider of content that can appear in any medium readers might choose."[33] Magazines are feeling the shock of the migration of advertising toward other forms of media, forcing the print business to think in terms of a more integrated multimedia platform. *Time,* along with titles such as *Fortune, People,* and *In Style,* is seeing a different kind of future for its brand and may also shift its business model away from advertising. So where are the ad dollars going to go in this new world? The answers are in the way wine brands like Ecco Domani are going—into people's lifestyles. For the publishing industry, this means rethinking how much people are willing to pay and how much fact-based news is worth. For readers interested in this content, paying a little more might be fine; for others perfectly comfortable with blogs, it won't make a difference. For advertisers it will mean rethinking how to reach people, and for ad agencies it will mean more creativity in bringing the content to the public.

The End of Advertising as We Know It

Businesses need to shift their attitude toward one of innovation and surprise, which makes people want *more* of the innovation provided by their brands, not less. I recommend that companies look into new product discovery and brand building, into initiatives that are meaningful and true, brand experiences that are memorable and inspiring. It highlights the fact that we currently under-leverage the power of design and design communication, the sensorial expression of the brand and the opportunities that exist to build trust through programs that excite and make consumers want to come back again and again.

To stand out, some ads don't have to be so similar.

Donna Karan, for instance, worked with an interesting concept using print advertising—an ad that looked like a movie poster—as a way to connect people to a Web site where they could view videos based on a narrative concocted by the brand. Instead of just glancing at a print ad for a few seconds among a mass of other ads, you were tempted to spend more time with the brand online.

Recently I was doing some research for a beauty brand, and as I was pulling ads and pasting them on a board, I realized that the ads of such powerful brands as Maybelline, Cover Girl, and Revlon, were vastly similar, probably the results of the same research techniques those three brands used. It showed the lack of imagination and brand relevance those ads were proposing. Very differently, Target stood out with a unique approach and visual vocabulary with an appealing message that celebrated its design belief in bringing new experiences in people's lives. An example of a unique magazine advertisement idea is what *Elle* did with one of its editorials. The magazine split pages that allowed readers to mix and match fashion products. The idea was soon endorsed by Gap in *Vogue*. A jewelry brand could make pop-up print ads, with paper jewelry pieces women could try on to see whether they wanted to buy them.

The transformation is about advertising media acknowledging that the spam-ridden world in which people live has trained them to select and recognize

any spam, even if it is advertising glut in traditional media. In some sense, the undesirable "commercials" have been deleted subconsciously in our mind, a trend in the outgrowth of a hyperconscious audience: today's consumers are increasingly attuned and resilient to all the devices of advertising.

How many millions watched with horror or glee as contestants on Donald Trump's *The Apprentice* created clunky advertisements for some brands such as Dove? Recalling this event, journalist Rob Walker marveled, "There is something remarkable about the way 'The Apprentice' determines where the line should be drawn between marketing and entertainment. Basically, there is no line; marketing *is* entertainment."[54] I agree with that as long as it is a "brand right" entertainment, not just a mad rush for the type of recognition that is out of place for a brand such as Dove.

How to Be an Experience

The new model for brand communication has the potential now to be more open and sensorial. Traditional broadcast and print advertising overload has eroded our appetite for "sound bite," repetitive communication; advertising simply must adapt to a new media reality and repurpose itself through new means of communications such as design and design experiences. Credibility is still

Traditional broadcast and print advertising overload has eroded our appetite for "sound bite," repetitive communication; advertising simply must adapt to a new media reality and repurpose itself through new means of communications such as design and design experiences.

perceived as mostly existing in the editorial sections of newspapers and television programs because people have always had a heightened trust in the perceived noncommercial information that supports a brand. Now in the mostly unfiltered form of spontaneous media such as blogs and text messaging also resides a credibility that affects a brand's acceptance. This journalistic filter provides the same sense of trust people have in the news.

Connecting what is known as a truly good product with a worthwhile message, such as citizen sensibility (see the section on Dove soap, pages 240 through 243), and engaging consumers in a dialogue is precisely the kind of courageous step a brand must take in order to get its promise across to the public. Brands that have something to say will break through, but the new rules of engagement require them to include some reality in their offering. These new rules might ask the brand to be judged by others, or to be transparent in order to be endorsed by the public.

The branding business, in a word, needs to focus more on proximity and consumer experiences either at the point of sale or in people's lives. New design or packaging needs to refocus toward being not a promotional instrument but a brand-building vehicle with a completely new twist. Design has changed the marketing landscape dramatically and is bringing a new layer of messaging that is less costly financially and more impactful in the long term. Companies need to forget the distinction between *message* and *experience*. If your message doesn't come in the form of an experience, then you've either got nothing to say or you are in sore need of a good designer. Design is not just a new "shtick," a new sales tool, or of-the-moment appealing language:

> **The branding business, in a word, needs to focus more on proximity and consumer experiences either at the point of sale or in people's lives.**

- Design is a way to build an internal culture of innovation inside a corporation.
- Design is a way to handle discovery as never before and a powerful opportunity to recognize, leverage, and bring to life new ideas.
- Design has the ability to improvise, surprise, and even suggest the seductive and scandalous that inspired jazz in the first place.
- Design leads to the unpredictable; it shows consumers the bold, the sexy, the sweet, the stylish, and the outrageous.
- Design touches the consumer directly.

In other words, design is a bold new form of advertising.

When the Promise Is Delivered

Great products lead to great advertising, but most importantly they lead to great emotions and trust. "When a good idea rings true, then there is a piece of truth in it," said the advertising great, Leo Burnett.[35] A brand's trust level is based on the fact that there is no disconnect between the promise and the experience. When the promise is not being delivered, the contract between people and the brand is broken. Most brands have been blinded by the idea that media tonnage and money will create sales for their generic or subpar products. Even the best communication will be crippled if the product does not stimulate people with an innovative proposition. When the product is remembered more than the commercial, you know you have a winner.

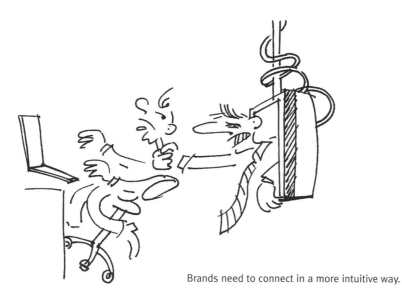

Brands need to connect in a more intuitive way.

What this means: *There are new ways to reach people with a powerful message—design is one of them. With a great product, there are more options outside of traditional media to create buzz for a brand and build loyalty. Consumers, marketers, advertisers, and designers should brandjam during the creative process—but don't talk about old products when you could be talking about new ideas. Stop being enamored with great TV commercials; they won't sell commodity products any longer. Advertising needs to be a message of promise that will be delivered or it will not work.*

SHIFT 4
Think Retail as Advertising

As advertisers struggle to find new ways to reach consumers, they have expanded their thinking to discover the power of retail as a way of extending the message and capturing people's attention by creating a more experiential relationship with the brand. Curiously enough, the retail industry, which owns the most powerful connection with consumers, is also looking for emotional design to inspire people and is striving to reinvent the retail model. Both brand specialists and retailers may be coming to a defining moment and learning from one another. Most importantly, they are learning that people love to shop, even if sometimes they are only shopping for *ideas* or *motivation.*

Pop Up Your Message

In daily articles about new brand presence programs, from a Nokia theater to Heineken bars to Lexus holograms and animated Coca-Cola signage in New York's Times Square, branding and financial writers are promulgating going beyond traditional venues to better reach consumers. These types of "presence programs" support the call for a greater role for design in brand communications. Brand retailing is the form of presence program I truly believe in and, if it is well done and the brand is consistent, it is the best new opportunity for brands. The opportunity, however, is not just about venue—a brand that is unwelcome on traditional TV will not be successful in any other presence program—but in leveraging a brand that people already trust in a more surprising and exciting venue.

Target and Levi's have successfully used the retail model known as "pop-up stores," a short-term appearance on the retail scene in iconic locations to prop up their image through innovative messaging. The pop-up becomes an invitation for people to rediscover the brand but also a topic to be covered by the national press. Levi's, for instance, rented space in a hip SoHo location in New York City to sell a limited edition of their famed 501 Jeans in five colors, and only for a limited amount of time.

Target once docked a "Target boat" in New York Harbor for shoppers to visit and shop at. It has recently made a powerful short-term retail statement in Times Square selling wares to support the fight against breast cancer. This Target "pop-up" store is a perfect example of a branding initiative that is far more effective than any billboard advertising could ever be. One hundred percent of the profits go to benefit the Breast Cancer Research Foundation. The store featured entirely pink merchandise—everything from cashmere scarves and umbrellas, to clothing, cosmetic bags, and flip-flops in a modest price range from $5 to $25. It was so successful that it was continued online long after the Times Square store was dismantled. Target was able to create a lasting emotional bond with a short-term initiative.

The best part of brand retailing is when it has an impact on the press that cover those events as news—a great way to get free advertising on news channels or newspapers across the country, and a sensible way to build credibility around your message. Design as advertising ultimately connects better with people and

Design as advertising ultimately connects better with people and in a richer way by bringing to life ideas that people can *feel*, ideas that generate community interest, and ideas that as a consequence are attractive to the media industry.

in a richer way by bringing to life ideas that people can *feel*, ideas that generate community interest, and ideas that as a consequence are attractive to the media industry.

Retail design as advertising is so powerful that the most successful corporations, cultural institutions, and government organizations are waking up to what an emotional identity that understands the language of design can do not only as a solution to people's lives but also as a "brand lab" for creating value and awareness.

Connecting Emotionally through Retail

As I mention in Shift 6, "Think Commodity Design (Not!)," the concept of Dove's Beyond Compare campaign was first repurposed in Canada in a specially created art exhibit in order to bring a powerful concept to the public within a limited budget. Redefining beauty from a more personal perspective was a shift the Dove team was interested in exploring. Such a powerful concept could have failed if not connected profoundly to women, and most importantly it could have failed to inspire Dove executives in adopting this new revolutionary way of looking at communication. Sensitive to the limitation of Dove's budget in Canada, Ogilvy & Mather proposed this courageous idea to be expressed in an art exhibit, as the vehicle to communicate the brand's new promise to Canadian women. Sometimes the lack of funds for a major advertising push can help generate some new and imaginative thinking.

The first step was to ask sixty-seven women photographers from around the world—celebrities such as Annie Leibovitz and

Mary Ellen Mark, as well as lesser known but talented women photographers—to donate photographs that represented what beauty meant to them in a real way and to comment on them. The response from the photographers was not only positive but overwhelming. On their own time and without a fee, most of the women photographers contacted participated in this exhibit because they felt that their contribution was of a higher order. The vast variety of photographic choices was so compelling that it connected the brand to women in a very profound and truthful way. The women in the photographs were not the prototypical "model stereotypes" that plaster fashion magazines and create a tremendous sense of inadequacy and self-esteem problems for a lot of women. The photos depicted ordinary women showing pride in their reality and daily life struggles—a powerful testament to life's diversity and ultimately to internal beauty. It was not advertising as we know it, but advertising as it should be, or to paraphrase Leo Burnett, the epinomous founder of the agency, "a campaign that gave something back to people to encourage them to watch the ad."

The traveling exhibition called "Beyond Compare" crossed Canada in 2004, connecting directly with women in public spaces. The photographs from the exhibit were also printed in a rare collector's catalog for people to buy and keep. The total program was a huge success and more than met the objectives of the campaign, which was to raise the credibility of the Dove products and their awareness in women's minds.

Celebrating all women

Dove, NEDIC working to change perceptions of beauty

Margit Geeslinke's photograph entitled Mirror, pictured above, is part of Dove's Beyond Compare: Women Photographers on Beauty. The photographic exhibit showcasing images of beauty by female photographers from around the world is touring the country as part of a partnership between Dove and the National Eating Disorder Information Centre.

Georgia Kokolis's photograph Woman, pictured above, is also part of Dove's Beyond Compare: Women Photographers on Beauty. Kokolis chose this photo because the woman has a certain look of ease and comfort and looking at her makes her 'feel good'.

Eating disorders in Canada

Dove promotes 'positive energies'

By Paul-Mark Rendon

Unilever Canada's Dove brand is going on a cross-Canada tour to promote healthy living to women.

Dove has partnered with the National Eating Disorder Information Centre, a Toronto-based charitable organization, to sponsor a photography exhibit highlighting the beauty inside all women–not just the ones on magazine covers and television.

"We really want to start to stand for real women, versus stereotypes, and helping women feel beautiful every day as opposed to feeling inadequate," says Erin Iles, Dove's master brand marketing manager.

Inhale your beauty.
Exhale your beauty. (repeat)
Love, Dove.

Ads preceded photography exhibit

Entitled "Dove's Beyond Compare: Women Photographers on Beauty," the travelling exhibit will visit six Canadian cities starting Feb. 25 in Toronto.

The showcase features works from renowned photographers like Annie Leibovitz and Sam Taylor-Wood, and will eventually move on to Europe.

Iles says the sponsorship marks Dove's effort to align itself with women who may be unhappy with stereotypical female imagery. She says the partnership came about as a result of a review of charities the marketer wanted to support.

The tour marks the latest phase of Dove's marketing to women. The brand recently began a campaign for its face care line, featuring card-sized reminders placed directly on weight and fitness machines at gyms across the country, with "uplifting messages" such as: "Inhale your beauty. Exhale your beauty (repeat)."

"It all ties together into what we're trying to do," Iles says. "Instead of making women feel like they have a lot of imperfections, make them feel like they're glowing and they're happy and get the positive energies going."

The gym advertising runs through to March, with a reprisal set for the fall.

Dove also plans self-esteem workshops for young girls as part of its empowerment efforts.

Most of the detractors would say, "But how could such a limited exhibit have the type of reach that is necessary to connect with a broad audience?" The answer is simple: if you have an idea that can move society in the right direction, you will get support. This campaign was covered by most Canadian print and TV media, creating millions in free advertising for a message that was relevant to women. The proceeds from the event went to causes to help women with issues of awareness and self-esteem.

The campaign demonstrates how advertising is not only about a screen, but about connection. This campaign shows that people love brands if the brands can make an effort to help them in their lives. Most importantly, it shows that less media could mean more if handled in a real and sincere way. Design in this case led the media. The design idea of the exhibit changed how a message can reach people and demonstrated how people will welcome brands into their lives if the message connects with their emotional reality.

Among the marketers that have envisioned retail as advertising with more than just your shop next door, Nike was certainly a pioneer. Beyond its traditional flagship stores, it also explores other ways to reach consumers. In 2004, the company commissioned two teams of architects to create invitation-only exhibits in L.A. and New York titled "The Genealogy of Speed." The objective there was a lot more than to present or sell shoes; they wanted to communicate the element of speed through design to a select group of opinion leaders. I was quoted in the article written by Jade Chang for *Metropolis* as saying that "to associate themselves [the Nike brand] with young designers sends a message of renewal. The fact that Nike is focusing on speed is very smart because it's an emotion that matches their core business."[1] With such an initiative, Nike is endorsing brand retailing itself as advertising in order to build more loyalty with people and surprise their customers with innovation.

While working on the identity for AOL, Desgrippes Gobé suggested that this virtual brand become a reality from a sensorial perspective. We discovered that few people knew about its music-downloading capability or its services and broadband opportunities that help customers send photos by e-mail to friends, colleagues, or family. We suggested a place to do exactly that.

The concept allowed for people to have their photo taken and then shown with their authorization on a digital wall, which helped people see the other members of their "tribes." Functionally the store helped to engage in a more real and sensorial way in the promise of the brand, and emotionally it brought a tremendous reality to the brand by giving it a warm, friendly, and approachable human face. I have pitched this concept to beauty companies and fashion

AOL's visual identity brought to life as retail.

groups, as I feel that, just as women like to share their newfound color makeup or dress with their mom or best friend (let's not forget a traveling husband), this technology could help create an interactive dialogue with friends and family around brands. I really do believe strongly in this idea.

The Hershey's retail store in Times Square began as a simple billboard design assignment and ballooned into an entire Hershey's-world experience: a fifteen-story façade and street-level shop that inside tells the story of Hershey's Chocolate, from its beginnings at the end of World War I to the present. Everything from the candy-themed songs playing on the sound system to the smell of chocolate in the air to the abundance of things to taste is designed for the customer's pleasure. It is now considered one of the most successful retail stores in the country, with 2.3 million people walking through its doors every year.[2]

"Design is not a plan for decoration. Design is a plan for action," says Brian Collins of Ogilvy & Mather who headed the Hershey's store concept, designed by Jon Greenberg and Associates.[3] The idea brings this once supermarket brand to life in the most personal, sensorial, and stimulating way. It helps to

reveal the undiscovered feelings people have about the brand and takes the consumers in unexpected emotional directions. "Millions of visitors are able to live the life of the brand and understand all of its promises. Furthermore, what you buy in the store becomes a souvenir that keeps the brand nearby in the intimacy of your own home," says Ken Nisch, president and creative director of Jon Greenberg & Associates.

"Welcome to Galleria Illy: A Gallery, A Library, A Theater, A University, and the Most Authentic Espresso in New York"

So proclaims the advertising for the Illy pop-up shop in New York's Soho neighborhood. "A Coffee Themeland, Temporary by Design" reads the half-page article on the store that appeared in the *New York Times,* a coverage anyone would die for and a credibility that no ad could reproduce.[4] In the case of Illy, the connection of advertising to a real experience, the promise of a brand experience and not just a vague promise, is but one of the many strategies that connects the brand emotionally to people. If you can bring them there, they will remember you forever. If you give something back, the brand will be trusted. That language is one of expectation and sensorial discovery.

Just read the following ad copy and you will understand what is missing in most other advertising communications—the pleasure of the senses:

"The Galleria is open. And while you're there enjoying a perfect Italian espresso or cappuccino, you can immerse yourself in the culture of a unique coffee brand. You can view a new James Rosenquist. Enjoy David Rosengarten's theatrical coffee performances. Read from a library of things coffee and things art. Learn about coffee from the university of coffee experts. Witness baristas prepare it the authentic Italian way. Experience how espresso cup art elevates the taste. So to stimulate more than just your taste buds, there is only one place to go."

The Natural Billboard

While in Tokyo I came upon a plant-covered wall standing in the middle of Omotesando, the city's main luxury-shopping avenue. Designed by Klein Dytham Architecture, a Tokyo-based architectural firm, the project reinvents the concept of decorated fences around construction sites, which are normally an eyesore for most people. Instead of surrounding a major real estate devel-

opment project with the prototypical "high graphic" barriers that are the rave among graphic designers, Klein Dytham created an organic barricade covered with plants, grass, and flowers that grow every day, bringing a sense of nature to an urban environment. This vocabulary is readily endorsed and appreciated by the city's inhabitants.

"The screen will be there for three years, so we were looking for something that would react to the changing seasons and weather, and would improve over time, not deteriorate," said Astrid Klein and Mark Dytham in an interview in *ID* magazine. The impact is truly stunning, with a vertical garden standing up in the most provocative way, making the identification of the site even more respectable and bringing a positive sense of nature to a purely urban environment.

People stop to admire this work of commercial art, as it fits nicely with the trees that line the avenue. The sense of pleasure and transformation is quite real, even for professionals like me. I was uplifted by this unique idea. From an image perspective, the positive message will stay in people's minds and will add value to their future experiences with the site. There isn't a single more powerful idea that could have delivered a message of this magnitude and helped to raise people's quality of life.

This might be far-fetched as a pure retail idea, but to me it has the same dimension and mode of expression—it is on the street, it is part of our urban landscape. What is inspiring is the fact that the nature process can inform great design ideas and revitalize a brand, a store, a signage system, by introducing a new vantage point of perception. When you don't have the millions to buy traditional broadcast advertising, being in the street in front of people and editorializing in the *New York Times* in front of the world is the new "fusion" communication at its best. There is another benefit to this, as more than 500 million people search the Web for information, the article will be there for everyone to discover.

Fusion Advertising at Last! A Jazzed-Up Idea

Between the Dove Beyond Compare Canadian effort, AOL's new virtual store, and Klein Dytham's natural billboard, we can see the way advertising will operate in the twenty-first century and the new model that is taking place. Advertising has now become involved in people's realities and participates in

That merging of the medias, this new postmodern "fusion advertising," will reflect a greater diversity of desires and ways to enjoy brands on the consumer's own terms.

bettering people's lives. That merging of the medias, this new postmodern "fusion advertising," will reflect a greater diversity of desires and ways to enjoy brands on the consumer's own terms.

As I say in all my presentations, not all brands are created equal and certainly not all brands are up to the task or even understand the challenge. Not all products are brands, and not all brands understand the immense possibilities that exist for them if they can only reach people's hearts instead of just their minds. There are still products with no meaningful messages to share, and they will continue to clutter the communication channels with more irritating messages. This is a shame when most people are willing to listen; they seek quality messages that will help them discover more about themselves or stimulate their imagination.

THE NEW ADVERTISING MODEL

The old model of advertising is based on media revenue, reflecting a century-old formula based on the almost exclusive control of traditional media and the commissions that come out of that relationship. The new advertising model must be based on the value of the ideas, on sales, reputation, and product innovation. If venture capitalists are spending billions on new ideas that sometimes will not make it to the marketplace, they just might invest in that one really good one that will change a brand's perception. After only a mere five years, Grey Goose Vodka was able to sell its brand for $2 billion. Businesses need to validate the creative process and its rewards. This is the only way for marketers to support brand organizations that make a difference. In these conditions people will stand up for their brands, fight in order to right a bad product, and push even harder for what they believe in.

Branded Architecture Is Advertising

I spoke in previous books about the success of Frank Ghery's Guggenheim Museum in Bilbao, a project that helped the community where it was built succeed economically by attracting millions of tourists from around the world. This emboldened Spain to add more such offerings to its traditional tourism. The exhibit on Spanish architecture revival at the Museum of Modern Art (MoMA) in February 2005 was like a sign of Spain's newfound democracy and its will to attract tourists and businesses to visit or live there. Terence Riley, the former chief curator of architecture and design at MoMA, is quoted in an article in the *New York Times* as saying, "Construction has eclipsed tourism as the largest economic sector in the country."[5] The worldwide media coverage of this exhibit did more than any ad campaign could do.

A BRIDGE AWAY: THE TOWN OF MILLAU, FRANCE

In 2005, the small city of Millau in southern France likewise got the world's attention when it hired the British architect Sir Norman Foster—known for bold and dramatic designs that are based on ecology, responsibility, and the environment—to build a much needed bridge that would bypass the city and alleviate traffic jams during peak traveling seasons. Foster's stunning bridge rises fifty feet higher than the Eiffel Tower. On the one hand, this initiative could have been fatal for the town's economy, since the bridge would by-

pass the city and not bring tourists into its center. But the selection of a world-renowned architect was a stroke of genius. And the quality, beauty, and imagination of the new bridge transformed the small town into a destination for what is now considered one of the most futuristic architectural pieces of our era. One of the workers on the bridge was quoted in the *New York Times* as saying, "This is a work of art that touches all of us."[6] Hundreds of thousands of people have already visited the town to admire this masterpiece—and nobody is worried anymore about the local economy.

This effort is not only about the construction of a bridge but a celebration of life: it has crystallized the aspirations of the townspeople, the workers, and all the tourists who will come to celebrate it. It is a design effort that has put this unknown town on the map. Interestingly, people look at the project in the context of the small town, from an intimate perspective; no one speaks about it as a "French project," but as that small town's vision, a much more approachable and human endeavor. To the question "Why bother?" the answer is quite compelling, and the economic results telling to the town inhabitants.

What can we learn from such a program? First, that no advertising money could have made the place more famous than a single piece of architecture. And secondly, that work that celebrates the power of our imagination is always celebrated by people, since we naturally gravitate toward the extraordinary.

I think a lot about Millau's or Bilbao's rebirth in the context of the tragedy that happened in New Orleans due to hurricane Katrina. For the first time in history, America has the opportunity to recreate what could be the model for the urban planning of the twenty-first century. The success of New Orleans as a reconstructed urban space and the numbers of residents and tourists that the town will attract and bring back will be exponentially stronger if the rebuilding of the city becomes a model of architecture and urban planning for the rest of the world, a manifestation of America's true inventive spirit. The city now has the opportunity to build itself as the most innovative city in the country. But whether city officials and urban planners will decide to take this opportunity, or whether they will be able to, still remains to be seen.

China is on the move, and the growth of Shanghai is one of those examples, a city that is building what will become the largest port in the world. The Yangshan Deep Water Port is being built on an island located twenty miles out to sea. To get to the island, Shanghai is building a twenty-mile-long bridge that at this point can claim to be the longest bridge in the world. With 6,000 workers on the project, the bridge took two and a half years to construct, almost half the time it would normally take to build such a structure anywhere else in the world. From a public image perspective, new nations celebrate their vitality with projects that jump forward to show how the future will look like. Countries are brands and need to be perceived for their values; will Shanghai also become a favored destination for people around the world?

Urban Art Is Advertising: *Groundswell* at MoMA

Cities are brands now, competing with each other to attract businesses and visitors. To show their best face, more than a pretty shot of an iconic historical building is needed. The quality of life is important for people living there and for new guests.

In the catalog foreword for the MoMA exhibit *Groundswell*, the director of the museum, Glenn D. Lowry, states, "Since the early 1990s the surge of creative activity in contemporary landscape design is evidenced by the fast pace with which cities are reclaiming sites and transforming them into new and compellingly beautiful public spaces." This exhibit portrays some of the most innovative urban projects from the United States, Europe, the Middle East, North Africa, and Asia. All of the projects are metaphors for an emotional experience and a drive to bring more humanity into our communities. Some rehabilitate old industrial sites, such as the Duisburg-Nord Landscape Park in Emscher, Germany, or the transformation of Crissy Field, a former U.S. Army airstrip, in San Francisco. And in Brooklyn, New York, the restoration of the Williamsburg and Greenpoint waterfronts—areas that used to be abandoned and somewhat dangerous dockyards and warehouse districts—into luxury houses and parks. There is no end to how much neighborhoods can be transformed.

In Beirut's central district lies the "garden of forgiveness." According to the *Groundswell* catalog, "This district, literally destroyed by the war, in the process of being rebuilt has brought to life the foundations of the city's past urban reality." Archeologists who were brought in discovered building and street foundations from several periods of history, from antiquity to the Middle Ages. Most importantly, those foundations revealed how the Lebanese diverse religious fabric lived side by side with buildings of worship built next to each other. In this way, cultural diversity has been brought to life in a city that wants to be reminded of its shared heritage. In New York, the Staten Island Fresh Kills lifescape is a project to revitalize a landfill area and turn it into parkland, restoring life to this area of the island for wildlife but also for cultural and social life.

If you can visualize a large artificial lake surrounding the city hall in Bradford, England, you have pretty much understood the new thinking that goes into revitalizing public spaces around the world. There are countless examples of people demanding more social interaction and natural beauty in their cities in an age when, ironically, there is so much burgeoning individuality. The lesson here is that people strive for engagement and participation in the discovery of new ideas that positively affect their well-being. The sensuality and the intensity of the emotions one feels when prompted by such beauty creates a new perspective in people's lives and brings optimism into their world.

Bradford City Centre master plan.

Our expectations of living and experiencing in urban environments are changing. The contexts in which we live are being transformed; people want to escape their reality. People want to feel like they are vibrating in settings that are stimulating and that bring meaningful change into their lives. As an analogy and to demonstrate how our quality of living is now brought to life in a postmodern way, one only needs to look at changes in our urban landscape. It is fascinating to see how much care cities put into creating habitats and environments that people enjoy sharing. Inner cities and public spaces are being rejuvenated in order to bring connections and sensations into our daily lives, and at the same time commerce benefits from this revitalization and can capitalize on it. In Paris every summer, artificial beaches are created along the Seine to help people who are not on vacation yet or who do not want to lose the sensory feelings they brought back from vacation.

Maybe Architecture Can Teach Us a Thing or Two about Branding

In the film *My Architect*, Louis Kahn is seen teaching his students that the material they use in designing their projects is alive and will become beautiful only if the architect understands a needed and profound connection with nature and the nature of the material. For me, this movie focused a new light on his intellectual beliefs and passion. It explained my visceral love of his work and the mystery attached to that attraction. Architecture for him was only possible if conceived through the perfect balance and communion of man and his environment.

Beach lifestyle in the heart of Paris.

Other architects, such as Zaha Hadid and Rem Koolhaas, "exude a social dynamism and freedom—a thriving democratic ideal," pronounced Nicolai Ouroussoff in the *New York Times*.[7] And this is what I believe branding should be about.

As Kahn famously said once to his students, "I asked a brick what it wanted to be, and it said an arch." The teaching here is that the humanization of design by understanding one's materials can lead one's environment to beauty.

The "Sensurround" Experience

"All the conditions of modern life—its material plentitude, its sheer crowdedness—conjoin to dull our sensory faculties. . . . What is important now is to recover our senses. We must learn to see more, to hear more, to feel more."[8] Those are the words of Susan Sontag, one of the most influential American writers and philosophers of the twentieth century. She understood very quickly in the 1960s that our modern life of commoditization would erode and dull the quality of our lives and our happiness. Brands' answer to delivering on sensory experiences so far has been to mechanically and scientifically offer solutions that fit our logic, while people are expecting what I call "sensurround" emotions that will uplift their lives, liberate their feelings, and reveal aspects of their personalities they don't know about yet.

> "All the conditions of modern life—its material plentitude, its sheer crowdedness—conjoin to dull our sensory faculties. . . . What is important now is to recover our senses. We must learn to see more, to hear more, to feel more."

You can't talk about the power of emotive design without speaking about the "unconscious" and the shift an artist's passion can bring to life through his vision and imagination. The American architect Morris Lapidus brought inspiring design and architecture to the people through his hotel work and store design. With original and unorthodox talent, Lapidus strove to understand human nature and the emotive language of forms. His claim for emotion in architecture may insult art historians who revel in modernism, but Lapidus expresses the postmodern spirit of people-inspired, playful brand design emblematic of a new breed of architects that built an entertaining factor into their work. Yet who knows nowadays that the infamous Eden Roc and Fontainebleau hotels in Miami Beach, Florida, were Lapidus's brainchildren?

Born in Odessa, Russia, Lapidus was the son of Jewish emigrants. In the 1950s, he created some of the first dream hotels in Florida for an optimistic nation enjoying its postwar prosperity. In her book *Morris Lapidus*, Deborah Desilets, who worked for Lapidus, relates the impact this architect had on his generation. Lapidus's architecture was described as an architecture of joy, a new concept that is well expressed in the title of his book, *A Quest for Emotion in Architecture.* "Lapidus," writes Desilets, "strove to understand human nature and the emotive language of forms."[9]

Recognized by his peers in later years, Lapidus was a postmodern architect before the term was even invented. He designed hotels, residences, and store experiences that put people and their dreams first—a concept that has become the most relevant topic in marketing today. Lapidus was a people observer and knew how lighting and shapes could create the most eye-catching and opulent architecture or store design and bring magic into people's lives. He knew how to create or recreate the Hollywood new glamour to make people feel like superstars. For him architecture could not leave people cold. In mixing commerce with art, he broke established rules and walked away from the elitist design theorists of the time. In a speech at Columbia University, he used these encouraging words: "Use your head, your heart, and your hands . . . feelings find form."

"Sensurround" experiences, the kind of experiences Lapidus was so good at creating, are boiling over every day in the fertile minds of designers. Design-centered retailers like IKEA are a good place to see this concept in action today. In an article in *USA Today* one writer noted that the store is all about "seeing, feeling, touching products, and having fun."[10] That's why 2,000 people waited for the opening of the Atlanta, Georgia, store with the promise that the first one on line would get a $4,000 gift certificate. Someone even waited for seven days. The store might just have become "a curator of people's lifestyles, if not their lives."[11]

Because of that unique combination of design, brand values, and unparalleled experience, IKEA is setting up a model that hosts 410 million people a year worldwide and where the "emotional response is unparalleled."[12] Praise for the concept is positive on their Web site, where the comments range from being about the life-transformation experiences people have to product descriptions, because the product innovation is one of the store's key assets.

To have access to what would normally be a more expensive design, people do not mind putting the products together themselves. We all know that it really is a chore, but in the end you feel like you have taken part in the design of the products and are proud to have accomplished something, to bring the inner carpenter in you out into the open. (I always thought that cars one day would sell their parts in kits for people to put together with minimum help and at a great savings.) The main focus of the brand, though, is to "design beautiful products at an affordable price"—a concept that really helps to advertise the brand when there is already an openness for a big idea.

I don't know if the founder of IKEA, Ingvar Kamprak, read Susan Sontag's literary work when he started his business, but the store indeed reconnects people with their inner "sensory" and at the same time liberates them from the pent-up frustration they normally experience when shopping in most department stores. The integration of the emotional experience in IKEA is not only physical but also spiritual; this is one of the few stores that have made citizenship a major part of their brand ethos. Design here plays a huge role in the brand promise and experience, as it is relevant and encompassing.

The advertising is socially sensitive, and connected to the brand promise. IKEA was one of the first brands to show same-sex couples, for instance, and its messages are always fun, beautiful, sensitive, responsible, and memorable . . . like the products in their stores. Design is also always the inspiration for the ads.

The Apple Store: How Innovation Connects to Every Aspect of Our Lives

If you are Apple, there is no type of distribution that will be good enough to fully showcase your products. Traditional distribution outside of the luxury goods is boring and unaccustomed to celebrating brands. So why not build your own? That is my thought when I go to any Apple store. I love going there; I revel in the discovery and continuous surprise the brand brings to me.

It therefore was not a surprise to me when Ronald B. Johnson, senior vice president of retail for Apple, was invited by *Women's Wear Daily* to be a speaker at its CEO summit, an exclusive meeting of top retailers from around the world. Reading an article in *WWD* covering Ronald's speech, I was truly amazed by how this former Target executive viewed the development of the Target stores as mostly a brand building and human connection tool. Apple's approach, expressed in the article as "a place to belong," sums up the attitude Apple innovated in ways that will always reach out to the lives of its guests.[15]

At the Apple store, you can buy products, get superior service, and learn all there is to know about your equipment at the "genius bar." More than just a place to shop, the store provides an environment in which you can explore different products and find the one that is right for you. Filled with light and a pleasing combination of green glass, modern gray tones, and the now-pervasive white products, from iBooks to iPods, the store makes you feel like you are spending time in the California home of someone who knows everything and then some about the next wave in computer technology.

The New York Fifth Avenue store.

The stores, 137 and growing in the United States, Canada, and Japan, start to represent a sizeable presence in the lives of consumer fans, but they also now represent a growing and substantial aspect of Apple's revenue with sales in 2005 of $2.5 billion and profits close to $150 million. With $4,000 per square foot in sales, Apple stores generate more profit than a Gap store does revenue.[14] But the philosophy of the Apple retail executive is intriguing in the way he mixes brand, emotions, experience, and pleasure in one offering that reaches people with a message that they want to hear. Apple is the intersection of reality and imagination—of what it might become.

This is clearly a part of brand building, when brick and mortar reinvents itself to showcase emotions more than information. From a brand where the CEO takes a total compensation of $1 not including options, you can see a lot of confidence in the way the company is operated.

The Brand Retailing of Cars

The automobile industry has best discovered the power of retail as a "vehicle" for promoting its brands, from creating museums that celebrate the magic of past models to reinventing the dealership to convey its message.

In Tokyo, for instance, I was surprised to come upon a multilevel Nissan dealership where the first floor, instead of showing new car models, exposed their service area. The intriguing idea though was that on the ground level where you would expect the car showroom, you had the service area for everyone to see. Mechanics were working on cars with clean uniforms and in the most pristine and professional environment—nothing to hide, nothing to be afraid of. It was a way to show the hidden and somewhat mysterious and scary side of what happens to your car in a time of crisis. Emotionally, this was totally reassuring.

The message was powerful and emotional, not unlike the restaurants that have open kitchens for everyone to see, and even sometimes offering a table looking onto the kitchen so that patrons can experience the beauty of cooking. Nissan was not merely revealing to customers the way its service department works but differentiating their brand by convincing them that its service was truly superior and worthy of showcasing. Brand retailing, in this case, was the entire message, and a powerful one at that.

On the Champs Elysées in Paris, one of the most desirable retail strips in the world, you can find a global array of car dealerships that operates as a mix of fashion and cultural inspiration. They host seasonal exhibits on everything from lifestyle to toys to innovation in the car industry as backdrops for eye-catching new car designs and offer some of the best restaurant experiences and boutique shopping in the world. They are memorable, influential, and above all prominently placed for everyone to see and remember.

By realizing the great amount of emotion attached to its vintage models, Mercedes likewise built the Mercedes Classic Center in Irvine, California, to service vintage models. However, this 27,000-square-foot center will also include a showroom for classic Mercedes cars and a boutique that will sell vintage accessories and automotive literature. Collectors and enthusiasts will be able to rediscover the dream associated with classic models and perhaps even young car lovers will visit and keep the dream alive so that they connect emotionally with the brand in their adult life.

Most interesting is Mercedes' entry into the cultural world with the building of their Stuttgart glass and steel museum: a space that will be "as tall as the Statue of Liberty and with nearly three times as much exhibit space as New York's Guggenheim Museum."[15] Celebrating the brand in such a fashion, bringing a sensorial and emotional quality to the brand experience, is what environment can bring in terms of a new perspective on brands.

BMW has not been left behind. It is working with the London-based architect Zaha Hadid to build what is now considered one of the most interesting post-modern architectural works, the new BMW plant in Leipzig, Germany. "Ms. Hadid's project is a powerful vision of a mobile society. At the same time she has rejected the regimented order that gave the machine age a dehumanizing quality," said Nicolai Ouroussoff in his *New York Times* article on the project. The fluid lines of the plant not only make for beauty, but according to Ouroussoff, "the Leipzig assembly plant is a sophisticated attempt at social engi-neering. By creating a fluid work environment in which management, engi-neers, autoworkers, and cars seem intertwined, Ms. Hadid is seeking to break down hierarchies that have defined the traditional factory. In this world, infor-mation flows freely."[15] The BMW factory at once keeps with the close, careful attention to design and engineering so characteristic of the brand, but also rec-ognizes the new importance of creating more dynamic cultures that break with traditional linear, hierarchical command in the factory. BMW at once leverages its past and innovates in the present. This is the achievement of the best design.

This plant project is only part of the sexy German automaker's investment in its brand, as it is also building a futuristic BMW world ready to accept 850,000 visitors at a cost of $130 million. The building will have shops, a bistro, and interactive exhibits that allow people to see, hear, touch, smell, and taste the "BMW" brand. (The chapter on sensory experiences in my first book, *Emotional Branding*, has not fallen on deaf ears.)

The concept is not new; Peugeot, the French car company, with its Peugeot Avenue concept—a retail experience idea based on the great avenues around the world where Peugeot is sold—offers the best in French cuisine, innovative exhibits and fashion shows, new futuristic inventions, stylish accessories, and interactive games. Volkswagen AG has also attracted more than 10 million people to its theme park in Wolfsburg, Germany, where car shoppers can scope out the latest models right in the factory while also enjoying museum tours, restaurant dining, and other leisure activities. It even has a hotel on site so that shoppers can turn their visit into a weekend getaway.

Creative retail environments provide businesses with a way to stimulate the brand context, which in turn allows them to humanize the experience.

Brand retailing has this ability to convey the positive aspect of a corporate culture, its tone, potential, and promise of the brand for the community and employees as well. Creative retail environments provide businesses with a way to stimulate the brand context, which in turn allows them to humanize the experience.

Luxury Brand Retailing

It did not take the luxury industry long to realize that if it did not invigorate its stores there would be no amount of advertising that would keep its customers stimulated. Consumers are constantly surrounded by sources of stimulation and brands need to keep innovating in order to be heard. When Target started to be perceived as an "affordable luxury brand," the luxury business had to preserve its price and emotional exclusivity.

The answer was bold and visible. The luxury brands would not be outbranded. Prada, Dior, Chanel, Louis Vuitton, Burberry, Armani, and now Hermès are taking stock of each other not only in terms of the quality and style of the

products that they sell but also in terms of perceived glamour through the sheer size and luxury of their stores. They hired the best architects to design retail environments, selected on their own notoriety and fame so the media would not miss covering their latest work, helping the brand build more exposure. By combining the intimacy of their exclusive status and the promise of their dreams, they rival the glamour and style of some of the most inno-vative cultural institutions, even museums. The rich and beautiful go there to see and be seen, particularly on those grand stairways that are very often part of the design. The new luxury stores are about visibility for the analysts, and some would also write off a percentage of their real estate costs as adver-tising expenses.[17]

The luxury brands understand that the way to keep their customers interested is to keep them always surprised and motivated. New stores become not only selling spaces but places for parties and socializing, places that are recognized in fashion and lifestyle magazines and mainstream media. They know that the extra notoriety those stores bring to the brand are worth the investment. These brands also understand that the best way to avoid being copied is to constantly change, to stay ahead of the curve in creating new design experiences.

Brand Retailing for Retailers: An Oxymoron?

You would think that retailers would have been the ones to think of brand retailing first, right? But there is clearly some soul searching that needs to happen if retailers want to compete at the brand level. The new goal of savvy retailers, in a market that has become more and more niche-oriented (see Shift 7, "Think Emotional Customization"), is to reach people individually in order to fulfill more of their emotional needs. The retail format becomes an idea lab, a kind of sophisticated, live R&D department that hands-down beats traditional methods of research and consulting because it connects directly with people in the most interactive fashion.

Generic retail stores and niche brands alike that understand the new con-sumer-retailer relationship are trying their hand now more than before at innovative and testable ideas that will help them understand where there is an appetite for new offerings. Gap, which had overextended itself into generic status, is coming up with a new brand concept called Forth and Towne for women over thirty-five, and is testing new stores that include a more colorful palette to change the bland look of their format, maybe as a return to their col-orful heritage. The Limited continues to reach out to people with new formats, including its new Bigelow store brand, a new beauty venture, and Pink, a new lingerie line for younger women. Ann Taylor has relied on its Loft concept, an idea that Desgrippes Gobé branded to reach out to new consumers and ener-gize the main brand.

Abercrombie and Fitch, American Eagle, and Aeropostale are also generating new retail ideas. Urban Outfitters is celebrating the success of its Anthropologie stores. Much of Urban Outfitters' success is due to the company's ability to create design concepts that resonate and celebrate the aspirations of the people who shop at its retail stores. They are cautious about building new ventures and take their time to evolve their concepts through retail labs in order to ensure that they are the right fit. In Sao Paulo, Brazil, I was impressed by Galerie Melissa, a store that changes its design on a regular basis.

Galerie Melissa, San Paolo.

In Japan, Celux—a private shopping environment created by LVMH, the French luxury group—caters to an elite customer base willing to fork over $2,000 for the privilege to buy pre-selected items in a stress-free environment.[17] The management views this concept, which is bound to hit other shores soon, as "a nice piece of direct marketing," reinforcing the point that brand retailing can be a potent communication vehicle for brands.

SMALL IS BEAUTIFUL
The idea of adapting a designed environment to a shopping lifestyle is finally emerging among retail chains. The notion that smaller is better and more

intimate applies to retail as well. Retailers are dropping their for-everybody formats to create smaller niche stores that cater to customers in a more personal way. Small feels more precious, more qualitative and considered. People are migrating toward trusted brands that do the "editing" for them, since too much variety can be intimidating. In other words, they don't want a million different brands to choose from; they want just one brand they can trust.

Best Buy, for instance, is experimenting with newer, smaller, and more intimate concept stores that customize their offerings to more targeted lifestyle groups. In a similar evolution to boutique hotels, boutique retailing that makes a more emotional proposition seems to attract more guests. By designing for customers beyond the store itself, Best Buy's two new concept stores, Studio D and Escape, bring a new level of attention to serving their customers, including providing them with rides to baseball games or allowing the space to be used for groups or private parties. What is interesting about this idea is the fact that the brand sees this effort as "more about what we learn than the economic model," affirming again that retailing is not only a way to do business but also a way to learn more about consumers and how to do business with them.[19]

Realizing the need for people to get service, Best Buy launched the "Geek Squad." Highly trained professionals—dressed in short-sleeved white shirts and black ties—drive black-and-white Volkswagen Bugs to support customers' needs. Those funny-looking professionals have been dubbed "intelligence agents," "double agents," and "special agents." The FBI connotation is quite humorous. Best Buy also tests concepts through its retail formats; for example, it is opening "lab stores" in China to learn more about

the Chinese customer. What could be more insightful than to have full experiential spaces in which to watch guests interact and explore the brand offering? All retailers can learn from their retail environments; they are a great way to find out about people's desires. In the long run, retail can provide companies with a richer form of market research on an ongoing basis.

However, one cannot leave this topic without mentioning both the plight and opportunity facing department stores.

BRAND RETAILING ENTERTAINS: THE NEXT STEP FOR DEPARTMENT STORES

Journalist Tracie Rozhon wasn't breaking news when she wrote recently, "department stores are no longer the queens of the shopping mall. . . . Consumers have been telling survey-takers for years that all the clothes in department stores looked alike and the clerks spent more time talking on the phone than waiting for customers."[20] One by one, the features that once made department stores design destinations have been whittled away, until only a big, bland box remains. Shoppers responded by moving first to specialty retailers, and then to the younger, hipper department stores like Target.

Their failure is not just about sluggish stores with wimpy wares. There has also been a shift in the mall itself: consultant Marshall Cohen explains, "It's no longer the department store that's the lure" at the mall. "It's no longer even a shopping mall anymore—it's an entertainment and lifestyle mall with play-houses, community halls and restaurants."[20]

The decline of the department store has been such a long, drawn-out affair it's almost hard to remember when the department store was something special. Many of the most highly sought-after consumers—between their early teens and late twenties—were in diapers the last time the department store was a high-profile design-destination for shoppers. Nike was so frustrated with the department store doldrums it actually pulled all its products from the shelves at Sears—just sitting in such an uninspiring environment was considered to be a liability! How depressing for department store aficionados like myself, who grew up watching films like *Miracle on 34th Street* and have long admired these old-time urban meccas of consumer experience and emotion.

However, as a designer, I try to look at the promising potential in the department store. I look for what the stores have now and how these assets can be jazzed up for the new consumer. Despite the rise of specialty boutiques, Internet shopping, and the like, I still believe that consumers are willing to respond to well-designed, exciting stores, particularly if they can offer added value features like entertainment, community, and scale, which are absent from other less sizable stores.

Selfridges, the U.K.-based department store, in a venture with the city of Birmingham in England, has created a new format for a department store that uses a unique architecture to promote not only the store itself but the town. The idea was that a retail innovation such as the one they have partnered with would allow the town to be finally on the map as a tourist destination. So far it has worked—the press has been covering this unique approach with a frenzy, and the retail concept has helped to revitalize the city.

Signs of life persist in the numbers at least: between December 2003 and December 2004, sales per square foot at department stores actually rose 4.2 percent. For example, in May 2005 reports, traditional department stores sales growth outpaced competitors like Wal-Mart, according to industry sources.

Although they have lost the prestige that once made them anchors of the suburban mall and major attractions for large cities, there is life in the department stores yet if they can shake off their nondescript slumber and replace it with design based on emotional zones that inspire. In order to survive and thrive, more department stores will have to reconceptualize. From a merchandising perspective, everything, from shelving to CDs to denim jeans, must be understood as a vehicle *designed* for cultural expression and celebration.

They have always been home to a wide range of retail-branding expressions, with enough energy and excitement to draw traffic. "Big box" department stores might provide the perfect opportunity for corporations looking to target a specific audience. In this regard, it is appropriate that Wal-Mart recently began offering home subscription DVD rentals—a disc arrives, entertains, and is then sent back. Once upon a time, consumers bought jeans that happened to be fashionably designed: today consumers buy fashionable designs that happen to be jeans. Once upon a time consumers bought jeans that happened to be fashionably designed: today consumers buy fashionable designs that happen to be jeans. The retail culture today is the business of retail. Through inspiring design it could become the business of joy.

Creating a Humanistic Brand Haven

More than simply a "less-is-more" approach, however, this new paradigm is also about brands embracing the consumer's need for relief. It is about allowing the consumer to play an active role while the brand plays a more passive role—that of creating an inviting, emotional place that the consumer can discover on his or her own initiative. The idea is ultimately to create something of value and meaning for the consumer—something that will actually be a contribution to the consumer's life. The idea is nothing short of creating a humanistic "brand haven" that reflects people's values and allows them to feel at home and experience a moment of relaxation from the harried demands of their lives. Now that takes vision. Retailers must keep searching out new ways to create buzz and excitement around their stores, designing spaces that correspond to the individual tastes and desires of their customers.

What if businesses started asking, "What types of brands do *people want to live with?*" instead of, "How are we going to ambush the consumer?" Retail environments, whether fixed or mobile, can be at the center of an inspired brand connection if coordinated with big ideas of substance and integrity.

Ambush marketing.

What this means: *Retail stores, not unlike other corporate communications initiatives, are an investment in the image of a brand. The amount of money it costs to build a store, either a specialty retail or a department store, is an investment in a "media" and needs to be designed that way. Generic products do not inspire even in the best environments. If IKEA is bringing out "your inner carpenter," then the retail format needs to be consistent with the offer. If l'Occitane is a complete sensory experience in the richness of the flavors and lifestyles of the south of France, then it needs to connect that way. If car companies want to woo us through a fashion style, then their dealerships need to feel that way.*

Retail environments need to create the mood for great design to shine and stimulate our buying. The design of an emotional experience is the best brand message.

SHIFT 5
Think Design Research

In his book *The 7 Habits of Highly Effective People*, Stephen R. Covey explains, "We see the world, not as it is, but as we are, or as we are conditioned to see it."

In a research sense, I interpret this to mean that asking people to rationally explain how they see a brand will lead most likely to what they are familiar with. Over the past thirty years, corporations have spent up to $7 billion a year on research in the United States alone. You might start to wonder whether the sea of sameness might not be the result of research processes that are missing the mark, and bring an expected set of information we already know.

Visual Research Leads to Imaginative Solutions

The most successful innovative brands have not been researched for concept, design, or graphic dress: Victoria's Secret's success was not based on focus groups. Red Bull, according to Dietrich Mateschitz, the owner of the $2 billion energy drink company, was a dismal test failure. "People didn't believe the taste, the logo, the brand name," he says.[1] The available insight tools used in focus groups—a technique that favors asking people what their opinions are on everything from brand creation to concept themes to communication and design programs—are limiting marketers in their jobs. The almost obsessive reliance on focus groups as a research technique limits innovation instead of fostering it.

Such strong reliance on research as the only source of insight has narrowed the brand opportunities and led to costly decisions to spend large budgets in manufacturing, advertising, and media buying. Existing consumer research that recommends asking people for validation of new ideas is being reevaluated or even discarded as a reliable source of insight.

"Shoot the Focus Group," an article in *Business Week*, is one of the manifestations of this frustration, as it recommends looking "at more intuitive processes to get into the consumer's head."[2]

Brand marketers have in fact disengaged from the decision-making process and have built their choices on incomplete and sometimes dubious insight. In some cases the focus-group model and other more quantitative techniques have obscured the way to brand innovation, costing corporations billions of dollars. They have become a smokescreen for indecisive marketers to avoid blame and helped push ideas that have subsequently become market failures. Research today, according to Censydiam Synovate global account director Christophe Fauconnier, "is about evaluation when it should be about inspiration. We are not measuring Benchmark but moving Benchmark. It is about human understanding, illuminating brands through human emotions."

Without this understanding, the formula for failure will continue because it does not allow room for approaches that support and encourage innovation. If you ask people whether an apple-scented fragrance will sell, you'll get a negative answer, until it is distributed in a surprising packaging and supported by provocative advertising by DKNY. If you ask people whether they would endorse a sleek and stylish yuppie Swedish vodka, the response is no—and *was* no!—until it shows up at a trendy bar in the hands of "cool" people. Sidney Frank, the creator of Grey Goose Vodka, might have the best answer for marketers' indecision when quoted saying in the in-flight magazine *American Way*: "Some people are afraid to put their money into something, even if it is something they believe in. But you can't be afraid in life, because fear will stop you from achieving success."[3]

In this chapter, I want to introduce a "brandjam" way to conduct market research that celebrates the power of innovation, instinct, design, and visualization—a new approach that celebrates the birth and power of innovative ideas and places the creative process at the center of a new partnership between consumers, marketers, and designers. As importantly, any research that does not consider the finished visualization of a product, a simulation of product's selling environment, or the cultural aspirations expressed by customers in that environment is destined to fail. Research in that context needs to repurpose itself to give marketers the conviction to be able to lead their brand to success by bringing to life ideas that will shift or differentiate their brand's uniqueness and relevance. Major books on psychology, social science, and marketing all agree on the fact that the best ideas are those that break an established paradigm, and that those unconventional ideas are too much of a shift to be created along rational lines.

Emotion, Imagination, Observation

This chapter looks into some of those new research approaches that bring insight of the richest kind by making designers part of the research process. This "brandjamming" research supports probing and observing people's subconscious interactions in life and the impact of their environments on their life experiences. Assuming that designers need to play a new critical part in "visual and cultural insight." I have always been fond of the power of visual and observational techniques as a way to see for oneself what will influence behavior and choices and to understand how people experience brands in their day-to-day reality.

Designers have the uncanny right-brain ability to observe people in their culture and scan information from their life experiences that later can push the limits of the creative process. I hope that after reading this chapter you will be convinced that the best research is one led by conviction first, the power of design, and finally a deep emotional connection with people.

Emotion: Design and the Subconscious

We live in a world of constant change, where the ideas of the past cannot be relied upon to make the decisions of the future, and where choices are unpredictable. Our insecure world makes people volatile and emotional in their choices and forces corporations to struggle for answers. The intuitive nature of decision making in businesses, its capacity to adapt to change, and the corporate need to be agile and versatile when competing must be based more on gut feeling and a brand manager's ability to respond instinctively. There is less time for research: time is of the essence when responding to a competitor's attack or a market change. But do we have the right tools, the right benchmark in an emotional economy?

> **There is less time for research: time is of the essence when responding to a competitor's attack or a market change.**

Life is random.   iPod shuffle.

THE MARKETPLACE IS RANDOM

Research should be about inspiration, not opinions! It should put ideas into motion and blaze new trails that inspire consumers. As Apple's iPod campaign says, "Life is random." P&G, Apple, and Target all owe their success to a shift toward design as a strategy and a priority in reconnecting with consumers in a differentiated way. Suddenly brand managers are now discovering ethnographic research, an ergonomically driven methodology that has always been preferred by creative people but kept on the sidelines for some time because it is not "scientific" enough. But how do you put observations into charts and graphs?

In order to repurpose a brand, emotion is one of the most important assets in marketing today, as most mature brands fail to stimulate people.

I have learned the hard way that research pleasing to accountants leads to disaster and stifles innovation. In order to repurpose a brand, emotion is one of the most important assets in marketing today, as most mature brands fail to stimulate people. Outside of the technology business, which demands continuous innovation, in the arcane world of commodity it is important *to repurpose* an offering to make it relevant emotionally. Switching from "fighting dirt" to "dirt is good and liberating" repurposes the role the brand plays in people's lives from a negative to a positive experience. (See Shift 3, "Think Advertising as Design Experiences.") Understanding the greater emotional truth about people's relationships with a brand can lead to imaginative work that elevates the brand's value.

Rick Warren, the new superstar evangelist pastor, is hailed as a branding genius. In his bestselling book, *The Purpose-Driven Life*, he took the "Christian" brand and repurposed it by activating new ideas such as fighting poverty, illiteracy, and AIDS in Africa as challenges for his church. By being visible on the humanity front, his church brought a new, contemporary purpose to people ready to find meaning in their lives beyond sin, salvation, and paradise. Whether we agree or not with some of this group's fundamental beliefs, such as its position on abortion, stem cell research, human cloning, and gay lifestyles, is beside the point. The lesson is that Rick Warren has brought new life and enthusiasm to Christian worship.

Unfortunately, observing transforming ideas in society has very little place in research processes today. When making a case for management approval on a new initiative, the rational approach of a global consulting firm is more credible than a group of creative thinkers or psychologists with "circumstantial" evidence. It simply supports the conclusion that there is stuff we know about, stuff people will tell us, and stuff that is out of reach for marketers until they reveal themselves unaided through the stimulation of new ideas. But it gets worse. Consistent failure with ideas vetted by unprepared consumer groups in the last thirty years has not even put a dent on the research approach, leading brands in a downward spiral to more of the same. The lack of research options marketers have at their disposal is staggering. It has led some to try initiatives based on the belief that people are logical and rational beings in a random, illogical, emotional world. Well, this is the wake-up call: people do not know how to tell you what they want until they see it and feel it. People have even a harder time telling you how they feel and what is brewing in their subconscious. Therefore, any research process that leads to innovation can only happen through the physical stimulation of realized new experiences and the motivation of inspired leaders in a willing partnership with their audience.

ARE INSPIRATION AND INTUITION RESEARCH?

New ideas are created by truly inspired leaders with a knack for innovation and who subconsciously have a deep sense of people's unknown expectations.

In this context, research is a subordinated act, one that reassures and supports. The challenge is that great ideas are generated every day, but it takes intuition and cultural knowledge as a special talent to recognize them. At some point marketers will only have their gut feelings and creative skills to rely on to make decisions.

I have taken part in many brainstorm sessions where some of the best ideas were left on the table. In one particular instance, Reebok organized a meeting with leading-edge sports-marketing types, athletes, and designers. After a solid day of work ripping magazine pages, drawing sketches, and participating in silly ideation, the group created hundreds of ideas for a new shoe. Problem: where do you go from here? One of the ideas was the concept of a shoe that would be "minimal," a second-skin type of shoe that would recreate the feeling of running or walking barefoot. A designer thought it was a great idea; he was the only one, and this idea was probably left in a bottom drawer for lack of support. Soon afterward, Reebok's competitor, Nike, launched a very similar concept, the "Nike free shoe." Some people are inspired by creativity and see the great ideas in a sea of designs. But few have the courage to execute. This is the talent that makes the difference.

Motorola's Razr mobile phone took three years to come to life. It invented the technology to create credit-card-thin cell phones in 1999, but from a consumer experience perspective, items such as a bigger screen, seven-hour batteries, and photo capabilities—suggested by the marketing department—altered the design so much that it made it too bulky and ultimately killed the original design idea. Then Motorola watched its worldwide lead diminish in the face of Nokia's design onslaught. It had missed its timing.

When Ed Zander, the new Motorola president, originally from Sun Microsystems, came onboard, he asked to see all the new concepts that had been developed by Motorola over the past few years. He could not take his eyes off that unique ultra-thin design and focused on the product. No research, no discoveries that would drag for months. Franco Lodato, the internationally known designer now with Herman Miller, had helped work on the program (he designed the beautifully innovative and intuitive etched keypad for the phone) and remembers how suddenly the organization "opened up to innovation." This leap of faith from their leader helped the risk takers stick their heads out and push the design process.

Why did Ed Zander see what others did not? To his advantage he had one of the best technology teams at his disposal, and more importantly—with Jim Wicks, the new VP director of consumer experience design—the creative power to deliver iconic products for Motorola. Great ideas were brought to life for him to challenge his competitors and give back to Motorola the "edge" that it needed to succeed. His decision was not based on obtaining research data and analyzing it, but on his belief in the importance of design.

The fact that the Razr boosted Motorola's sales to new heights and gave it the number-one position in America is further proof of how transforming design can be for a brand culture.

The ability to see breakthrough products through the clutter and discover a great idea is a talent in itself and most often necessitates this huge leap of faith that many brand professionals would rather avoid. Research is more than asking people what they want; it is also about intuitive skills and continuing to experience for oneself what the market is all about. Research is best when it helps make those leaps of faith. A lot of ideas originate as worded description or sketches, but this is just a preliminary step. "You have to have the guts to believe in what you're doing and what your brand stands for," said Wicks in a *Fast Company* article.[4]

THE NAKED CONSUMER

Some of the new research can be a way to go deeper into understanding people's motivations, as long as the methodology is one of *probing*, not validating. Recently, the Gallup organization in Princeton, New Jersey, embarked on a study in Japan to measure brand preferences and loyalties by using brain scans. What came out of the study is that brains process strong emotional feelings differently. In fact, according to an article in the *New York Times*, areas of the brain associated with visual memory *and* emotions—the orbitofrontal cortex, the temporal lobe, and the amygdale—light up when properly stimulated.[5] So emotional interaction is clearly not based only on rationality, but on the deeper mental experiences people have with a brand, justifying the reason why stores or products that rely on design to separate themselves from the expected have a much more superior attraction rate.

Dr. Daniel Kahneman, the 2002 Nobel Prize winner in economics and a psychology professor at Princeton University, says that emotions are important determinants of economic behavior, *more so* than rationality. I have always felt as a designer that only the emotional relationship between a brand and people makes a brand special; the bond is one of connection in a neurological and philosophical way. (My first book, *Emotional Branding*, was influenced somewhat by the work of Antonio Damasio, one of the first neurologists who connected neurology to people's well-being and happiness.)

The frenzied search for "big ideas" in consumers' brains.

Corporations are rushing in droves to spend substantial amounts of money to be able to read people's minds, or in this case, their brains. A psychologist friend of mine mentioned rightly that it is critical that marketers do not confuse the wire with the light bulb. Seeing how information is connecting in our brains does not necessarily lead to the next "big" idea or show the impact of those outside influences on decision making, such as peer influence, environment, or a particular moment's psychological state of mind.

In their book *The Naked Consumer*, about why consumers really buy things and what it means for marketing, Censydiam Synovate partners Jan Callebaut, Hendrick Hendricks, Madeleine Jansens, and Christophe Fauconnier ask the question, "Why are there so many marketing failures if market research is so compelling and insightful?" Their answer is that most research companies ask *what* people buy when they should be asking *why*. And that "why" can only be answered by digging deeply into the unconscious of the human mind and uncovering what really moves people. As an analogy, the partners at Censydiam Synovate love to share the following story: If you ask consumers if they are interested in consuming a powder composed of ground-up modified hair cells from a fairly unsanitary source, the answer will most likely be *no!* But, if you explore the average consumer desire to improve his or her love life and relate that human motivation to some mystical aphrodisiac properties found in a rhinoceros's horn, the story is quite different in some parts of the world. Christophe Fauconnier goes on to say that the two most powerful forces or motivators that "move" people's behaviors, and therefore consumer behavior, are common human strivings and people's assumed beliefs. Both human strivings and human beliefs are functioning beyond consciousness and can be quite irrational in nature.[6]

Consumers' behaviors are indeed not truly rational, and those inconsistencies are based, Censydiam Synovate believes, on our attempt to satisfy deeply held needs from a physical, psychological, and philosophical perspective. To therefore find the "why," Censydiam Synovate uses a "psychodynamic" research approach that instead of providing numbers provides a richer understanding of consumers' motivations and satisfaction in relation to specific products or brands and within a certain context of human manifestation. The process includes consumers' observations in the context of their own culture, as culture greatly influences how people buy products.

Take ice cream in Europe, for example. In Britain the notion of pleasure is associated with reward: "I worked hard, I have been good, I deserve it!" This leads to ice cream containers that are big and rewarding. In Italy, pleasure is about intensity; therefore, the containers are smaller and jewel-like to communicate slow, deliberate, and delicious consumption. Culturally driven psychology applied to branding is one of the most powerful ways to probe a person's unconscious desires.

One of Censydiam's formulas worked very well in helping Unilever with a new mission statement and visual-identity positioning. In a company that believes that people make a difference and that a multinational presence is a bridge to solving people's needs, Unilever's "face" did not fit its projected worldview or its wish for growth. The project was fundamentally to understand the role of multinational companies within society and what kind of bridge the company could build with both their internal and external partners. This approach is really postmodern in nature, aligning a business culture with a market's reality in a practical but also emotional way. As Christophe Fauconnier explained to me, the research showed that "research can and must go beyond research" by understanding the role brands play in people's lives. The Censydiam Synovate research provided an excellent platform for the design of a new Unilever logo and turned out to be an insightful and actionable piece of research for the company to use in the future.

Great Philosophers Who Influence Marketing Today

Carl Jung (1875–1961)

Among the philosophers who have contributed great insight into building brand perceptions is Carl Jung. His theory is that we are all connected to the culture we are born into and that our early childhood impressions leave indelible imprints on our minds. This can be used to shed light on new brand research techniques. The Jungian science of creating emotional profiles, called archetypes, has been one of the few philosophical theories that has influenced the research business in a profoundly fresh way.

According to Synovate Censydiam, brands can be expressed as "primitive mental processes that are converted into images that consciousness can understand. Even if by way of symbols and metaphors, archetypes are the self-portraits of the instincts and emotions." In probing consumers' unconscious, deep-seated desires can be brought out through visual and symbolic stimuli. Jung's theories have helped research consultants connect psychology to consumers in terms of the meaning of brands, leading to a truer and deeper insight into the emotional relationships people have with the brands they use. Jungian psychology has also revealed the impact visual iconicity has as a way to help crystallize an emotion or help its manifestation.

An analysis of the instinctual abilities of our brain and the importance of the "collective unconscious," Jung's phrase for what I call "cultural wisdom," reveals what people in aggregate know and feel. In most research I have done, I have been amazed by how quickly a conclusion can be reached when a small group of people expresses its collective unconscious without rational layers of thinking.

The psychodynamic Jungian philosophers are in sync with designers, first because visual symbols are at the core of what designers do and second because they share the belief that beyond aesthetics visual symbols must have meaning. People love myths, and myths need symbols in order to connect emotionally.

Baruch Spinoza (1632–1677)

Baruch Spinoza was one of the most influential thinkers of the seventeenth century. He was a Portuguese Sephardic Jew whose family had moved to La Haye, Holland, escaping retaliation, forced conversion, being burned at the stake, and other such atrocities of the Spanish and Portuguese Inquisitions. In Holland, his family found religious freedom and a democratic society that was open to a diversity of cultures.

This element of freedom that creates security and joy in people's lives was something that Baruch Spinoza focused on in most of his work. His belief was that joy based on freedom was the ultimate path for personal growth and creativity, a situation that helps people transcend their reality through creativity and invention, the perfect terrain for dreams and progress. This philosophy did not go unnoticed. Many intellectuals have found in Spinoza a theory that empowers the individual. The French writer Jean-Paul Sartre based his existentialist movement on Spinoza's theories. More recently the world of science and neurology, through the research of Professor Antonio Damasio, has found in Spinoza's writings a rich platform for understanding the human mind and curing some of its illnesses. In his book *Looking for Spinoza*, Antonio Damasio states that "Spinoza's has seen that joy and its various expressions lead to a greater functional perfection," while sadness, on the other hand, leads to bad health.

From a branding perspective, Spinoza opened a tremendous window on the positive impact brands could have if they work at making their relationship with people one of joy and balance. More than that, we can assume that people will gravitate toward those brands that will improve their lives. How many times in a focus group have you heard the question, "Does this design make you happy?"

Alfred Adler (1870–1937)

Alfred Adler's philosophy was to offer hope in a time of widespread disillusionment. Not unlike Baruch Spinoza, Adler celebrated the individual in a free society. This powerful idea connects the democratic ideal with that of the individual, as those values are then spread to others. But Adler's most powerful concept is that we are born as empty shells and that we spend the rest of our lives struggling to fill that shell, looking for solutions to our lives that will bring us answers in a physical, psychological, and spiritual way. This gives us from birth a sense of inferiority that drives our behavior and makes us motivated to always search and explore. Brands have become objects of that search from an emotional perspective as they help us fill some of those lifestyle voids and feelings. In Adler's approach inherently resides the power of the will, the free will in active search to complete oneself.

This is one of the most powerful insights in "psychological branding" because it opens up a greater understanding on why brands can help us discover and fulfill our most intimate emotional and physical cravings. Red Bull, for instance, tapped into the need of people to find energy to enjoy life more, the need to feel alive at any time and most importantly at will, which is the essence of freedom.

Wilhelm Reich (1897–1957)

Wilhelm Reich, remembered as one of the inspirations of the beat generation, made sexual fulfillment for personal well-being the core idea of his philosophy. This made him a hero of the sexual freedom movement in the 1960s, illustrated by that generation's motto, "Make love, not war." The learning of Reich's philosophy for branding is that sex is the most powerful motivator in our society; sex sells and always will, particularly when it is kept on a tight leash by society rules or religious dogmas as it becomes an escape and psychological relief. Food, for instance, has been proven to be a way of diverting those inhibitions, and violence, too, in some cases is motivated by sexual frustration.

Brand narratives have always been successful in tapping into this powerful emotion. Fragrances, for instance, are most of the time telling sexual narratives that allow one to live these kinds of stories safely without penalty from society. *Playboy* was a magazine that could sell nudity along with "serious articles" that legitimized its racy style. With the advent of the Internet and particularly an expanded access to pornography, the tension is heightened, mostly among males, and understanding the meaning of these stimulations is important for brands. Through their advertisements, Abercrombie & Fitch and Victoria's Secret have been able to corner the emotion that connects the anxiety of sexual desires to fashion edge. This is not to say that A&F buyers are only interested in buying the products for sexual relief, but the sexual point of view of their material emphasizes freedom and promiscuity, which are relevant to college students open to a culture of hedonism. People are buying the unconventional positioning of the brand because it allows them to express a personal but acceptable rebellious message.

The branding world is paying more attention now to people's psychology by seeking and understanding people's deep-seated concerns and life aspirations. In parallel, design more and more reveals itself to be a true catalyst between people's psychological aspirations and the delivery of a brand's promise.

Imagination: Design through Visualization

Visualization is the new language for creative people, a way to brainstorm the pursuit of powerful ideas around the same language. In jazz terms, visualization is the music and the language that connects emotionally. For creative firms like us, this is how we get to innovation or the "light bulb" faster based on the quality of rich emotional visuals and sensorial inputs created by this process.

WEBSUALIZATION

Michael Solomon, visiting professor of marketing at St. Joseph's University Haub School of Business, is so sanguine about involving the right people in a new research process that he developed a unique visual approach online. For research purposes, people can access hundreds of pictures that help them gain unusual insight through the process of visualization.[7]

Speaking of traditional focus-group research, he believes that there is little effort today to involve customers in the decision-making process in a substantial way. "In some cases, [corporations are] just content to settle for a few focus groups to validate ideas in which they already are intellectually or financially invested."

Solomon's theory, articulated around the idea of "participatory marketing," is based on the fact that consumers need to be full partners in the research process, as a guide to corporations and sometimes as sounding boards. "Consumer empowerment offers new opportunities," he says, and he is absolutely bent on representing the true voice of the consumer to those corporations that hire his services. His process employs a multi-method, visually based approach to explore the underlying meanings associated by consumers with brands from an emotional value perspective or sensory experience, meanings such as "freshness" or "well-being."

By visualizing the sensory and emotional needs stated by consumers, the process allows for:

1. Visualizing concept and meaning dimensions for specific products and usage situations.

2. Exploring the most relevant sensory modality in which those concepts can be delivered.

3. Addressing product categories and usage situations where consumers prioritize each emotional or sensory value.

Participants from around the globe can interface on the Web through collage creation approaches in which they select key images across visual categories. "Participants are recruited from national, statistically representative panels according to the needs of each individual study. The Web site presents them with images of products in a range of product categories that they then arrange into collages," says Solomon. This provides visceral, unfiltered responses to the products tested, including the social contexts most relevant to them.

Mind/Share Inc. did an interesting project for Invista performance fibers, formerly Dupont apparel and textiles. The company that owns brands such as Lycra, Tactel, and Coolmax is largely engineering driven, and Invista wanted to do research that would be based on consumers' needs. Mind/Share Inc. developed a sequence of three data-collection steps to build data. Mind/Share's first step involved the use of traditional focus groups to gather consumers' ideas about a latent concept, such as freshness, and to get a sense of how they tend to visually represent the concept. The next step was an online survey that asks respondents to link various product concepts and usage scenarios and to share their reactions in terms of the desirability of these. The final step, also in an online format, focused more specifically on the product that respondents prefer and also on those new product ideas for which respondents are willing to pay a premium.

"This allowed us to take a 'market-back' approach by identifying unmet consumer needs and then developing fibers to meet those needs, in contrast to the typical 'molecule-forward' approach of inventing a new fiber technology and then trying to find one or more applications for it," says Solomon. This approach had a huge impact on Invista's product development initiatives as it opened the door to new opportunities based on how people felt about a category. The Internet format, unlike traditional focus groups that minimize people's interaction, added a freer form of response for people, since they could not be judged by their peers and could participate in a less formal environment, which allowed them to open up more with fun, new visual stimuli.

For designers, those new types of research discoveries based on human sciences are great tools for uncovering the hidden aspirations of people and their emotional reality. If a campfire always conveys the meaning of discovery and friendship, then when the visual of a campfire is selected to express the personality of a brand, we know how people truly think of the brand. Unconsciously, people are passing information through visual communication that would never be articulated in the rational context of a focus group.

VISUALIZING EMOTIONAL PORTRAITS

Vincent Van Gogh was an artist in the Impressionist movement who was not just painting what he saw, but how he felt about what he saw. Branding for me as a designer has always been about asking myself, "How do people feel about a brand?" not just what that product is going to do functionally. Visualization is about feelings if feelings are probed.

For my speaking engagements, I have created a visual presentation portraying a stereotypical suburban woman, her car, her house, and a photo of her husband. Then I ask, "What's wrong with this picture?" Most people in the audience don't know what I am talking about. I then show the same woman wearing more exciting clothes and ask, "What if she wants to feel this way instead?" I follow up with pictures of a dream car, a much more beautiful house, and the portrait of a cool-looking, handsome young man who, as I like to say, "she would rather be with." Although the first photograph represents how marketers and researchers usually visualize their customers' profile, the image does not reveal the hidden emotional aspirations of this "perfect" customer at all.

For instance, seemingly conservative middle-aged women buy very sexy lingerie in Victoria's Secret. Being naughty is a transforming experience even if the product you wear is hidden. The movie *In Her Shoes* is about the interaction between two sisters whose personalities are defined by their love of shoes. Actress Cameron Diaz discovers her (more successful) lawyer sister's shoe closet, and while eyeing her sister's vast shoe collection with envy tells her, "These shoes shouldn't be in your closet, they should live a life of scandal." Her sister (played by Toni Collette) justifies her purchases later on by saying, "I get something out of them. . . . Clothes never look any good. Food makes me fatter. Shoes always fit." Shoes are safe, fun, and pure gratification without the negative psychological baggage. Beyond the fact that this is partly why the shoe industry is such a booming business, in this dialogue one finds beyond style and fit a much more interesting insight into how women feel in general—information that is only available if you take a closer look at shoes in an emotional context.

Visualizing emotions gives us deeper insights into people's behavior than the superficial physical portraits of consumers. It demonstrates how complex and conflicted we all are and how we want to activate or experience all of our emotions in order to feel alive or different. Emotional customer profiles are key to better understand people's motivations and aspirations particularly in regard to self-esteem and peer relationship. The five emotional profiles I established in Shift 1—Citizenship, Freedom, Status, Harmony, and Trust—are a great way to start identifying and crafting a consumer emotional portrait.

THE PENTAGON AND VISUALIZATION

Thinking like a terrorist is something the Pentagon is very keen on these days. People who can visualize planes as weapons might see vehicles of destruction in other forms that are not yet written about in military books. Terrorists are agile, mobile, imaginative, and unpredictable. The army has always used creative thinkers, alongside more formally trained military professionals, to bring a different perspective. Jeff Baxter—a former musician who joined the Doobie Brothers in 1974—uses his out-of-the-box ideas to help the Pentagon anticipate terrorist tactics and strategies. The Pentagon is taking initiatives that are outside its comfort zone.

By contrast, businesses are not doing this; they follow a limited approach to branding that takes the inspiration out of the process by avoiding the tough questions that would challenge existing conventions. How is our competitor thinking? Who is going to be our next competitor? How do we react and protect ourselves? The answers lie in bringing out scenarios that are based in our imagination and expressed through visualization. This kind of approach is more powerful than any probing through a third party, particularly when it comes to set a new course for a brand.

Major business pioneers such as Leonard Lauder or Andrew Grove, the former CEO of Intel, have used visualization techniques to anticipate a business success or jump start a major turnaround of a company. As Andrew Grove explains in his book *Only the Paranoid Survive*, "To make it through the valley of death successfully, your first task is to form a mental image of what the company should look like when you get to the other side. This image not only needs to be clear enough for you to visualize but it also has to be crisp enough so you can communicate it simply to your tired, demoralized, and confused staff."[8] Leonard Lauder, as quoted in his mother's book *Estée: A Success Story* says, "I've visualized success, then created the reality from the image." Both express their use of mental visualization to anticipate the future of their business and their brands.[9]

Olivia Fox Cabane, author of *The Pocket Guide to Becoming a Superstar in Your Field* and executive director of New York–based Spitfire Communications, believes that visualization works so well because our subconscious mind does not distinguish between imagination and reality. "During a movie, when we see blood and guts on the screen, our subconscious sends us straight into 'fight or flight' mode, even though our conscious mind knows that it is fiction, because the subconscious mind—which controls most of our bodily functions—believes what it sees to be real." This is why, she says, professional athletes will spend hours visualizing their victory: their subconscious mind will accept the victory as real and will have the body act accordingly.[10]

This is the reason why the power of visualization around emotional states or feelings should be part of any brand ideation. Designers are very adept at this process and practice it every day, but they are still a vastly under-leveraged resource.

Observation: Research through the Designer's Eye

Nearly twenty creative executives from our firm went to Japan for one of our global meetings, and as usual, time was reserved for visiting new places and exploring new trends and ideas. The best form of research is to take into account the designer's power to observe and filter outside information and stimuli for creative purposes. These days in the branding world, the designer's visual sense, the fruit of years of emotional connections to culture, art, and people, is put to test rather than looked upon as a complementary research approach.

> In the branding world, the designer's visual sense, the fruit of years of emotional connections to culture, art, and people, is put to test rather than looked upon as a complementary research approach.

Tokyo is the right place for this. The Japanese youth in particular seem to escape from the rigor of a very homogenous and demanding society by expressing their individuality through brands. Parallel to this is the affirmation that Japanese youth find in iconic foreign brands. You also discover a childlike fantasy world of comic strip characters, accessories and fashion paraphernalia that is unique in the world, making Japan a laboratory to observe new ideas and trends. This need to escape by borrowing foreign influences and iconic brands has made Japan a cradle for innovation.

Many products around the world have been created based on Tokyo trends, such as the L'Oreal hair-color brushes, for instance. The audit is therefore mandatory but also challenging. The Japanese market is always busy with too many new products and ideas, some copied but many original; the search is continually on and requires serious digging and editing. The people in the group that traveled to Japan are considered the creative leaders at Desgrippes Gobé. They can pick out the "Wow" ideas, even when they are surrounded by an overwhelming environment where everything looks good! Our creative directors will return with key observations that are revealing of a society or a trend, observations that inform the rest of the company about a cultural shift from a design-anthropology perspective. These team members have the unique ability to go beyond the obvious and identify the special.

One of the discoveries that made recently in Tokyo toy stores was "Gloomy" the bear. Gloomy is a small, cute bear with paws that, on closer look, have real claws. The bear *seems* cute until you go deeper into his story. Gloomy, it turns out, is a nasty little fellow—in his cartoon strip he actually attacks children, punching them or slashing them with his sharp claws. It is pretty intense as blood is splattered all over. Once you've experienced the initial shock of these images, however, you learn that Japanese teenage customers are enamored with this violent toy.

For Japanese teenagers, Gloomy's extreme story is perceived as funny, far less disturbing than it would be for Westerners. The powerful realism of the story by contrast makes it unreal in Japanese teen's eyes and the brutality in this context is considered hilarious. Teenagers absolutely adore this little monster, which was the humble creation of a street artist before it gained the fame it has now. Of course, violence has always been a part of teenagers' lives, whether Eastern or Western—guns, army vehicles, war toys, and video games based on killing and destruction are not new. But violence associated with an ultimately "cute" toy—the teddy bear—enters into an unexplored territory that is emotionally more challenging. A teddy bear just doesn't do things like this!

In a world in crisis, this rejection of the unreal, safe, and cuddly is important to understand as a trend. It shows that the world is perceived by younger generations as dangerous. Teenagers have reached their point of confrontation with reality and are finding ways to escape it through humor. From a psychological perspective, it is well known that horror stories help children exorcise their fears of the night and the unknown. Teenagers around the world clearly want to affirm their identity through eye-popping product associations or symbols that digress from the uniformity of their lives and parent's expectations. They are the best group at innovating or reframing reality to fit their anxieties, such as making something that is funny scary, and vice versa.

That type of information filtered through the eye of the designer is one of the most powerful ways to analyze a market or comprehend the vast mosaic of people's life stages. I don't know if in the future we will see more products or brand strategies that mix the realistic with the dramatic and repackage the outrageous in quirky humor, but the way to reach people will certainly be to go through their psychological mind states, and creative people are well equipped to do that.

The ultimate emotional impact on brand messages from that point of view is already present in the marketplace. The success of reality TV might be trading on the adventurous and dangerous side of life without the risks. The Gothic look in fashion is clearly reminiscent of children's books in which ghosts, monsters, and villains horrified our youth. Our unconscious works in peculiar ways, and designers can help brands understand these unconscious shifts as they seek to reach their audiences in the most meaningful way.

Our unconscious works in peculiar ways, and designers can help brands understand these unconscious shifts as they seek to reach their audiences in the most meaningful way.

Creative people in general do not believe that there is a relevant process today for evaluating a new design or a new idea. And they might be right. Why couldn't the instinctive and creative process not be considered as research, since it is often the source of most breakthrough innovation? Why couldn't we observe people and their environments to unearth their dreams instead of asking them only practically minded or expected projective questions? When researchers are designers or people from the creative field, you add another layer of insight that is intuitive and future-oriented. When creative people express opinions on new ideas, colors, graphics, or shapes, they bring to life a new vision for the brand, a new point of view, a new take on the world we live in. It's not only about the product but the brand and its emotional connection.

DESIGN OBSERVATION
Design research is the "new, improved" research. It's what happens when you mix the power of understanding with the spark of inspiration, which is when creative people use their imagination to predict the future, either of a company or of its brands.

The most feared phrase for designers is "focus group research," when it is used as the ultimate tool for judging design, new ideas, or concepts. Asking consumers to be the final judge of a new design concept or suggesting that they would be the only inspiration for new ideas is totally unfair. Consumers don't have the benefit of the information we have on the brand, the brand strategy, or the challenges it faces in a highly competitive world.

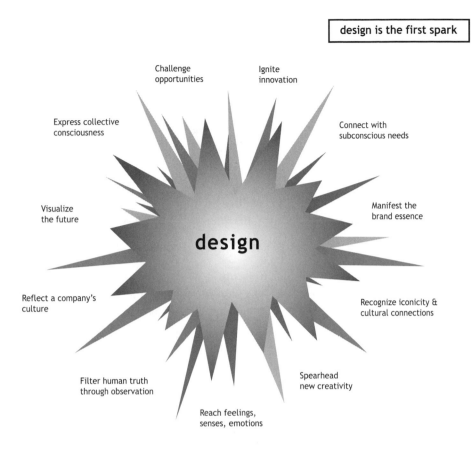

Challenge
opportunities

Ignite
innovation

Express collective
consciousness

Connect with
subconscious needs

Visualize
the future

Manifest the
brand essence

design

Reflect a company's
culture

Recognize iconicity &
cultural connections

Filter human truth
through observation

Spearhead
new creativity

Reach feelings,
senses, emotions

Design as research: Corporations now rely on design as a source of inspiration beyond pure aesthetics.

In doubt? Go to the market; see with your own eyes. For instance, according to an interview in *WWD* with Stacey Cartwright, Burberry's COO, the company is putting in place a new software system that will allow it to understand what products its customers are buying and why. The brand will be able, for instance, to know "if bags sell better when displayed with a dress or analyze why customers at the Moscow store buy trenches with their eveningwear."[11] The best design research process integrates observational studies of consumer's motivations and unconscious desires. Effective research today is based less and less on asking people what they think about a brand and more on observation of them in real-life situations.

This information again supports the idea that the experience created around the brand can change someone's perception and that testing or researching design ideas out of context or in isolation immediately limits the understanding of the emotional interaction that could be created by, for example, a great window display.

When Benjamin Nissanoff and his wife started their bath soaps based on ice cream flavors (see also Shift 4), they wanted to test out the idea but did not want to use focus groups, which are usually held in a bleak environment, so they decided to go to people directly by setting up a booth in several farmers' markets in the Midwest. That's certainly the more gutsy way to do it—being there, listening to people's comments directly, as well as the sound of an opening wallet (the final proof of success).

To their delight, the product did well, but it was in casual conversation with people that they discovered the idea that launched their business and ultimately made it successful: farmers' market visitors saw in their round soaps the look and feel of a scoop of ice cream! It did not take long for these entrepreneurs to shift their brand focus from bath soaps to "bath ice cream," a concept that has opened doors to some of the best spas in the country. Emotionally, what people saw in the idea, says Benjamin, is a fresh new

Testing new "concept" soaps at a farmer's market.

concept, connecting the feeling of pleasure and guilt associated with ice cream to bath products, which in turn provides a guilt-free pleasure that reminds people of childhood. The live **The live research Nissanoff and his wife conducted in farmers' markets led to a real dialogue between their customers and their brand.** research Nissanoff and his wife conducted led to a real dialogue between their customers and their brand. The environment was conducive to dialogue and the response was real and genuine. It helped build their business.

THE EMBEDDED DESIGNER

The death of a good idea for research reasons is a designer's nightmare. My company had developed a new packaging for a major company. After six months of relentless design exploration and consumer probing, the final solution was almost identical visually to the original design. After exploring hundreds of innovative ideas that could have moved the brand to a better place, we were back to where we had started. "Opening to innovation is outside of most people's comfort zone," says Franco Lodato, VP of Design Exploration at Herman Miller, "and I truly believe that some research techniques have adapted to support the brand's fear."[12]

I recommend that every company appoint an innovation captain, someone whose role it is to say, "No, it's ugly" or "not differentiated enough," someone who understands the power of design and its impact on society. It is not the role of marketers to lead a creative exercise; only a few can do it, people like Steve Jobs of Apple. To make a difference, marketers and researchers can help their perception greatly by partnering with creative people.

Designers, architects, art directors, and stylists think and feel at the same time. They are incredible observers of life and generally see what others' untrained eyes do not. They find the unusual in the most ordinary places—that unique color, a unique typography, a trend, a texture you want to touch, structures that tell a story, objects that in any other context would have a different appeal, the magic of the eternal partnership between man and nature. A sound, a smell, a moment in time with others becomes a defining idea to share.

Think about fashion shows; they are a good benchmark of where fashion designers are redefining culture. The fashion show attracts top buyers from the retail world, media, even suits from Wall Street who are interested to see how their investment is doing. You can tell by the mood and attitude of the audience if a collection has hit the mark or not, and what the trends and innovation will be for the coming year. The fashion world evaluates and reviews their collections on a seasonal basis, understanding that change is key to creating customer interest.

For trend discovery, one of the most visited fashion events is "Premiere Vision." Held twice a year in Paris, this 60,000-square-foot weavers' trade show presents the latest and most creative fabrics. The show attracts not only fashion professionals but also designers, marketers, and visionary executives such as Michael Dell. In this show you can find what the colors of the future will be and the textures that will inspire fashion designers in their next collections. It is truly a place that excites your senses and imagination, a crossroad of creativity and a picture of the styles and designs that people will wear. There you can feel the mood of the world expressed in the most creative fashion.

In the mass-market, consumer-goods world, some brands have realized that change is key to building loyalty. Coca-Cola, Pepsi, and Cadbury have moved toward seasonal strategies inspired by the fashion world. Fashion shows are about inspiration and a sensory way of presenting the brand in its total visual expression. This is also the ultimate test, with professionals as judges of a designer's creativity and vitality. Why not emulate this format instead of using traditional focus groups? This would force brands to expose their creativity and be reviewed by people who bring a more informed and discerning judgment to the table. It would also force marketing professionals to think of their brands as an important event when launched.

A few years back, Proctor & Gamble (not a client of mine at the time), paid me to assess their different beauty brands. I was told to be as candid and truthful as possible. P&G's top management wanted an outside designer's "eye" that could look in with a fresh perception. I found the process courageous and smart. Now P&G is leading the new industry transformation. Design and the creative process have taken on a real role within the organization as an agent of change[15] (see also Insight 2, pages 17 through 25). P&G has named Claudia Kotchka vice president for design innovation, but such a role is still absent in most corporations. J&J has hired Chris Hacker, a well-known designer who revived the Aveda beauty line to take charge of the visual vocabulary of all J&J products. But in most corporations these positions are not given the authority they deserve or the freedom to be creative, and the brands are suffering. "Design used to be an afterthought with the company focusing mostly on the graphics of the packaging. Today it is evident that good design can help a brand differentiate itself in the marketplace," says Claudia Kotchka.[14]

From a research perspective, what P&G has discovered is what *Newsweek* called "Going Home with the Customer." The P&G designers go to the homes of consumers to gather firsthand information. One result of such exploration is a new design for Kandoo toilet-training wipes for kids. Based on research that showed that kids want to be empowered to do things on their own, P&G embarked on the design of a new box of wipes that helps kids use the product by pressing a large, easy-to-identify button on the lid. "Kids went nuts for it," says Kotchka.[15]

This approach certainly has become an inspiration for others, but one should not lose sight of the fact that new product ideas will be more memorable and preferred by customers if they *transcend* the functional and also create a beautiful aesthetic. Style makes a brand feel more friendly and approachable and touches people's emotions in an unforgettable way. Research needs to include searching for the creative inspiration to better inspire designers and marketing professionals. Case in point: at the NRF (National Retail Federation) convention in New York City, the most savvy retail-relevant electronic products

We are often testing the wrong things: products instead of behavior, acceptability instead of experience.

were presented. One booth showed a handheld electronic device that a customer could use to find the merchandise they like faster, review the kinds of products he or she bought previously (which is very useful when buying products like books), learn what promotions there are, and check out while in the store without waiting in line. For the retailers it is a great way to integrate supply and demand and to streamline costs. But the handheld electronic device was bulky, heavy, and not that compelling, a far cry from the sexy look of most cell phones we are familiar with today. The experience was not organic, sensual, and emotional; it was hi-tech, processed, and inhuman, in effect turning humans into machines. This was an unfortunate drawback to the program, which sought to empower people by saving them time. Research into consumers' behavior around a certain product can be a huge opportunity for marketers. But we are often testing the wrong things: products instead of behavior, acceptability instead of experience.

DESIGN DISCOVERY

Designers have an uncanny ability to find or create beauty in chaos. Scottish artist Andy Goldsworthy is foremost in inspiring the world to look at nature in a different fashion. He redefines the language of nature in a responsible way. What he does with found pieces of our natural environment is a celebration of the core foundation of our lives and our relation to the universe. Nature understands his language and has guided him in some amazing discoveries, such as when he found stones in a New York state river that produce a magnificent red color when crushed. "I want to get under the surface," says Goldsworthy. "When I work with a leaf, rock, stick, it is not just that material in itself, it is the opening into the process of life within and around it. When I leave it, these processes continue."[16] Goldsworthy's work is instinctive and primal, transforming into human art another form of natural art that we are familiar with. Guided simply by his hands, he creates a new natural language that we are close to but misunderstand sometimes. It allows us to see familiar things in a new light, unfamiliar things in an unforced way. He knows how to celebrate life by celebrating our environment, how to make us rediscover the essence of what and who we are. Designers have this inner sensibility, to create visual and sensory work that makes our hearts pound.

The best designers live in a world of intuitive sensibilities driven by imagination. Some have tried to imitate, bottle, or deconstruct those kinds of thinking, but most designers find in their discovery a gate to freedom, away from the expected to the magical. Freedom is the ultimate emotional state for a designer, and it is heightened when others open up and understand their own reality and world. Branding can offer a door onto the process of life if we open our eyes and let our minds be open to new possibilities. The ability to extract the truth hidden behind mass information, to translate that innovation into products that challenge people's reality but at the same time respond to their deeper aspirations—that is what design research is all about. Designers translate visual information into architecture, new products, and communication tools that compel people to experience a brand. We respond to brands in the context of our environment, not in the clinical "dark rooms" of a focus group, where all sensory stimuli are dimmed as much as the light. Testing out graphics, breakthrough commercials, or any other communication tool that is supposed to be transformative, but it just sets the stage for revolutionary ideas never to see the light. Research needs to enhance the creative process, not take away from it.

Design research is all about the ability to extract the truth hidden behind mass information, to translate that innovation into products that challenge people's reality.

THE DESIGNER IS THE CONSUMER

And why not? I would challenge the branding world to reconsider consumer research and even to adopt design as research. This is revolutionary, but I will go even further and say that designers are really "the consumers." As visual anthropologists, designers understand visual communication better than anyone. By integrating the imaginative power of design into a true partnership between consumers, creative professionals, and innovative marketers, you can:

- *Jazz up* your ideas and challenge preconceived formulas.
- Set the stage for marketers, consumers, and designers to be partners in innovation from the beginning of the branding process.
- Validate the hypotheses of marketers and designers in a richer way.
- Put on equal footing the power of logic and the inspiration of the more visceral creative process.

This would signal the end of the top-down client-researcher relationship as the main axis for brand development. I am not saying that every design idea will fly and that designers are some kind of infallible gurus. Some ideas influenced by designers might not make it, and might even fail the same way other ideas are failing right now. But in a dollar-to-dollar comparison, the direct financial impact of the rate of failures from the old method compared to the huge successes of those new ideas that build brands emerges to be vastly positive on the brand side. Designers get all the blame for one weak idea, while the research industry remains immune to it, and this false accountability needs to change.

> In a world where consumers are looking for pleasure and innovation, ideas that they can *see*, you can't rely on focus groups to bring forth what they can't even imagine *could exist*.

Marketing today is led by people who have tremendous managerial talent who need to be challenged and exposed to the best ideas. This is not happening; the dialogue does not exist. In a world where consumers are looking for pleasure and innovation, ideas that they can *see*, you can't rely on focus groups to bring forth what they can't even imagine *could exist*. The goal is to transform a world of sameness into a world of exciting and relevant beauty.

Brandjam: Finding Insight through Collaborative Discovery

Brandjam is an insight process that Desgrippes Gobé has developed from Brand Focus, an evolved approach to branding based on years of consulting with

225

major corporations (see also my first book, *Emotional Branding*). It is proving the power of collaborative thinking between designers, marketers, and consumers, around a new set of emotional aspirations and the power of visualization as a new language for innovation. Brandjam helps to create naming solutions, address consumer insight, bring to life corporate cultures, and foster the creation of new product opportunities and innovative visual identities.

Brandjam lines up management teams behind fresh, consumer-driven creative visions and stresses collaboration over individuality. P&G is leading that charge by reengineering its management model to encourage greater involvement of employees with consumers[17] while at the same time promote collaboration at all levels. James P. Womack demonstrates that the weakness of the overall American automobile industry versus its Japanese counterpart is the lack of a really good business model: "GM and Ford can't design vehicles that Americans want to pay 'Toyota's' money for," adding that their business model does not encourage interaction and dialogue with consumers the way Lexus does.[18]

We have learned that these diverse brand teams spend most of their time working as silos, without a clear understanding of the brand's ultimate impact.

Sometimes, the perception of a brand is not vastly different from the corporate perception, but the real insight is in the emotional nuances. In one of our sessions we were intrigued by how a leading brand saw itself versus their clients: as a father figure, a protective force. Accordingly, they selected a visual showing a child looking up to "Dad." Their clients did not have a problem with the Dad figure, but they selected a visual with a sitting dad talking eye to eye with his child. The brand's clients were actually expressing their trust but wanted less arrogance from the brand itself. Same idea, different emotional perceptions.

Unfortunately, more often than not a brand is managed by a host of dynamic players. Most typically, the team consists of a CEO, a CMO, a creative director, a director of product development, a lead engineer, an advertising agency, a branding firm, a research firm, a PR firm, a promotional consultancy, the IT department, and the list can go on from there. Brand teams tend to craft their own personal versions of what their brand can stand for. Individuals use what works for them personally, creating initiatives in isolation that work against consumers' perception of a brand.

Most brands also have reams of research data that either tells them what they already know or brings them contradictory material to execute against. Companies pay extraordinary sums of money to track much of what they think is pertinent information. But they often do not address how a brand may be shoving complex and confusing communications in consumers' faces.

Brandjamming helps bring the brand home, what we call "landing," by bringing all the decision makers together to focus on its internal meaning as well as its face to the world. By crafting brand emotions through narratives, brandjam acts as a compelling brand-building and innovation tool designed to build a brand's emotional identity and address these four core issues:

1. Team alignment around a clear brand vision, language, and platform.
2. A visualized and sensorial declaration of what your brand is about.
3. A go-forward brand story that is brand-right, timely, and strategic.
4. A tool to indoctrinate your internal team to make believers out of them.

WORDS ARE FIXED—VISUALS DON'T LIE

The brandjam process entails researching thousands of visuals to find the one that best represents a brand's core characteristics as well as introduce new shadings or evolved brand values. In a day-long, structured, game-like setting, senior management brand teams select and comment on these visuals to create a new brand portrait. Brandjam has helped reposition major brands right down to the selection of a distinct visual language, tone, message, cause, relevant spokesperson, core colors, and typographic style.

We have conducted these types of brandjam sessions for more than fifteen years with Fortune 500 companies in the United States and major groups around the world. We have talked to more than a thousand of the brightest, most qualified people. The process was even covered by the *New Yorker* as we were repositioning the venerable clothing retailer Brooks Brothers for a younger audience.

THE PROCESS HAS BROUGHT US A NEW SENSE OF THE BRAND

When we initially pitched Brand Focus, the precursor to the brandjam process, the reaction was, "Well, we don't know if we fully understand this tool, but just in case we are missing something, let's try it." That was the booming 1990s. The budgets were there, but not a strong commitment by brand teams to embrace and execute our findings and recommendations.

The early years of the new century were tentative. No one could figure out what brandjamming would bring to the corporate culture, and the mood was for cost-cutting rather than innovation. The brandjamming process was used as a way to get to solutions more quickly and cheaply. Post-9/11, reality set in. The concept of reinvention became a strategy for growth. In a tough economy people were holding tight; in a tough reality people wanted to fight to survive. The era brought us out of our comfort zone (high-image beverage, beauty, fashion, and jewelry brands) into the world of universities, esteemed newspapers, banks, pharmaceuticals, insurance companies, and consumer services. All of these entities were now more concerned than ever before with what their story, look, and vibe consisted of, and they wanted to understand what the outside perceptions of their brands were all about.

THE GLOBAL CORPORATE VISUAL PORTRAIT

The most interesting discovery for us during those years was what we learned while interviewing and brainstorming with the top management of major global corporations. We saw an unconscious demand for innovation and freedom. Teams of talented people were paralyzed by red tape, vested players, company politics, layers of management, fears about change, alienating an existing core consumer, mounting competition, and on and on. The desire to move forward was pent up in people's corporate lives, and we thought the frustrations were bound to explode. There was no strategy to address a rapidly evolving consumer landscape and a marked difference between how the Controlling Baby Boomers, the Experiential Gen Xers, and the Brand-Disconnected Generation Y saw life.

TEAMS USED VISUALS TO DISCOVER THEIR OWN STORY

Out of thousands of visuals, corporations always seemed to choose what we call a few "jackpot visuals" to be their "face," or emotional portrait. They revealed profound issues such as generational differences and an overall frustrated corporate mood. Here are the top three:

1. **A woman's hand opening a white curtain to look through a window onto a lush green forest.** This most chosen visual begged for a new way out of a current situation, and the message was one of hope for change, clearly indicating that the management wanted a green light to go out of bounds and find the next inspiration for creativity.

2. **A hand with thumb and index finger touching in front of the sun, as if trying to capture a piece of radiant sunshine.** This visual is an emotional message that tells us about the need to find the next idea, to capture the impossible, to discover the unknown and leverage a brand's connection with natural resources.

3. **A dynamic red sculpture made of differently shaped pieces that fit together to make a perfect square.** This was a message about diversity and multidimensional partnership. Cohesion among all the different pieces to arrive at something coherent reveals the challenges in our global world to meet the aspirations of a diverse work environment. The fitting together of these pieces screamed the need for recognition and the beauty that comes from people of different backgrounds and personalities working together to make sense out of chaos through innovation and integration.

The brandjam process showed us that people in corporations had the talent and wherewithal to effect change but that the existing business model did not offer that opportunity. In an emotional economy, there is no model to follow up on, no benchmarking that allows room for emotional analysis. As we would deliver our findings to executives who had participated in the workshop, the challenge was how unprepared corporations are when facing an emotional economy. You could feel how tough it would be to implement those findings and the lack of internal freedom to try new ideas out. The emotional language to communicate those ideas internally was absent, and the models to connect new emotional ideas with the outside world did not usually exist within a company.

There was a vast difference between traditional companies and more innovative ones. Banks, insurance companies, industrial corporations, or traditional consumer goods companies were about opportunities to be defined, selecting visuals such as structures and objects with a sense of craftsmanship, while retailers and Web-driven businesses were about ideas to be implemented, selecting visuals such as a light bulb or a multicolored artwork. You could really see what stage of innovation a team was at and assess their tolerance for change.

Some of our clients have made major, exciting changes and some are still considering them. But brandjam is an intuitive process that is most powerful when it demonstrates the human drama within corporations and shows how to embrace a new language and dialogue to connect big ideas to the reality of a dynamic marketplace.

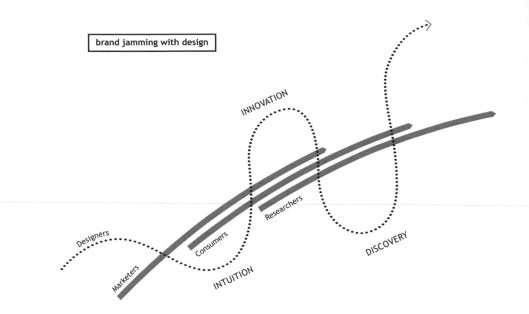

Design, not unlike music, benefits and inspires the creative process.

Research Designers Crave

When it is repurposed to probe cultural, psychological, emotional, and anthropological perspectives, research can provide deep insight into people's motivations, behaviors, and lifestyles. I love research when the questions posed are based on how people *feel* about a design, not whether or not they like the graphics, when it uncovers unknown realities and emotions, such as the fact that many people will buy a brand because it is socially responsible. I am inspired by the way Jungian archetypes can help define the visual expression of a corporation's gut and soul. When applied to a company and evolved to fit today's marketplace, Jung's inspired psychological portraits can lead to some of the best, most focused work. I love all research that helps me get a better understanding of people's emotional desires and cultural aspirations. I love to know people's anxieties and pressures; I like to have an emotional profile of the person for whom I am designing.

Sometimes the best research comes from smart observation, putting yourself in the shoes of the consumer you want to reach. If mass marketing is dead, then understanding the different niches of people and their expectations can bring new insight if this understanding is emotional. The reality is that research can't be institutionalized: Sometimes the best research comes from smart observation, putting yourself in the shoes of the consumer you want to reach, and having the courage to follow through.

What this means: *There is so much people would love to tell us about themselves, and then there is the information that is hidden in their subconscious. The gate to that subconscious can only be unlocked through the power of intuition and imagination, giving people a new language to express their emotions. Visualizing brands through narratives in a collaborative way, with stories that stimulate people's dormant emotional states, creates a new level of understanding of people's unmet desires.*

SHIFT 6
Think Commodity Design (Not!)

There is no bigger idea than design.
—*Steve Hayden, Vice Chairman, Ogilvy & Mather, New York*

If there is one country that understands design today it is China. In its Asian edition of its November 21, 2005, issue, *Business Week* titled its cover "China Design: How the Mainland Is Becoming a Global Center for 'Hot' Products." The article emphasized how Chinese companies, not unlike those of their successful neighbor and inspiration Korea, are seeing their future through the lens of design.[1] Young talents now from China but also from around the world are participating in or moving to this new emerging economy to experience the thrill of innovation and invention. As design is now a favorite major in Chinese universities, a movement is taking place to support the worldwide opportunities that exist for new Chinese brands worldwide.

China Invents

Lenovo Group Ltd., which bought the IBM PC division in May 2005, "is focusing on design as a way to establish worldwide credibility for the brand through innovation at a breakneck speed," said Deepak Advani, SVP and CMO of Lenovo, at a Columbia University Conference that I attended.[2] He knows well that once the almighty IBM logo disappears from its products as a signature, the new Lenovo brand will need to stand out successfully.

Yao Yingjia, Lenovo's lead designer, already runs a team of more than one hundred people worldwide and is even changing the way IBM in the United States used to look at managing the formidable equity the IBM "Thinkpad" had established. Innovation through design is not even an option for countries like China; it means survival. Yao also brings a particularly Chinese version of the jazzed-up approach to creativity. To inspire his team and the company's executives to

understand the power of creation, Yao takes them on retreats where they build rafts from scrap material and then sail across a lake.[5] This is brandjamming at its best, making people share and participate in the creative process with a purpose in mind but also the freedom that sparks their imagination.

Lenovo is moving up the brand ladder with impressive energy; their vastly successful new cell phone, according to *Business Week,* is the only electronic device that, among other things, emits a sweet fragrance as the batteries heat up. Pushing the limits of innovation to be sensorial and provocative is not an option for this brand to succeed, it has to do more and experiment with passion.

It is not a coincidence that in this same *Business Week* issue there also appeared an article on "The End of TV," meaning the end of advertising-sponsored TV shows. In a media landscape that is losing the attention of its audience, the emergence of a new communications power—design—is becoming more and more clear; it is what connects with people best, and it is filling some of the void left by the retreating TV advertising business.

In a new world of communications empowerment (see Shift 1), the product has to work harder to convince; it is now not only the proof of a brand promise but also an engagement to new discovery. The product is the hero. The strategy is design. Let's face it: we live in an iPod economy based in rapid innovation transforming not only brands, but inviting brands to transform their surrounding environment. Our commercial, personal, and public spaces are designed spaces. By emotional branding we understand people's aspirations. As Oprah Winfrey mentioned in one of her shows on home decoration, "You deserve to have something beautiful."

> **By emotional design we design our way into a courageous and inspiring future of promise but also an engagement to new discovery. The producer is the hero. The strategy is design.**

The IDSA: A New World of Design

The Industrial Design Society of America (IDSA) invited me to be a judge for its 2005 Industrial Design Excellence Awards, where I got a chance not only to sit with jurors of immense talent and reputation from the United States, Europe, Asia, and South America, but also to review industrial design entries from around the world that captured the look and feel of their different societies' self-images, corporate values, and ideas of progress.

In these competitions, you get a broad bird's-eye view of the impact of design on society, a sense of how design will influence the future, and how designers can shift consumers' expectations. The designs ranged from the most advanced macro-medical technology to a completely recycled corrugated "flip-flop" that expressed "spa and craftsmanship" in the most simple way; from a sexy, racy car to a baby bottle; from a power drill to a digital camera; from the subliminal to the pleasurable. I could see great innovations penalized by bad design, and great design that came across as fake given the poor quality of the products.

Most fascinating, however, was how the best ideas and visual codes in one category could inspire another category in major ways. For example, we found inspirations in the washer and dryer entries that could have been relevant and inspirational to the digital projectors. There are also leaders in their categories that do not show their vitality while small emerging brands—such as Method, a new line of cleaning products successfully sold through Target—have utilized design as a competitive advantage.

The medical category had the most innovative design. The scary procedures and severe-looking equipment—MRI scanners, X-ray machines, heart stabilizers, cardiogram equipment, and surgical instruments—are becoming more ergonomic, friendly, and approachable.

During the judging process, I wrote down my observations on the impact design has in society and its role in strengthening brand strategies. My four strongest impressions were the following:

1. **People are the focus.** Designers' work will impact people's lives. In certain products focus on users' experiences, the sustainability values of the products, and their impact on the environment and society.

    Nike was one of the brands at the forefront, presenting technologically advanced products, such as sunglasses that monitor your health and performance by providing information, such as heart rate, that you can read inside your glasses while you work out. Another product included search-and-rescue jacket with mikes and radio holders. Nike is looking to broaden its product lines within specific categories, like sports gear, and in areas where it could imaginatively see itself as an asset.

2. **There was an imaginative response to lifestyle needs.** Many products were meant to go on a wall—a diversion from tabletop or desktop products that helps solve the problem of a lack of space in offices or apartments.

    There were also increasingly more products sensitive to an aging population (and to women in particular, who live longer and need more physical support), like a user-friendly contraption for securing a kayak to the roof of a car and a tennis racket designed to prevent tennis elbow. NASA-like technology brought whole new meaning to fitness for all ages. These "transgenerational" products promise a great future.

3. **Designers are creating emotional experiences.** Product quality is now paired with good design and sensorial elements. Design vocabulary hearkened back to the ideas of the arts-and-crafts movement, which offset the sterile and somewhat elitist design of modernism. One juror called the result "homespun, crafty, and emotionally beautiful products."

Designers are no longer working in a vacuum but from an emotional standpoint. IBM presented truly breakthrough lip-reading technology; Lexus's new hybrid car oversold at a huge premium before it was even put on the market. Fitness machines were designed to be in harmony with people's bodies and emotions. All of these designs help solve human challenges, but mostly they are attempting to communicate with people's souls.

4. **Corporations are discovering the need to leverage design.** There was evidence that the corporate world now views design not as just an aesthetic element, but as the message itself. It is now being understood as a witness of our progress as a society, an expression of changing cultural phenomena and life values. (I was particularly impressed by the visual language used for the Mini car accessories designed by Yves Behar; I could tell which brand they were for without seeing a logo.) Products with the potential to influence behavior impressed the jury most: organic, intuitive, simple designs with a new purpose.

> There was evidence that the corporate world now views design not as just an aesthetic element, but as the message itself.

It was not surprising that the foreign country that sent the most entries, given its size, was South Korea, in line with its competitive spirit and appreciation of design as a viable edge. For example, Samsung enters more design competitions than brands from other countries (see page 273). It pushes the limits of its offering by challenging itself to reach out to people through innovation. New South Korean conglomerates are seeing the possibilities through product design and are using the opportunity.

The jury was both internationally and professionally diverse, comprised of product designers, a journalist, an advertising executive, a furniture retailer of high-end European design, and design stylists like myself. I could feel cultural tensions in the jury: some preferred a mostly modern, minimalist aesthetic; other politically driven judges wanted to make a statement to the world; and the postmodernists focused on emotional and sensory experiences. After hours of preparation, two days of grueling judging, and more than ten thousand entries, the judges were commenting casually on the gold selections of each category on one table. We discussed the results, the process, and what it all meant to us as individuals. The best moment was when, on a hunch, Tucker Veimester, a renowned product designer and the president of the jury, asked everyone to take a yellow Post-it note and at the count of three place it as a vote on the photo of the entry we thought was the best of show. Given the wide variety of entries and their incredible quality, I thought the votes would be spread out all over the place. To my surprise, a huge majority of votes went to the elegant Nike "Considered" shoe—an environmentally friendly product that solved numerous styling and manufacturing challenges. The handcrafted look was a far cry from the processed look of so many products. "Substance leads style," said one Nike designer, and I thought this was a great statement about where design is headed. The Considered shoe crystallized an idea, a hope, and an emotional aspiration—that a product without a human soul is just a product.

ARE WE LEARNING THROUGH THE DESIGN MOSAIC?

The designs in the IDSA showed that competitive forces are at play, pushing corporations to differentiate themselves, and this may be where the opportunities lie. But in their rush to reach the new design El Dorado, brands forget that simple functional differentiation will no longer suffice: they must differentiate themselves from an *emotional design* perspective as well. That is why design is such a powerful tool.

Some entries in the same category had identical "visual style." In electronics, most products looked streamlined, used black and silver, and the "Apple-ization" was obvious, in more or less desirable ways. Industry leaders in all categories find themselves faced with competitors using *their* visual language, approved by the same research techniques. Design must be unique and courageous in order to succeed. Creating just another, albeit better-looking, generic product wastes money and can go against initial objectives that could have brought in a fresh spirit.

Design in the twenty-first century is defined by culture, not by designers, and that might be the greatest message of all. The best and the most comforting news to come out of the IDSA competition is that the notion of "lifestyle products"—products that look right and more importantly feel right—are a rapidly growing phenomenon. A design transformation is occurring. As one juror commented, "Everyone gets it; it does not need any explaining." This is good design versus bad design. Relevant design simply has a purpose and expresses an emotional reality created by a new set of experiences. Design in the twenty-first century is defined by culture, not by designers, and that might be the greatest message of all.

The Marketing Shift: Branding Needs Courageous Design

Courageous design needs courageous people. At a time when constant changes in consumers' behavior and aspirations impact perceptions of brands, design rises above the clutter, delivering a clear and consistent message. Design shifts the brand from commodity status utility to an emotionally inspired offering. Brands that adapt the right design, tailored to the culture of their corporation and consumer, can thrive amidst the forces fracturing the consumer base and multiply consumer expectations. As the rules of branding change to be more personal, design is an increasingly important way to survive and thrive amidst these changes.

I have interviewed several designers and marketers who, through collaborative techniques, created a new set of positive brand experiences by **In a branding world of cynical advertising and manipulative messages, it is refreshing to see that some executives with courage and belief are giving a good name to branding.** leveraging their sincerity, personal beliefs, and passions to meet people's expectations. Through the minds of these innovators, their personal visions, and the ways in which they see their brand's role in society, we will discover the profound truth that drives the success of the professionals who care for as well as want people to trust their brands.

"The shape of the Dove bar is iconic and a very important part of the equity success."

Why is Dove—$3 billion-plus brand—more successful than Ivory, when both started as just a plain bar of soap? Not quite, according to Silvia Lagnado, senior vice president at Unilever and global brand director of Dove. "The shape of the Dove bar is iconic and a very important part of the equity success," asserts Lagnado. "The real success comes from the shape, the promise (of beauty), the reason to believe (mildness and moisturization), and the powerful recommendation of dermatologists (in the United States and Canada)."

According to her, the design of this bar of soap had already resonated emotionally and "sensorially" with women in a way that helped the franchise become the beauty powerhouse it is today. The defining Dove Campaign for Real Beauty resonated with customers and media in one of those rare combinations of a "commerce meets culture" approach to building great global brands.

Building on the attachment women had with that little bar of soap, Dove became inspired to create a new skin- and hair-care offering. In an effort to create a powerful brand identity that would support such a business, Dove went back to celebrating that wonderful emotional connection of trust that

□ wrinkled?
□ wonderful?

Will society ever accept 'old' can be beautiful? Join the beauty debate.

campaignforrealbeauty.co.uk 🐦 | *Dove*

already existed. For most women who are intimidated by the portrayal of luxury beauty and fashion brands by professional models, the promise to always feel more beautiful needed to be attained through a more sensitive language. According to Lagnado, the brand could differentiate itself through inspiration rather than aspiration.

After Dove conducted a worldwide ethnographic survey regarding women's perceptions of their own bodies, they were amazed to find out that as Lagnado puts it, "too many women develop low self-esteem, form hang-ups about looks in their younger years, and, consequently, fail to reach their full potential in later life." Women were unhappy with the unrealistic expectations of beauty promoted by "luxury" brands.

Fortunately, when Lagnado took over the responsibility for Dove's brand management in 1994, she understood the potential her brand offered, but also intuitively realized that women like herself had changed. Unilever's corporate approach to having a "brand point of view" about the world inspired her to create her own point of view about women; and she felt that Dove could deliver that message. Women wanted to be reassured and told the truth in a real way.

The story would be just another marketing success story except that making a statement about the world is easier said than done, since it almost always creates debate and controversy, topics that marketers would rather avoid.

Lagnado admits that powerful brand messages conveyed by other brands such as Nike and Apple have paved the way by helping her sell her conviction to the company and bring meaning to the message behind her work.

For her, the most encouraging part of the journey was seeing how passionate and convinced her close team became about finding a message for women that could transcend the superficiality of most current marketing campaigns. She also understood that she would have to fight for her vision and struggle to sell her idea to the Unilever management. Realizing that no research would ever give her the back-up she needed until she had a fully realized campaign way down the road in post-production, she knew that only her own belief and passion would help make the project a reality.

Generally speaking, I am not fond of "guerilla marketing," a term often used with "ambushed" when speaking of strategies that will help grow a brand. On the other hand, this type of strategy works when trying to sell a great idea to higher ups in a corporation. In Lagnado's case, it meant doing the most taboo of all things: bypassing a few supervisors who doubted her (while they were on vacation!) and going directly to the top. And it worked, as the top executives at Unilever had already accepted the important role of brands in society. I see this more and more, where brand managers fight for their brands and their customers, becoming real activists for branding in general, and society in particular.

Lagnado's close relationship at the time with the Canadian team gave her the platform she needed to test and launch the wildly successful Campaign for Real Beauty. Still, although the thought she had a clear vision, the concept still needed to be articulated successfully. It took "a year of agony, a struggle to find the right answer." It took a creative director at Dove's agency Ogilvy & Mather. After talking to his wife one night about the campaign, he found out how little he knew about his wife's own feelings toward herself and the issues she had about her own body. This gave him a renewed—and now personal—interest in finding a solution for the communication of the brand.

The Campaign for Real Beauty was the answer. It started as an international photographic exhibition, *Beyond Compare: Women Photographers on Beauty*, to open up a discussion on beauty. (Read "Think Advertising as Experience," in Shift 3, on how the idea was launched.) Based on its success in Canada, this idea became an inspiration for Dove's global brand presence, a campaign that used models whose bodies were closer to those of ordinary women. And though it was not always consumer-tested—and actually rejected by focus groups in Brazil—it subsequently became a huge success throughout the world. The success of this branding initiative shows how reaching out to the unknown, the intuitive sensitivity, and people's skills can connect a brand's strong belief in a very effective manner.

"My group was looking to plant a stake in the ground," mentioned Lagnado, "and wanted to communicate a sincere and opinionated message of truth for our brands that resonated with ourselves first." Women's strong emotional response to this truly innovative idea could have only been achieved because of that "little bar of soap." That iconic little bar first brought joy and pleasure to women, setting up possibilities for the successful expansion of the business. And yet it also built a trust and empathy that made the connection to culture possible. Not unlike the "dynamic ribbon" that marks Coca-Cola cans, the Dove brand is, first and foremost, the expression of a design style that connects the sensorial and emotional values of the brand with a wide audience. It is one of the most successful brands in the world, with a potential to be a $5 billion business in less than five years. The best story is that the brand's emotional success with women has had a serious impact on the brand's bottom line. Overall, Dove sales are up 15 percent, and in some countries even more.

After my interview with Lagnado, I was thinking: don't give up ever; success is always there for opinionated people who care. I also thought about the importance of what started it all, a great little design that created the opportunity for the brand to build a powerful sensory and emotional connection with women. What could have been just another bar of soap set the stage for a credible and life-transforming ad campaign.

What this means: *Product design is important in establishing the first bond with an audience. The first emotional sensations people will experience with a product will help establish the personality of that brand in the consumers' lives and support the brand's marketing programs.*

VERONIQUE GABAI-PINSKY:
LAUNCHING DKNY'S BE DELICIOUS AND SHIFTING
THE PERCEPTIONS OF A FRAGRANCE

"Don't over-intellectualize, the success of a brand is based on the absolute consistency between product and brand heritage, the consistency between the product quality, the relevance of the brand narrative, the right price, and the sensory and emotional connection that comes through design when reaching a consumer's aspiration."

I was truly surprised by a new fragrance concept launched by Estée Lauder for DKNY (Donna Karan New York). Named "Be Delicious," the fragrance's tag line, "Take a bite out of life," at first threw me off. I thought, What is this fragrance trying to communicate in a market that has always been about scent and sex? I knew the apple was a widely used New York symbol and consistent with DKNY, but I found the hidden meaning behind this story even more compelling and exciting.

I was so intrigued that I decided to find out more about the concept, whether it was successful, and how the brand had been created. Be Delicious had all the right elements needed to reframe a category—using language that connected to people's sensory needs and desires. It walked away from the customary sex and celebrity used in the fragrance world—a graveyard of failed concepts and vain aspirations.

Be Delicious, I found out, is a huge success. This was something less obvious, more subtle and emotional. The consumers create their own fantasy. The Donna Karan brand has had a less-than-stellar success record in the fragrance category and its new association with Estée Lauder brought a heightened professionalism that seems to have paid off. Who was the brand manager behind this idea, and how was this person able to tap into the immense inspirations of Donna Karan as a designer and bottle it so compellingly?

That's how I met Donna Karan's team at Estée Lauder, the beauty company that help Donna visualize her creativity and talent with Donna Karan's fragrance business. Leading that team is master interpreter Veronique Gabai, senior vice president and general manager of designer fragrances at Estée Lauder, and the person who has been able to manifest the magic that lies in the Donna Karan brand and its founder. From a brandjamming perspective, you have here one of the best fragrance houses, a mythical designer and a team of marketing experts who are real magicians in bringing a brand to life.

Gabai is not at all new to the industry. She has also created the Acqua di Gio men's fragrance for Armani, one of the single most successful men's fragrances in the world. My first question for her was whether she had a secret formula and whether this marketing approach could be applied to other brands.

"Don't over-intellectualize," was Gabai's reply. "The success of a brand is based on the absolute consistency between product and brand heritage, the consistency between the product quality, the relevance of the image, the right price, and the sensory and emotional connection that comes through design when reaching the consumer's aspiration.

"Most brands that are failing are missing one of those points; they are splintered in their vision. The image might be right, but the product is not connected to the emotional heritage of the brand. Conflicting messages that are not consistent confuse a brand's offering."

Be Delicious is so appealing to the taste buds you feel you could drink it as well as smell it, but at the same time it also resonates with your gut. Not only is there the connection between the apple image and "the Big Apple," but there is also an emotional connection to the symbol of the apple itself and what it means.

Gabai is very serious about the verbal and visual process, which she says is a way to establish the territory of the brand from an emotional perspective. An apple could mean many different things: an orchard, nature, health, fruit stands. In the context of New York, it could even mean the forbidden fruit, or sin, or Broadway, luxury shopping, and wealth. It could also mean New York as an ambition and a destination, a place that allows you to reframe your life dream. Both Gabai and Karan felt that the underlying theme/feeling of New York was starting over again, doing something more in life. Both women shared the experience of success thanks to the energy and opportunity New York gave them. They wanted to communicate that spirit to their customers.

In their hands, the symbol of the apple brought the essence of New York into fresh perspective. And not just as a tourist hotspot. New York exudes life: in the downtown galleries, Chelsea Market, Harlem, New York glows with glamour. It's where the rough lives side by side with the sleek and the modern. Remember, "ugliness" can also be remarkably beautiful. The brand needed to reflect New York as a place where the memorable and defining events happens—ones that last forever, or for "a New York minute."

Deep is a word Gabai uses often when speaking about brands. Karan is passionate, creatively energetic and sensual, authentic, and intuitive. The Be

Delicious concept is about her, about her vision and soul. "When I worked with Giorgio Armani," she said, "I knew that the brand was about perfection, austerity, discipline, authenticity, sensuality, and purity. I went to his country house on the beach in Italy; it was so beautiful in such a simple way. I wanted a bottle for his fragrance that was modern and the advertising to be direct and authentic, a sensual young man on the beach feeling the wind and the sand, enjoying the perfection of a pure, simple but powerful moment."

So Veronique, I asked, how do you create and execute? (I was thinking of the Italian proverb, "The one who creates must execute; the one that does not execute does not create.") Is there a formula?

Gabai had prepared a presentation of Be Delicious to her management with packaging, advertising, point of purchase, and PR fully realized. "You can't disconnect the different parts of the brand expression; to be real it has to be fully executed, then you get a true reaction. The quality of the design is absolutely something you can't compromise on. We even gave a presentation to our sales associates, the ones who meet with our customers on a daily basis behind our counters in department stores. In this case, everyone cried! We knew we were reaching out."

"We are in a world in full transformation," says Gabai. "We are living the end of an era, our social structure is being challenged, our role in the world reconsidered, our relationship with religion and family structure debated, and our political and economical models challenged by technology and the impact of globalization. Redefining who we are and our mission in life in a world in movement is a working project, not a predefined solution. The consumer market is shifting every second, influenced by conflicting cultural, social, and political forces; former protocols and business models do not work anymore, you have to rely on your intuition and own observation."

In other words, the age of ivory-tower marketing is over; you have to use your instincts about people in order to innovate. You have to own an idea and see it through to completion, make your decisions by following your vision with a visceral compass. "Everyone is afraid of change; consumers react to concepts based on what they know, and this is not the information that will help create new ideas. The best research connects with culture." Talk individually with top thinkers, visionaries, architects, designers, or even perfumers that have created the types of innovations that were successful in the marketplace.

"We all want to be happy, to find a mate, find balance in our lives, self-fulfill-ment in our activities, and escape from our reality," Gabai continued. Successful branding is touching people in ways that will make them feel they can accomplish some of those dreams.

The Be Delicious program does just that. The bottle design was created by Hans Dorsenvelle of Laird & Partners, with the help of Chad Levine. It is a sophisticated design that expresses both the modern and the glamorous aspects of the city, while the outer packaging and the displays are reminiscent of fruit crates you would find at a fruit stand in the markets downtown, adding a raw and fresh sensuality. The photograph under the line "Take a bite out of life" shows a woman biting into a green apple, a clear appeal to our senses, but also to Eve.

The consistency and tightness of the concept is clearly here to build the story in the most compelling way. The fragrance itself is one of the most sophisticated I have ever experienced. First you smell the top of the apple, which gives way after a few seconds to reveal a more complex floral fragrance, a combination of white muguet rose and violet. The advertising, created by Laird & Partners, avoided the expected visualization of skyscrapers or iconic New York land-marks and instead focused on the feeling of a "city ripe with possibilities," an emotional idea that is translated by a woman of "natural beauty" biting into an apple just as she would "bite into life."

Most importantly, the whole concept works: it works together as an idea, it works together with the brand's fundamental values, and it delivers on a beau-tiful design and exciting fragrance. The dream is there to share, the provoca-tion is there to experience, and the feeling is one that only Donna Karan can promise, a mouth-watering DKNY.

What this means: Gabai was quick to say that you can avoid disaster, but pre-dicting success is hard. Be wary of any formulaic research or process. A branding strategy needs to be simple to be understood, to build on common sense, and feel right. You know when it is right; there are special moments when you can feel the vibe of a concept, and you know it is right when it touches people's lives around you. The main hurdle to branding innovation is all those ideas people can't see, concepts that are not fully realized to be truly appreci-ated, research that informs the wrong emotions and creates resistance to change.

ANNE ASENSIO:
WHY THE CAR INDUSTRY IS THE MOST INNOVATIVE
PLACE FOR BRAND DESIGN

"I had to go where there were no references, to find seduction and beauty in the unexpected, even if it meant creating a car in the shape of an egg."

Anne Asensio is the executive director of advanced vehicle design for General Motors. She started at GM after being part of the team who designed one of the most successful family cars for the French automotive company Renault, the "Megane Scenic," a funny egg-shaped car that won the hearts of European buyers.

In speaking about Renault, Asensio passionately described the fighting spirit that existed in this small company whose survival was dependent upon being imaginative. "We were the Davids against the Goliaths," she asserted. "Renault's future depended only on our ability to change. For us, risk was the only solution." With survival comes the notion of necessary risk and team spirit; she felt she had both there. It was not a star system but a management that supported a "roll-up-your-sleeves" approach to understanding what would excite people about a car; the type of culture that exists in small corporations such as Renault that need to fight to survive.

The fascinating part of this effort is how the Renault car really connected to the French public in ways that could not have been found except through a design methodology. To start with, the scenic car is not designed in the image of the traditional car "archetype" of a stylish outside as the main expression of the design. The Scenic was quite the opposite; it was designed starting with the people inside a structure and then building the car around them. This led to a new stylistic expression that focused on the soul: the inside of the car; its intellect and humanity.

The result was a look that puzzled people at first sight since it broke a few rules of engagement in how one judges a car—mainly by its aesthetics. The car was . . . let's say it, a bit unexpected, unconventional in its proportions, "out of codes," but it was clever! This intelligent, new inside-out design humanized the product.

An intelligent car certainly is a new idea, and it worked in France where beauty, according to Anne, is not necessarily linked to social success. The brain is often admired more than physical attributes. Renault was connecting with people through the car's "intelligence," not its superficial aesthetics: "the seductive, easy to love," says Anne. People started to understand and experience the car from the inside out; it transcended beauty and traditional stylistic expectation. People fell in love with a "concept" of beauty and the benefits the car would provide.

"You had to go where nobody went," Anne said. "You had to bring solutions that would surprise and take people where they had not been before, to places that would stimulate their minds. And design needed a free rein to do this; intuition was key. How could you design a car in the shape of an egg if you had to rely on research?" she asked. "Approaching a market with number-driven research is artificial and often slanted; everyone knows that you can make the numbers tell you anything you want."

This seemed to ring true with what other innovators I interviewed have said about traditional marketing research: that research provided either a false sense of security or a kind of slow, bourgeois process that only helped to fatten the amount of unused data that reassured management teams but did not help innovation. During her career, Asensio has been flabbergasted by the number of marketing professionals who select car designs without seeing them, relying solely on research results. I know of many companies that only look at their products or their brands through the eyes of focus groups. "Marketing represents the customer," as Asensio would say, "they have to *see* the product and get excited about it." Not only that, but you have to see for yourself how the product is experienced in real life.

Anne confessed that she loves cars so much that she indulges herself by sitting in an open restaurant or café terrace not to people-watch, but to watch cars in a real environment. She thought her little indulgence was a secret until one day when her mother, a bit tired of seeing her daughter pay attention to the street instead of her, said, "Anne, stop working."

When Asensio came to the United States to work for General Motors, she wanted to expand her talent with a new multi-brand company. She settled on the one that owns powerful brands such as Buick, Cadillac, Pontiac, and Saturn, among others. I talked with Asensio and tried to get her thinking about being not only a design professional, but also a woman in—let's face it—what is still a man's world.

As a European looking in at American culture from an outside perspective, Asensio has an interesting viewpoint on the American psyche, particularly since she works in a category that is all about emotions. She talked about the American fascination with nostalgia, the almost compulsive urge many Americans have to relive the 1950s, a time when the country was safe, economically dominant, and prosperous. The success of the PT Cruiser is only one example of certain products that have connected emotionally with the American psyche over time. Design sometimes follows social trends and sometimes precedes them, but most often, it works alongside of or parallel to them. In this case, the automotive industry might send us a message that is clearly fascinating. Is America ready to move forward to compete in a world that it can no longer control, or should it find short-term relief in looking back at its history through the rearview mirror?

According to Asensio, when she joined General Motors, she encountered a culture that was different from her previous experiences. It was more rational, numeric, and not as humanistic. Intuitions needed to be legitimized, they reasoned: prove them! This was the challenge she wanted to tackle and, in fact, the very reason why GM brought her onboard in the first place.

The car industry has an interesting design culture; an entire institution has been built around what a car *should* be. For instance, the American car culture can't seem to shake the need to return to the 1950s aesthetic, which was so innovative then, but not relevant anymore when looking at what makes a car a car. "In France, we were always going back to the 1930s, when French design was at its peak with the Voisin, Delahaye, and the Bugatti style—long hoods, dash to axle proportions, big wheels. The 1970s defined the Italian car design and is still dominant in the European car landscape today." Anne believes that American designers' fascination with the 1950s is an emotional connection to a time when creativity was unbridled and magic was an everyday event. The Cadillac was then the standard for an unparalleled dream!

So why is it always "back to the past" instead of creating desires that are yet to be formulated? "To break away from tradition is very difficult," says Asensio. And this has led her to probe the emotional and physical relationships people have with car brands and the motivations that drive their acceptance of a product. This, in turn, led her to a better understanding of the sensorial elements of a car and how it could change a person's life; it highlighted the importance of sensory design inside the car—after the first rush of adrenaline or seduction is over and reality sets in. After falling in love with the outside appearance of the vehicle, there is a "marriage" that happens mostly with the interior.

Not unlike the other innovative design professionals I have spoken with or read about, Asensio talks about branding in a very humanistic fashion, linking brands to people's emotional realities. This dialogue requires a corporate culture to change. But how? Asensio best answered: "by leveraging what you've got." Find the creative force within the people who are ready to "jazz." Her preconception joining GM was that the team of designers she would be leading might not have what it takes to innovate. On the contrary, she found talent that had not been leveraged—a talent that could play "real music" if given the right stage and, like jamming, the capability of creating magic together.

There has been a disconnect in our industrial economy between people who thrive in science and math and are trained to handle complicated supply-chain manufacturing strategies for growth and profit, and the groups that understand creativity and a connection to culture. The silos are real and complementary, but they need to work together. For instance, the business executives of the fashion brand Chanel, I was told, have to go through three days of creative education. In a postmodern economy, the human factor has become a large point of differentiation; brands need to bring the math/science minds closer to the creative process and its affinity with the emotional.

Suddenly, the supply-chain process that began with a factory creating products is superseded by an emotional chain of events that promotes people's individual desires and emotional well-being. This new approach has to rely on both reason and passion to reach a vast variety of individual choices. "We have to work as tailors," says Asensio, "manufacturing with flexibility."

Suddenly, the supply-chain process that began with a factory creating products is superseded by an emotional chain of events that promotes people's individual desires and emotional well-being.

Therefore, the role of the creator is looming large, creating designs that add value by bringing in new concepts with a twist. How do you revive the Buick brand, for instance, which only appeals to men sixty-eight years and older? How do you make a paradigm shift that can make Buick relevant the same way Dior did with John Galliano or Gucci with Tom Ford? Those are some of the issues Asensio will face. "The future is the present tomorrow," Yogi Berra would have said. The future is the result of all the decisions made today; it pertains to the right response to a new cultural shift that is happening in the world right now. Nostalgia is in the American psyche in a profound way. Is the Western world too focused on aesthetics? While we try to find comfort in the style of cars from yesteryear, countries like Japan compete by reaching out to our beliefs instead, with futuristic concepts such as the hybrid car. The appetite for change is different in many cultures, but you can't go in a direction opposite that which the world is going in without some serious plans. Change can't be escaped.

GM saw Toyota take the emotional lead in "clean" technologies with the Hybrid Prius, a huge marketing coup for Toyota's brands. They now own the discourse and are showing that new spirit with an advertising campaign that mimics the Target graphic look, standing out from the undifferentiated visual language of their competitors. The majority of the automobile industry, except for the Japanese brands, could not rationalize the Hybrid, and still automotive insiders will tell you that the positive financial and environmental impact of the hybrid technology is very insignificant, if there is any. "People think they want hybrids and they'll buy them, even if a conventional car would make more sense," journalist Jamie Lincoln Kitman writes, "just because a car has so-called hybrid technology doesn't mean it's doing more to help the environment or to reduce the country's dependence on imported oil any more than a non-hybrid car," journalist Jamie Lincoln Kitman writes.[4]

The missing point from most car brands is the fact that the hybrid concept humanizes the brand and connects with people's beliefs; it is an emotional proposition. You might want to be nostalgic with a PT Cruiser or powerful with a Hummer; but you'll feel responsible with the hybrid. People are looking for emotional experiences that bring meanings to their lives. Oil prices have created new perceptions of the world in which we live. First, we need to become less dependent upon oil by limiting our access to foreign suppliers. Second, we all know that our impact on the environment is our responsibility for generations to come. The car industry has been hit by the hybrid concept head on—it has been a huge wake-up call for the industry. We are at the beginning of a new trend.

For a long time, GM has been developing new technologies for clean energy. In Brazil, the company developed vehicles that run on ethanol, a fuel made from sugar cane. But the problem for GM is that such news gets lost in the middle of all the communications they send out about their large portfolio of brands. The result: almost nobody knows it. From the brand perspective, GM has not understood the profound emotional ramification of these concepts in people's psyche today, and they have not capitalized on that particular know-how.

Anne sees a magnificent challenge in "new technology vehicles." Through them, she sees a new future for the car industry and a way to redesign the car around a new set of values. Anne is inspired by how Gillette recreated the woman's universe with the color and new shapes of their female razors. "Gillette has been able to manifest through design a new invisible technology they created for people to feel." The designers' power is in resisting any temptation to over-intellectualize, and to rather let their hearts speak out.

Anne sees an "open freeway" for innovation and a bright future for the industry to recreate the car experience around new technologies and connect the cars with people beyond just the look of the vehicle. It is true that nothing has changed for the past seventy-five years. As Anne likes to say: the hand brake is still at the exact same place, and we are still using keys to start an engine at a time where you can "remote" almost anything, even your car.

There is also an almost tragic denial by mostly male car designers and marketers to hang on to the cars they loved as kids and keep on recreating the archetypal "beautiful car." Women, she says, have a more emotional approach, one that is iconoclastic and for the benefit of people: a car that would find a new space, that of a new era.

Asensio's point is this: "With the new-technology vehicles, we don't have any physical limitation. We don't need big hoods for major engines because those engines are different and located at different places in the car. There is an opportunity to literally reinvent the look and experience of the car. Do we need a dashboard like before? Are we going to design the new-technology vehicle to look like any other car, as if we had designed propulsion jets to look the same as the old propeller version? How much expectation and opportunity exists in the market to see the future in such a concept? For once, the car industry has the possibility to create and innovate without bringing the baggage inherent in other models; as everything seems to be going miniature, from cell phones to electronic equipment, how would that translate into a new car experience?"

The new-technology vehicles are Asensio's next project, and if she has her way, we will see just how car design can bring the future into our lives in new ways. It will also help expand the emotional niche opportunities inherent in a multi-brand company such as General Motors. The challenge for Anne in this new endeavor is to bring the GM executives along for the ride. Her belief is that new design ideas are always shown to them way too late in their iteration. The brand decision-makers are then faced with limited choices, forced to either approve or discard a new concept without the proper insights. Anne's new approach is taken very seriously by GM as a key program to create innovation and turn around their brands. With the top management of the company involved in the workshops (Jon Lauckner, VP of product development; Bob Lutz, vice chairman of product development; John Smith, group VP of product planning; Edward Welburn, VP of global design; and Jim Queen, VP of engineering), the company participates and everyone is an avid participant and contributor. Anne's team of creators and designers develop concepts that will shine in GM's automotive showrooms.

"When everything goes well, the corporate world is less inclined to celebrate innovation. But it is in times of struggle that business discovers its true genius, driven by a strong sense of survival." Her "innovation" strategy is built around three main vectors:

1. **Have an "ideation review" every six weeks with decision-makers**. This takes pressure off people and helps them participate in the creative process. The idea is to help the executives be exposed to innovation in a non-threatening way, without the commitment to make a decision yet.

2. **Show those multiple ideas from a different angle**. For instance, if in the previous six weeks you have used physical models, the next time you might use a video on large LCD screens. This helps keep the same ideas but repurposes it to be provocative and motivating. "I change everything in the way we propose ideas, but the ideas themselves stay the same."

3. **Continue to stimulate**. Standardized approaches based on predictable or established presentation formats lead to expected reactions and canned responses. Keeping people involved, but on their toes, will help an idea grow on them.

General Motors' Advanced Design Centers are hubs for innovation.

"If you take people outside of their comfort zone and destabilize them, if you submerge them in a lot of prototypes to help them imagine, then they can't expect to see what they would normally expect to see. This allows you to stimulate their brains and surprise them with new, convincing arguments that will help your ideas make their way into reality."

Her experience is that the design process needs to be a team effort, consistent with innovation. The creative approach can often lead to creative accidents, such as an idea that gels around the right timing. An idea presented at an earlier stage might not be relevant then, but a month later could suddenly make sense. The seeds previously sown are being reintroduced by the group who has grown into a concept—a concept that has found its relevance at a particular time. Everything then converges to the point of "why can't we do this now?" It is possible because the germ of the idea is already part of everyone's source of possibilities.

This ongoing process of imagining and searching through design innovation finds its true power in the continuous, even incremental evolution of the process over a long period of time. But everyone is armed and prepared; everyone speaks the same language around the same shared ideas, a mental idea bank that can help spring to life new concepts in a timely manner and with everyone knowing the opportunities. That type of creative research and development is at the core of innovation: the idea of challenging and nourishing everyone's brains with new thoughts that can be activated or resurrected at any time.

To support this effort, GM Advanced Design Center is part of a large network of eleven GM design studios across the world, including Shanghai, China; Seoul, Korea; Melbourne, Australia; Russelsheim, Germany; Trollhattan, Sweden; Birmingham, England; São Paulo, Brazil; and the United States. Anne's own design team represents the diversity of every single continent. This provides a source of rich thinking and discovery that not only brings a richer global inspiration but also helps the understanding of the diversity of each market and their different aspirations.

What this means: From a brandjam perspective, this novel approach brings another aspect of decision making, which is, according to Anne, "common sense." The tendency for management is to rely on traditional research as a back up for decision-making. This is why Anne is working hard to find new, design-driven ways to integrate managers into the design process. This will help bring perspective to what Anne calls "the research sanction," by giving managers the tools to make informed decisions. "If traditional research is expressing today's feelings on tomorrow's cars," Anne likes to say, "then we won't find the answers with traditional research. We need to bring a new set of filters that will help decision makers have more liberty to interpret and act on the right decisions when judging innovation."

JEAN WIART:
REFURBISHING THE STATUE OF LIBERTY

"You can't make love mute. The difference between beauty and ordinary is in the love you put in what you do and the care you take in crafting an idea."

When New York decided to refurbish the Statue of Liberty in 1983 in view of its centennial celebration of 1986, the city contacted Les Metalliers Champenois, a group of French craftsmen that specializes in the art of metal-work, thinking it would be able to restore the famous flame in an authentic fashion. Les Metalliers Champenois is not just a newcomer to this work: most of its artisans are members of a guild with a tradition and expertise that dates back to the thirteenth century and the construction of the great European cathedrals. To this day, LMC's knowledge has been passed down from generation to generation by craftsmen who dedicated their lives to their trade. Working with copper, the original metal that covered the torch, was something the company was very familiar with, but recreating such an iconic and complicated form was another challenge altogether.

LMC won the project based on its tremendous track record, but the team knew it would have to invent a new method in order to complete the project. The torch of the Statue of Liberty is not a simple shape: *it is a sculpture*. It has curves and complicated angles that are a challenge to the shaping of copper plates. Adapting a large piece of metal that has been pre-shaped to cover the complicated form of the torch in this case was not possible due to the fact that it had to match precisely a sculptured plaster model. A new technique and approach needed to be created.

Jean Wiart is an artist who believes in the human connection between the material and the artist, not unlike Louis Khan, the great American architect. I have met many people in the creative profession who draw their inspiration and creativity from the relationship they have with the tools they use or the materials they transform. Jean explained to me that he talks to his tools sometimes, or the material he is working with, so that they will deliver what he wants. He told me a story about how, after a few months managing his business took him away from the atelier, he returned on a weekend to work on some ideas and felt that his tools were not "happy with him." This was not a good situation, as he had to sculpt a foliage ornament for one of the iron entrance gates gracing an historical mansion in Long Island. "So, I talked to my tools. I had to get friendly with the tools again." For the first hour, he would ask them not to let him down, then he would talk to the material so it could transform itself into the form he wanted it to become.

In branding, it also seems that the best designers have a tremendous respect for the projects they work on and the impact their work has on the environment. Their personal commitment to the work seems always to resonate with an audience. Innovative solutions are unpredictable and eluding; they don't exist yet and are not yet in anyone's mind. That solution-finding "mindset" is something that creative people are dealing with every day; there's no process, just an inspiration based on a relentless probing of sources of inspiration in sometimes the most unlikely places.

The belief that kept them going was that, as Jean puts it, "we would show our pride in being among the *privileged* ones working on the most powerful symbol of our time, Liberty." The insight came while arriving with his partner, Serge, at New York's Kennedy Airport. As their plane was moving toward the gate, they had plenty of time to look at other airplanes taking their positions for takeoff. They both suddenly turned to each other and exclaimed out loud, "The nose of the airplane!" I wouldn't want to know what the other passengers thought about two crazy Frenchmen giving themselves a high-five over an airplane nose, but for Jean and Serge it was a moment of revelation. They had just found the solution to their problem.

The "Ah-ha!" was in the small pieces of metal that make up an airplane's nose, one of the most intricate and complicated shapes to reproduce in an airplane carrier. The solution the airline industry found was to build a mosaic of little pieces of metal that would nicely fit together in a flexible way to cover this complicated shape. This was exactly what LMC was looking for to solve the challenge they had with the torch, and it made the quality of their work and their time management more efficient after that discovery.

What this means: *The ability to find answers and inspiration in the observation of one's surroundings is something creative people are especially adept at doing. Finding real solutions that make a difference is something that is of value; it is research, visual research. Innovation is a feeling sometimes, a feeling in your gut, that comes only from a true passion to create messages or work that will connect with people emotionally. It is a feeling and belief that somewhere out there, if we are committed, exists that information that will then be the basis for informing the design of products or the making of a masterpiece.*

DEBORAH ADLER:

SOLVING LIFESTYLE PROBLEMS BY RETHINKING MEDICATION PACKAGING

"Thoughtful design can have a real impact on people's lives. Drug corporations spend billions on advertising, but that doesn't always translate into a patient's individual experience."

Deborah Adler, the inventor of the new Target ClearRx Prescription System, is a graphic designer who believes that her design expertise can help people. One day, her grandmother misread the label on a prescription bottle and took her husband's medicine (he: *Herman*; she: *Helen*) instead. Her health took a dangerous turn for the worse. This experience motivated Adler to find a way to make the packaging of medicine safer and easier to use. What she found out was devastating—up to 60 percent of prescription drug users have taken their medication incorrectly. And, according to an article by Gardiner Harris in the *New York Times*, "Medication errors harm 1.5 million people and kill several thousand each year, costing the nation at least $3.5 billion annually."[5] "Bad design can hurt people," Adler says. Yet nobody focuses on that aspect of the business.

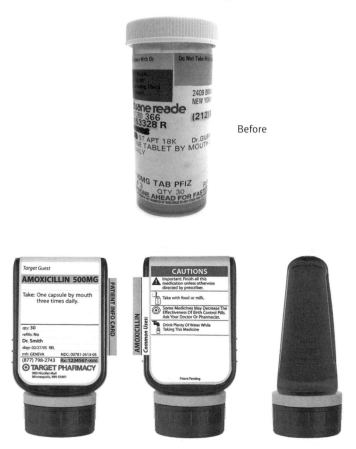

Before

After

It took one determined graphic designer to solve an issue that should have been of greater concern to any manufacturer—the safety of its clients. These days, marketers and ad agencies are mostly concerned with avoiding competition with Tivo by bringing ads to major retail environments through LCD screens; spending millions to show people ads they don't want to see on TV anyway and ruining their shopping experience. Why not instead spend a large portion of that money going back to home base, thinking about the total consumer experience?

"It's important to take a broader view and look at the landscape in which a product or idea exists," said Adler. Her example is how a museum—such as the Guggenheim in Bilbao or the Brooklyn Academy of Music (BAM) in New York—have changed those two cities. When creating an identity for a museum, she explained, why not look into the impact this change could have on the environment, the neighborhood, restaurants, and people's experiences overall so that a change such as a new identity could trigger a more integrated, memorable, and human impact? I thought about how many hospitals are proud to have a new name and brightly colored logo while the rest of the experience at the hospital has not changed. Wouldn't it be great if a change of identity could also mean a change of experience for people?

Many corporations have the power and opportunity to use design as a way to help people in their lives but haven't yet found a way to make it happen.

After first showing her work to the FDA (who loved the idea but, due to varying state regulations lacked the jurisdiction to create a national packaging system), she took her idea to Target. And while this project could have potentially been shelved at another corporation (along with many unrecognized great ideas), it found a home there. It is interesting when you consider that neither a pharmaceutical company nor a packaging company were first in line—but Target!

This is an important point to make because Target has become one of the most integrated design-centric businesses in the world. It shows that great design ideas can be a source of revenue and positive image in a way that no advertising commercial can. The result was staggering, and the PR was dazzling. The story, endorsed by the medical world, made it known that Target was in the pharmaceutical business, and that it's design philosophy doesn't stop with aesthetic—it's also about problem solving. "Target is committed to great design," says Adler. "It's central to its core proposition."

What impressed me most was how much observation and discovery she did to get to her final design. First, she studied the supply-chain process to see how the products are packaged, shipped, and displayed. Then she looked at the source of medication errors. She observed what most medicine cabinets look like and how the products are shelved and sent a questionnaire to two hundred people to find out how they experienced their treatment routine. After she brought her design to Target, she worked with more than one hundred Target team members, pharmacy professionals, and industrial designers to create the current Clear Rx system.

Most medication bottles today are similar and generic, hard to read and difficult to open, regardless of your age. The more medications you take, the more prone you are to making a mistake. The challenge was great, but Adler helped solve the most obvious issues through typography and ergonomic design. She researched medication-taking schemas and studied how people perceive information and the intuitive habits that we all have in processing written information, from the Web to print.

Her conclusion was that the following medical information needed to be clearer:

- What is the drug?
- Who it is for?
- How do you take it?

By creating a flat panel in the back of the prototypical circular container, she was able to present a clearer area for information. This also made it impossible to turn the bottle, making the face always visible to the user. She also created a color-coded system that helped differentiate the products. That color-coded system works "like toothbrushes; you know which one is for whom." People are better able to recognize their right medication when it is differentiated by color.

Adler's feeling is that too much money is spent on frivolous research and communication when more attention should be focused on ethnographic research, on people-driven product innovations, and on lifestyle solutions—responsibilities that designers are quite able and equipped to take on. Responsible brands are seeking to understand people's interactions with commercial products from a safety and control perspective. How do you manage product information in packaging but also public spaces, commercial spaces, and roadside information? How children, babies, and older generations interact with the environment is a crucial consideration for brands.

Adler's story is one of creativity but also one of courage and conviction. It is a message for businesses in general, since most have become disconnected from people. People love businesses that have the basic decency to bring good products to the market and that realize their responsibilities include helping to improve people's lives.

What this means: *"Empowering people is a good idea," says Adler, "solving people's life challenges is even better." The branding world is populated with opportunities ripe to be solved. Through smart design, the positive impact a brand can make on people is the best way to build brand relationship and trust.*

CHRIS BANGLE:

GREAT IDEAS ARE NOT ALWAYS UNDERSTOOD AT FIRST

"An automobile is what I use; a car is what I am."

I had the opportunity to meet with Chris Bangle, director of group design for BMW, after he gave a speech at a major innovation conference. I wanted to talk to him not only because of his success with the design of the new BMW series, but also to find out what he thought about the importance of the true human connection design creates with buyers, that invisible emotional vibe communicated through design that makes people trust a brand more because they feel the brand cares.

I spoke a little about the effects of the postmodern world in which we live, one that promotes an emotional contact with people through the craft and care brought to a design. He seemed intrigued and quite readily endorsed the idea. "You are right," he said, "in a postmodern world, people need to feel and believe your conviction in the design that you create. This is what I always try to achieve."

That answered another question: how could he have made *me* buy a BMW after seventeen years of faithful attachment to Mercedes? I was the prototypical Mercedes customer. It resonated with me through its virtuous design, subdued classic sense of status expressed in a modern way, and gravitas that signals longevity. I am a distance swimmer, a faithful partner, and a fan of long-term plans that build values. The Mercedes is me; and here I am with a bloody BMW! I felt like I was leaving Coke for Pepsi.

Still, the fact is that, as most Mercedes drivers already know, the service (at least where I live) stinks! But this was not the only reason for changing brands. I was drawn to the new BMW design; it emotionally reached me in a different way. In buying the BMW I felt freer, more liberated, as if I had unchained myself from a dogmatic, imposing brand.

I think Bangle was amused by my story. I mean, here I was talking to the guy who literally took the risk to create the new, vastly successful BMW design, and I'm getting sentimental about a car. But Bangle is passionate about what he does, and you can't help but open up to him. He puts you at ease, and you can feel the sincerity in his connection with people and the passion that drives him to reach out.

But, Chris, I asked, why do people get so emotional about the cars they drive? "An automobile is what I use; a car is what I am," he answered, making a clear definition between those two words. In the dictionary, a *car* is defined as "a chariot of war or triumph," while the *automobile* is defined as "a passenger vehicle . . . typically having four wheels and an internal combustion gasoline engine."

This is what Bangle does: he designs cars, not automobiles. He designs in order to reach people emotionally. I thought of how many brands could use or need to use this type of approach. If a product is a reflection of who I am and supposedly who I will become, why is the packaging in supermarkets still the same year after year? Why are soft drink cans the same shape for most brands? Why are milk and orange juice presented in the same format? Why are beer bottles so similar? Why are so many products still undifferentiated?

Our last piece of conversation centered around the freedom Bangle has at BMW to experiment with new ideas and the openness he finds there to create the innovation that will woo people like me. He gave credit to one of his designers, Jogi Nagashima, a visionary whose innovative ideas sometimes raise a few eyebrows. "He is crucial to the process," says Bangle. "He is an inspiration from which other ideas will emerge, the needed 30 percent inspiration we all seek to progress."

"He is crucial to the process," says Bangle. "He is an inspiration from which other ideas will emerge, the needed 30 percent inspiration we all seek to progress."

Bangle said, "People need to feel your conviction" as he revealed his attitude toward design creation. "First you need just 30 percent with inspiration and innovation, then you go to 70 percent in keeping with the consumers' expectations, and from there you arrive at 100 percent of the design execution, once you have integrated the limitations of the manufacturing process." His process first starts with the power of the idea, not the fear that limits its expression. Ideas need a spark to inspire; the challenge is to protect that spark and cultivate a project further by protecting the purity of the concept.

Bangle was able to fight for what he believes and has helped BMW think as he thinks. On the abundance of ideas that could frighten a design neophyte, he explained that people need to understand "if there is so much horseshit, there must be a pony in there. Listen, a few years ago it would not have worked, a lot of those great ideas would have been thrown out too soon. Now we can at least fight all the way to success."

What this means: don't give up on a far-out idea; it is the beginning of the discussion. This was the first time I heard such a great rationale on how to integrate the most advanced design creativity into the innovation process. Indeed, instead of taking those "precious fragile ideas," as David Ogilvy would say, to the graveyard of some focus groups, why not use them to jump-start a project in the right direction, with the right innovative spirit attached to it?

NATURA

"A business can be a powerful engine for social transformation."

Customizing with regard to people's sense of responsibility is both compelling and challenging. It takes tremendous integrity and absolute consistency in delivering on a promise. Natura has transformed this fragile emotional vision into a powerhouse of innovation where nature has become its most important partner.

For some reason, when you speak about "green" companies around the world, Natura, the Brazilian direct sales cosmetic company, never comes to mind. Natura is nowhere to be found in the 2006 seminal issue of *Vanity Fair* where the who's who of the "green" industry is being celebrated. Yet this is perfectly fine with the company; its financial results and consumer satisfaction speak for themselves.

Founded in 1969 in a small store in São Paulo, Natura is now a public company with a turnover close to $2 billion, 4,000 employees, and 500,000 representatives; but most importantly, it is a perfect example in demonstrating the way a business can be successful by contributing to the success of society as well. From inception, the company has been founded on two principles and passions, which were fascinating to me since they are based on human respect and life understanding:

1. The product as a powerful resource to develop well-being and knowledge anchored in the passion for cosmetics in the broader sense of *cosmetiques*, not just makeup.
2. The power of human relationships and their potential.

But how do you manifest such a strong focus on people's well-being to recruit employees, build your reputation, or create innovative products? Natura integrates all those objectives in expressing the brand values either through its packaging, headquarters, Web site, catalog, stores, or its communications material. The entire branding program speaks with one powerful visual voice. Natura believes in providing sensory discoveries or product perspective as it relates to people's experiences with the brand. And for that inspiration, the company relies on the rich Brazilian tradition and diverse culture, ethnic heritage, and love of nature. At Natura, the promotion of technology and science goes hand in hand with traditional knowledge. The core value of the company is to create and contribute to improvement in society at large and to the quality of human relations.

The offices in Cajamar and in Itapecerica da Serra demonstrate how Natura perceives the need for quality of life. The corporate offices and manufacturing buildings promote socialization and interaction. Every aspect of the brand vision comes to life in these buildings to foster creativity and well-being. There, in the middle of the countryside, you connect with this brand's ability to contribute to a positive progress in society and its sustainable development. You can't leave this place and not be in awe!

There I met one of Natura's founders and co-chairmen, Antonio Luiz da Cunha Seabra, who can speak very eloquently of Malraux, Beaudelaire, and Teilhard de Chardin; and in the same breath tell you that the only reason why Natura went public was not to raise money! It wanted to add scrutiny and expertise in its operation to see how it compared to the rest of the world

Imagination, design, and emotional customization are at the core of this company, which derives 63 percent of its revenue from new products launched in the last twenty-four months. Its reputation is so great that for some forty positions that the company needs to fill, it might get 40,000 résumés, allowing it to accept only the best talent in Brazil. The 2005 annual report (printed on recyclable paper) talks about beauty as the genuine aspiration of every human being, saying that it must be free of preconceived ideas and manipulation. They also promote the company as a living organism, a dynamic set of relationships that value longevity and the contribution to the evolution of society. Why wouldn't you want to be part of that?

Natura's recent product line "EKOS" is probably the most significant in expressing its core values as it shows that it is possible to use natural resources conscientiously to influence a movement that can help create work for everyone in Brazil. EKOS is made from Brazilian biodiversity in sustainable ways. The concept of EKOS is to let your life be guided by your senses as the products are based on the traditional rites of bathing as practiced by the indigenous population of Brazil. Natura asked the major fragrance houses to go back to the source and work with certain fragrances to bring that tradition into the new products—a new way to explore fragrance ideas straight from Brazil's indigenous heritage. By using the products found in nature without destroying them, you can find sources of inspiration and innovation that are limitless and sustainable.

Priprioca, for instance, is inspired by a legend: a group of tribal women, who were in love with a particular man, tied up his hands and feet while he was asleep. In the morning, the man was gone but in his place was a plant (the priprioca).

Breubranco is the resin of certain trees in the Brazilian forest that help protect them when its skin is broken. The essence of this resin was used to protect indigenous tribes from bad spirits and also has tremendous moisturizing properties.

The EKOS packaging has a simplicity and grace that breathes authenticity, honesty, and advocacy. Some of these products were actually *tested for* emotional impact. Stress levels are indicated by the level of cortisol in our saliva; our immune systems are monitored by levels of immunoglobulin. The EKOS products had a positive effect; people tested after using these natural products all said that they felt better afterward.

What this means: *Natura understands both the nature of man and the spirit of nature, connecting them to be one and the same. For Natura, design is the ambassador of that subliminal message through its convincing expression, a message well designed to inspire us even more.*

Do You Speak Design? *Parlez-Vous* Design? *Sprechen Sie* Design?
Throughout time, product design has articulated historical change. During the early years of the twentieth century, design brought modernism and industrialization into an exquisite language. Immediately after World War II, as a deluge of new suburban dreams and consumer goods swept the nation, design reinvented our kitchens and led to the famous "kitchen debates" with Eisenhower and Kruschev. Think of that: Cold War policy articulated against the backdrop of toasters! Kitchen appliances were our most potent weapons—the justification for democracy!

Design is always a prevalent form of communication, introducing differentiation and identity into the midst of uncertainty and change. The designer Raymond Loewy was a precursor in this domain, bringing newness and magic to people through streamlined products. Post–World War II is a particularly interesting period to study as design expressed a new prosperity and the promise of the industrial revolution and globalization for American brands in particular. Today, design has become the universal language of joy, the language of innovation and progress, the language of pleasure and fun for consumers and profit and success for corporations. Through design, brands have found a unique way to connect with people and break the grey sky of commodity, but do we know how to speak that language?

The word *makeover*—as in the reality-TV's *Extreme Makeover*, on which people change their physical looks through plastic surgery, better diets, and serious exercising—is becoming a flagship word for drastic change. A headline in the *New York Times* reads "City Backs Makeover for Decaying Brooklyn Waterfront."[6] The term *makeover* expresses what people are striving for: real change in their lives and in their environment, a drastic break from the past, a new image of the future. *Makeover* is linked to revitalization, the old becoming new, and the tired becoming hip. Everyone wants his or her life made over! Design permeates all aspects of our lives, on the personal level and in the world around us. Design has become a metaphor for individuality and freedom. Change in our physical appearance, home environment, and social situation happens by design. We want to make our lives over to feel better, to *live* better.

WHERE ARE THE IDEAS?

Most marketers have not been trained to think "visually" in business school, though this is changing. Universities now offer classes in design or interdisciplinary programs, such as the Sloan School of Management at the Massachusetts Institute of Technology and the Rhode Island School of Design. Harvard offers courses that "position technology as an enabler of design and as a tool to broaden design inquiry, and highlights emerging fields and innovations impacting design, design research and practice."[7]

The solution is to bring the design process upfront as part of the initial consulting and research process, involving designers and their ideas in the brands people will love.

The problem is not the lack of ideas, but the know-how to identify and evaluate good ideas, to have a better understanding of the visual process.

The problems are ignorance, as far as design is concerned, and a lack of guts. The solution is to bring the design process upfront as part of the initial consulting and research process, involving designers and their ideas in the brands people will love.

Victor Seidel, a lecturer at the Said Business School at Oxford University, says that, unlike traditional strategy firms such as McKinsey & Bain, "at the design firm there is a richer engagement that designers have as a starting point, and what's more, the designers' visual capability gives the capacity to expand rather than reflect."[8] Visual research done by designers leads to tremendous insight into innovation and the world of emotions, the only place where brands live (see Shift 5, "Think Design Research").

THE LANGUAGE OF ORIGINAL THINKING

A hamburger is the same everywhere; a hotel room is the same in every country. Once, in Taipei, I woke up in the middle of the night and could not remember which country I was in. I could have been in Tokyo, Helsinki, New York, or São Paulo!

For every person who buys an apartment in the residential part of a major city, there is someone else who will pay the same price to live in an emerging, run-down city neighborhood simply because it is more cutting edge and better defines a personality. Some people want to fit in; others want to stand out. Real estate promoters look for opportunities in places that are cheap to buy but can bring cachet and discovery to buyers who want to avoid the mainstream.

Luxury hotels around the world increase the number and size of their rooms and their amenities all the time. They are built in the most desirable places in major cities and provide a service that is close to perfection. But a great number of travelers prefer the intimacy of "boutique hotels," which tend to have smaller rooms for similar prices, but make guests feel unique.

Just as SUVs are getting even bigger—a military tank–like vehicle—you also see the rising success of the tiniest car in the country's history, the Mini. And just as the soft drink industry proclaimed higher health standards—much less sugar, less caffeine—Red Bull, with its new can design, decides to bring out more energy-boosting components, sharing with coffee the energy-booster category—right under the nose of Coke and Pepsi!

When a concept seems like it has become generic, it automatically becomes familiar and uninteresting in the minds of consumers. There is always a fringe of the population looking to stand out—performers, fashion designers, photographers, musicians, artists, intellectuals, academics. Pioneers and visionaries who prefer to craft a life of individuality. They are less encumbered by tradition and have a great sense of self-confidence. These trendsetters tend to spread their influence on those too afraid to change. They take the risks for others to follow. They are the early gallery owners who moved to SoHo—and then went to Chelsea when Soho had grown too mainstream.

For most brands, the issue is not the product itself or changes in people's habits, but a lack of innovation on the simple levels, like changing packaging design. Commodity is the ultimate insult! We are surrounded by mediocrity, and it takes brands down with it. "Don't underestimate me," says the consumer, "I am an individual and need to be considered as such. I hate generics, and I won't pay for them. I buy Martha Stewart at K-Mart; I want my detergent to look stylish; I am looking for the best and the most precious in products and services for my friends and family. My world is not made with linoleum; it is not synthetic; it is not messy in a way that will make me feel awful about my life. It is inspiring and innovative, fun and differentiated."

DESIGN MANIA

In a November 2004 article in *Advertising Age*, Gary Conya, a Yale University School of Architecture graduate turned strategic planner at Berlin Cameron in New York, wrote, "Design, in general, can communicate a sense of beauty, elegance and prestige by triggering memories and emotions." In the same article, Peter Arnell, the famed advertising creative, predicted that "product and industrial design will deeply contribute to a whole new mindset in marketing and communications that will say, why not invest your money into building and asset instead of spending your money on advertising?!"[9]

Communication is shifting from advertising to design, and nobody knows it yet except those on the receiving end—the customers! (See also Shift 3, "Think Advertising as Design Experiences.") Design offers ideas you can love and own and give and talk about and recommend. Instead of the latest commercial, people talk now about the latest product design or store experience, redesigned restaurant, or even the Seattle public library, designed by Rem Koolhaas. What about the new vodka bottle by Frank Gehry or the new Kronenbourg beer bottle or hotel by Philip Stark? Have you been to a party recently where everyone was talking about the latest hilarious or transcending commercial? No! But everyone will talk about a new boutique hotel or furniture design. Baby strollers, for example, are no longer just for the comfort of the baby but must also fulfill parents' uncompromising pursuit of the balanced life. New strollers are built like mountain bikes to work on all types of terrain so that parents don't have to compromise their running regimens. Generation X, the world's first multitaskers, would not lose valuable exercising time while taking their little ones for a stroll. (They can even get a bit competitive, the faster runners overtaking others while their babies cheer them on!**)**

In this particular case, design adapts and helps transform objects to fit the consumer profile and lifestyle. It follows the familiar aesthetic cues provided by sports equipment, such as for cycling or weight-lifting, in order to convey emotionally that a stroller can also be a piece of sports equipment. Parents will often dress in their running clothes when they take their children out in strollers, unable to transform themselves into the passive, slow-moving parents who flock to the park to stand around the sandbox.

Brands like Campbell's Soup and Coca-Cola have recently explored new designs that have caught consumers' attention. Campbell's distributed 300,000 multicolored cans of tomato soup with labels inspired by the now-famous paintings by Andy Warhol, showing that brands are willing to test themselves along design innovation. Coca-Cola in France asked Kenzo Takada, a well-known Japanese fashion designer, to create a new look for Coca-Cola Light, and he responded by painting the famous coke bottle contour in silver for selective distribution, such as at Collette in Paris, a fashion store for the well-heeled and people in the know.

Design is so pervasive that even a brand like Samsung advertised the number of design awards it had won at the IDSA awards competition, sponsored by the *Wall Street Journal.* Under the headline, "Bright Ideas," Samsung leveraged its design skills to influence people in their buying choices of its products.[10] In New York, the architect Richard Meier has designed towers on the far West Side that are sold like art, according to a *New York Times* headline. A number of celebrities have paid a fortune to live there. People are willing to trade comfort for adventure if the adventure is in style.

The 2005 Los Angeles auto show wanted to get some press and "respect" and so it partnered with Art Center, a design school known for car design in nearby Pasadena, to create a design competition where designers from different car companies showcased their products. The show was a contest created to pit automakers' designers against one another to create "the ultimate L.A. machine," as Phil Patton wrote in the *New York Times*.[11] The concepts were truly innovative and aimed at tantalizing buyers. The trend toward newness and individual style is clearly here to stay.

Many of the designers were frustrated because car companies do not have the capabilities to manufacture most of the new ideas. This is where design and production come into conflict. Design moves faster than manufacturing, and those brands that are able to solve the problem will discover the Holy Grail of branding success. New companies, like new nations, unhindered by antiquated production facilities, will be able to compete with more flexibility and speed. The "Swatch car" is already a reality, and like the swatch watch it will most likely be a long-lasting trend. The MCC smart city car is made with injection molded panels that can be replaced if damaged or change the color of the car if the owner wants. The demand for disposable models will hit the car industry as it has other industries; the expensive will leave a place for the inexpensive and stylish that can be changed often. Innovation paired with flexibility will generate ideas that can also be produced.

Design moves faster than manufacturing, and those brands that are able to solve the problem will discover the Holy Grail of branding success.

Is It Over Yet?

We might think that what is happening is design overload; the design press, the general press, and our peers are probably sick and tired of the renewed interest in design and its promise. Some people find design self-centered, over the top, and overblown. Some see in it a design bubble that will die out of consumers' exasperation with too much design and an over-stimulation of our senses. Are there limitations to design or is design just another indulgence of rich nations in need constant stimulation?

I don't know the answer, but I do see in design a much larger message. I see the end of the industrial age with its rules and dogmatic theories. I see creativity as the new fuel for a much-needed competitive approach to our future, and ultimately, the source of solutions to problems that need a creative mindset.

Design as it evolves to create emotional experiences is bridging the gap between science and business and innovation and marketing. Tomorrow will never be the same, and only the creative mind will prevail. Design is the expression of a social movement that is looking for more experiences in people's lives and a testimony of hope and progress.

The Individual Touch

One thing is certain, the age of mass marketing is dead and the age of production for the masses is obsolete. We will see more flexibility and customization, more choices, and easier access to personal choice. The competition in an age where technological differences are not that great will be on image and reputation, on how a brand understands the emotional landscape, and how we want to live our lives.

There is still so much to learn, so little we know about our own motivations and cultural backgrounds as they influence our consumption. In a global world, a flattened world as Thomas Friedman likes to call it, we need to move up the ladder on the innovation scale; if you are not any more the best producer and manufacturer, you can't lose the high ground, the intellectual property and knowledge. A country like Slovenia has a biannual show of industrial design that attracts the best designers around the world. Ljubljana, the capital, does not want to miss the creative boat. So no, it is not over yet. As long as there is an appetite for the future, a strong economy, a competitive point of view, and a continuous development of new ideas, materials, and manufacturing techniques, we'll soon see products that bring a new level of excitement into people's lives.

People Are Ahead of Design . . .
And in most cases, still waiting!

Designers work best for people and brands that celebrate design as a marketing tool, as a promise and a vision. "Design for all" has become the slogan of Target as it strives to differentiate itself from Wal-Mart. Crate and Barrel's new "art of the table" continues to bring magic into the home through fresh colors and shapes for its dishware. Olympus has designed a camera for food aficionados that emphasizes food tones and increases color saturation by reducing the flash impact. (That way you can bring home a souvenir of a delicious plate you had at your favorite restaurant!) Ginger, a faucet brand, will "enhance your water delivery and your soul," sing advertisements. Design now permeates all walks of life. The kitchen and bath industry is presenting what the *Wall Street Journal* calls "Alternative Looks," turning to the virtues of design as sales soften for refrigerators, dishwashers, washers, dryers, and freezers.

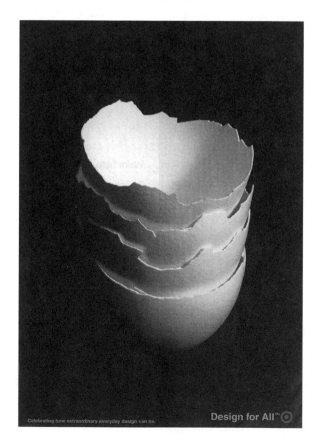

Celebrating how extraordinary everyday design can be.   Design for All™

Designers help people understand their unmet needs, and people are willing to participate in the creative process. With the help of psychologists, ethnographers, neurologists, and anthropologists, Designers dig into people's minds. The field of semiology has also become an interesting way to discover the meaning of shapes and visuals that surround us. Designers, in a sense, are also visual anthropologists who identify through an innate sense of observation new trends and emerging ideas.

Designers, in a sense, are also visual anthropologists who identify through an innate sense of observation, new trends and emerging ideas.

WELCOME TO THE EMOTIONAL ECONOMY
The old rules of marketing do not apply; traditional business approaches miss out on the greatest design opportunities.

WELCOME TO A WORLD WHERE DATA RESEARCH CAN'T PROVIDE THE ULTIMATE INSIGHT
Too many brand managers have been buried in so many market segment numbers and statistical regressions that they have altogether lost sight of the emotions and design expressions that are the foundation of branding.

WELCOME TO A STATE OF MIND THAT PROMOTES INTUITION
Products need to *look good* and *feel good* before they can *do good*. This is a world that celebrates the great partnerships between marketers, designers, and people; a new level of thinking in brand creation that allows for brandjamming.

WELCOME TO A WORLD WHERE DESIGNERS SPEARHEAD RESEARCH
They create the spark that ignites the fire of innovation; they lead our way through a world that's visual and sensorial, where the intuitive perceptions guide our entrée to culture and the consumer's heart.

BRANDS ARE NOT ABOUT MATH BUT ABOUT POETRY
Consumers don't need a better washing machine, a faster car, or another T-shirt. We are nearing the apogee of rational production and distribution. People need transforming emotional experiences.

DESIGN IS THE PROOF AND THE MESSAGE
Product design is the direct reflection of a company's culture, vision, and imagination. Design sends long-lasting messages that will be very difficult to

change. The promise of advertising if met with poor products that are badly designed will be wasted beyond repair.

A Competitive Edge

As long as consumer markets grew faster than the competition, industrialization, corporatization, and efficiency had room to expand. Notoriety was critical to success; visibility and exposure were the name of the game. The consumer was an end goal in the production process, not a creative partner or a defining factor. As long as consumers' rational needs were fulfilled, brands competed in an environment where choices were few.

The brands that still think they're selling tangible commodities to rational consumers are falling behind. Customers today seek innovation, personalization, and performance on the level of product and emotion alike. There are other reasons for this ongoing design revolution: an improved economic climate; an expanded global market; an inspired crop of young designers; and revolutions in product distribution, manufacturing, and technology. Design is enhancing a company, or even a country, to compete in a consumer world. Design will be one of the most potent business solutions. A nation must create to survive and renew its vital brainpower, and the job of executives in the twenty-first century is to imagine, to create, to innovate.

HERMAN MILLER:
BUSINESS DRIVEN BY DESIGN

To understand design as a business vision, one can't bypass Herman Miller, the world-renown Zeeland-based (that is, Michigan) furniture manufacturer. Not unlike most companies today, Herman Miller was faced with a changing market, new competition (cheaper manufacturing in the south of the country), and a more and more expansive distribution system in the 1930s. The furniture industry was in a state of shock, short on solutions and long on guessing,[12] Ralph Caplan says in his book on Herman Miller, *The Design of Herman Miller.* (Caplan is also the author of *By Design* and *Cracking the Whip, Essays on Design and Its Side Effects.*) Herman Miller, which specialized in ornate period residential furniture pieces, saw its business lose market shares and profit margins. The company was one year away from bankruptcy.

The new president at the time, D.G. De Pree, observed what he called the "ear-to-the-ground" attitude of the furniture manufacturing, which was to seek "reliable tips on whatever arbitrary changes buyers were going to seek in their quest for novelty and then gear production accordingly."[13] This meant, as Caplan writes, "that the industry was literally reactionary; it initiated nothing but merely reacted to circumstances." This was one of the four major evils De Pree saw in the state of his industry, the others being:

1. The strength of a buyer market.
2. The pressure of a seasonal model.
3. Lack of control in selling products as a manufacturer.

In hindsight it is interesting to see how the company started to observe the tyranny of a new consumer democracy and at the same time its magnificent potential. Connecting with people's imagination in showrooms that the company could control became the business plan and the vision. A commitment to the full brand experience consistent with the excitement of design never seen before became the futuristic trademark of Herman Miller and an inspiration for other companies to follow.

The new vision from Herman Miller came from Gilbert Rhode, a designer that impressed D.G. Depree with the subject of modern furniture. His vision, most revolutionary at the time, caught the attention of D.G. Depree, who, as a very religious person, saw in modern design a mirror image of Christian sincerity. By focusing the company to understand a new breed of users, Gilbert Rhode opened up the company to design innovation and consequently a new set of products such as modern storage and seating. It shifted the Herman Miller business from a provider of classical, ornate, high-priced seven-piece bedrooms to what has since become the concept behind the company success: a way of life.

Rhode's influence went beyond design to also train the sales force to understand design and what it meant for the company: a point worth mentioning is the fact that Jimmy Eppinger, their East Coast salesman, occupied a desk in Rhode's studio. Clark Malcolm, a senior writer at Herman Miller, believes profoundly that "Rhode is the one who really established design at Herman Miller, introduced the concept of the showroom idea, and attached customer education as a part of sales."

The business principles are what fascinate me about design—how do you manage a culture of creativity and risk in a continuous way and still stay fresh and competitive? In Caplan's book, you find that many of the answers crafted at Herman Miller are the same ones that brand managers need in today's new world of invention. I want to share the ideas that govern the growth and notoriety of the Herman Miller brand; visionary then, and visionary now:

• What you make is important.
• Design is an integral part of the business.
• The product must be honest.
• You decide what you will make.
• There is a market for good design.

With these five driving principles, I can rest my case. Those principles make the designer an integral part of the brand process on par with research, marketing, or distribution. It also demands a huge amount of courage and passion, and most importantly, a true belief that people will appreciate beauty, sincerity, and innovation they don't know about yet.

In Caplan's book, De Pree, while speaking of the huge success of the Charles Eames plastic chair, likes to say, "None of us ever asked where we fit into the market or what competitive products were already there." If you look into the depth of human desires through the eyes of a designer, you will get answers that will transcend the reality of what you know, but at the same time you will uncover the magnitude of all the possibilities for you to answer to. Herman

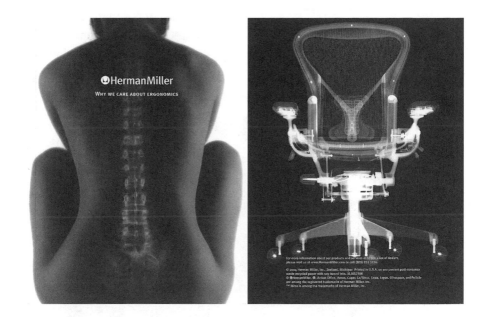

Miller had financial discipline and focus. It also understood its mission in life and how to connect with the emotions of an audience. It went where its audience would find the best experiences with the brand, and it never compromised. Herman Miller's mission, at the end of the day, is to humanize its brands to make them compelling for an audience and responsible for the environment. Its commitment to ergonomics and other human factors fits this human view of design that is unbending. "They spent eleven years studying how the human body should sit comfortably and healthfully before creating the now iconic 'Ergon chair,'" says Clark Malcom, during my visit to Herman Miller's offices, surely reemphasizing what counts when creating products: people.[14]

Herman Miller continued the legacy to attract America's best designers—the most challenging, the most visionary, a strategy that made their success. Talents such as George Nelson, Alexander Girard, and Ray and Charles Eames became the creative forces behind the Herman Miller brand. What they created was a company shaped by designers, led by an innovative design spirit and a tight set of company principles that could support the sustainability of such a concept. In the 1930s, design was mostly a craftsman's idea and the results were one-off pieces for collectors or wealthy patrons. With the emergence of a new middle class in America, Herman Miller understood that a new design language needed to be established to meet the aspirations of these new dreamers.

What this means: *Herman Miller had a lasting corporate philosophy, but it also had a vision that placed creativity and innovation at the core of the operating process. Most importantly, it was able to set free what makes our world what it is: our imagination.*

SHIFT 7
Think Emotional Customization

"Design is all around us, of course, but there was a time when most of us didn't notice it. Not anymore. There's a revolution in progress, and it's having a real impact on how people see and use and think about consumer products," Allan J. Magrath writes in *Across the Board* magazine.[1]

A study published in the *Journal of Product Innovation Management* further proves this point. It polled "138 experts on the 'industrial-design effectiveness' of 93 companies in nine industries, and then correlated the design results with the companies' financial performance over a seven-year period. The bottom line: On almost all measures, the manufacturers with highly rated design had stronger financial performance."[2] According to Clay Dean, design director at General Motors, "When a company gets desperate because quality doesn't push sales and incentives don't push sales, then all the business people realize they've exhausted all their ideas and look at design and styling."[3]

In the new marketplace, those companies who can harness the power of design in order to make products that are better suited to their customers' unique needs and desires—in other words, to customize its offerings so that they won't be turned down—will, without exception, outperform their competitors. "Providing a broad array of customized services adds complexity to any business. . . . Smartly customizing services for major retail customers can translate into several points of greater organic growth and an increase in net profitability of 10–20 percent," says Matthew Egol, Karla Martin, and Leslie Moeller.[4]

> Those companies who can harness the power of design in order to make products that are better suited to their customers' unique needs and desires will, without exception, outperform their competitors.

Customizing an experience for millions, often billions, of people is no simple task. How exactly do you make each and every person feel as though you are speaking directly to him or her? In my first book, *Emotional Branding*, I explained that the very first commandment of emotional branding is a shift from consumers to people because: "Consumers buy; people live." This insight is essential to understanding effective product customization. Companies must get out of the "mass consumer" mind-frame and build their brands one customer at a time. In this chapter, I will explore how "customization" is not only about multiple choices but providing selections that successfully appeal to diverse personalities, emotions, and preferences.

Better Living through Design: Personalizing a Brand by Giving It a Function

A shift is happening in product categories based on the concept of providing solutions. "The traditional marketing technique of simply offering another standard product under a 'brand name' is no longer capable of locking in customers," wrote Nirmalya Kumar in *The Financial Times*. "Today, customers are time-starved, impatient, and demanding. . . . As IBM observed during its transformation from a seller of products to a solution provider, many of its strengths, such as a decentralized organization, a technology focus and strong product divisions can become precisely those things that stop the company from making an effective transition."[5] So what, exactly, is a solution? Let's explore. . . .

In the jeans category, for instance, I was very intrigued by the seeming anonymity of jeans brands whose strategy was to focus on a small group of people who are "in the know." Those new "cool" jeans brands such as Earnest Sewn, Acne, Paper Denim & Cloth, Edition, and True Religion have become insider brands that are not supported by splashy media and national advertising. True Religion, which can be found in most department stores and in more than six hundred fashion boutiques,[6] is promoted exclusively through word of mouth, fashion editors, and blogs.

Customization as expressed in this chapter is not about superficial line extensions or do-it-yourself kinds of offerings. I am intrigued by how customized a brand needs to be in order to connect emotionally with people and bring a message of truth. Looking at customization from that point of view opens the field of compelling opportunities that can then be manifested powerfully through conceptual ideas that make sense for people if well understood. I have explored five types of customization worth looking at in the context of how people view brands:

CUSTOMIZING BRANDS EMOTIONALLY BY GENERATION

BABY BOOMERS (39-55)
"The Connoisseurs"

- Comfort
- Ergonomic Functionality
- Premiumness / Exclusivity
- Artisan Quality Craftsmanship
- Established Classics
- Childhood Nostalgia
- Elite Status
- Customized—Homes, Gardens, Jewelry, Cars
- Scientific Innovation
- Life Simplified Technology
- Safety Protection
- Artsy-Crafty
- Authenticity
- Antiques / Collections

◀ SHARED VALUES ▶
- Beautiful Cuisine
- Luxury Goods
- Exclusivity
- Following Designers
- Logos/Brand Centric
- Whimsical Chic
- 20th Cent. Modern
- Global Artifacts
- Animal References

GENERATION X (27-38)
"The Chic Seekers"

- International Luxury
- Limited Editions
- Cool Technology
- Natural/Organic
- Sensory
- Chic Factor
- Fashion
- Destinations
- Boutique Hotels
- Statement Cars
- Graphic Pop Art
- Celebrities/Stylists
- Graphic Design
- Interactive Media

◀ SHARED VALUES ▶
- Self-Expression
- Retro Vintage
- Creative
- Homemade/Handmade
- Design Form Factor
- Expressive Accessories
- Smart Design
- Tattoos/Piercing
- Environmental

GENERATION Y (5-26)
"The Creatives"

- No-Brand
- Ethnic Influences
- Playful / A Wink
- Illustration
- High Design / Low Price
- Personalized, My Design
- A Political Message
- Integrated Technology
- Entertaining
- Deconstructed
- Repurposed Objects
- Animation / Anime Characters
- Embroideries Embellishments Ornamentation
- Grass Roots, Hippie, Bohemian

ILLUSTRATION PROVIDED BY PETER LEVINE.

285

CUSTOMIZATION THROUGH DESIGN STIMULATION

If we look at the evolution of the Gillette razor design over the last eighteen years, you find a company that has integrated the need for consumer stimulation and discovery in their products development. The Chanel or Estée Lauder portfolios of fragrances keep on evolving to reach new younger groups while protecting their classic heritage. The evolution is stimulating and always provocative, refreshing the perception people need to have about the brand. The luxury brands have also "redesigned" themselves to wow their audiences with new offerings, such as Vuitton and its new flagship stores or new redesigned bags by Takashi Murakami, the famous Japanese designer. Target's evolving visual vocabulary supports its ambition always to inspire different groups interested in the new and in design aspiration.

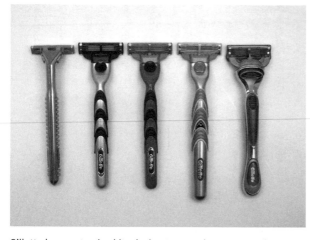

Gillette has customized its design to meet its customers' changing expectations.

Shoe personalization, although still in development, has the potential to become a huge trend. The custom programs "Converse One" and "Custom Shop" by Vans, "Nike ID," and "Mi Adidas" allow customers to construct and personalize their own shoes using an array of design choices over the Internet and have their creations subsequently built and shipped directly to them. Timberland.com has capitalized on upgraded technology and an expanded selection of footwear. Now shoppers can choose from multiple Timberland boot styles and specify so many product details, including color, hardware, laces, and typefaces for monogramming, that more than one million combinations are possible for any one base style. With a speedy product-configuring tool that instantly updates images as a consumer designs a boot, the site not only allows for instant gratification but also quicker buys. The customization process becomes fast, seamless, and satisfying—and so does the shopping experience.[7]

Even in the arcane world of fly-fishing, one can find examples of branded product customization. If you watch a movie like *A River Runs Through It*, you might think that this is a simple, old-fashioned sport that can be handled with basic traditional equipment. If you speak with any fly fisherman, however, you realize that this is not the case. It would be like thinking that people still play golf with the same clubs their ancestors used in Scotland at the beginning of the last century. Fly fishermen will passionately tell you about the numbers of lures or artificial flies that they have to buy or make themselves in order to match nature's real flies that hover on top of lakes, sea sides, and rivers during different seasons. Some of the insects trout are fond of only live at certain times of the year or even times of the day, and if you don't have a similar-looking fly as the ones that congregate around your favorite watery spots, you will not have a chance. Studying nature and the attention to detail in making bait, therefore, are important. The success of the sport is based not only on the love of fishing but on the personal involvement of the fisherman in preparing for the success of the event.

The Scott Fly Rod Company is one of the rod companies that understands the importance of craftsmanship (their rods are handmade), the bonds that unite all fly fishermen around the same passion for the sport, and the need for the most valued expertise. When you read the sales material, you will find that Scott likes to celebrate the fact that the members of the company are a community that "is held together by tight bonds." The company also likes to com-

Scott fly rods collection.

pare its business to the details of preparing a great meal, such as the best ingredients, the right tools, and a chef and team with experience and creativity that is exactly what fly fishermen are all about.

At Scott Fly Rods, this challenge is not an issue. You will find more than 131 models of rods and at least seven types of cork-finished grips, pretty much any rod you want for any fishing situation or skill level. Customizing the rods to the fishermen's emotional attachment and the fundamental values of the sport is what interests me and connects well with what needs to happen in brand customization. The design of the rods is magnificent from a technological or aesthetic perspective, only using the most advanced fibers, and the packaging is also on par with the expectations of this type of company. Fly-fishing is about nature, craftsmanship, dexterity, diversity, ethics, discipline, precision, and instinct, and the products and the brand need to match those values. Using design to manifest the brand's promise of making an experience even more memorable for a client is most intriguing.

CUSTOMIZATION THROUGH PERSONALIZED SERVICES

Catering to the personal attention and support that you need can be customized and manifested in all kinds of ways: Nordstrom and its unbending commitment is a model of service excellence. The boutique hotels cater to the emotional hipster. Air France builds the context in which people find a touch of French hospitality. Travelocity focuses on the support and trust of a great vacation.

This approach has been exemplified by Starbucks, proposing 19,000 ways to offer a coffee, or Hotel Indigo in Atlanta, which serves favorite drinks to loyal customers before they even order it.[8] Companies have also found ways to use up-to-the-minute communications venues to showcase their brands. Absolut Vodka sponsors a text messaging service through which dodgeball.com recommends places for socializing . . . in this case, places that serve Absolut. Other brands use the language of text messaging when they advertise in more traditional media, helping them to connect with younger audiences, for example, Dorritos' outdoor campaign "inNw?"

Credit card brands are also an interesting model for innovative ways to humanize an offer. In order to compete in today's market, all card companies offer very similar APRs and benefits—so how is the consumer supposed to choose which carrier? Inevitably, lifestyle and emotional differentiation has been the key:

Speaking your customer's language.

- **The "Do-Gooder" Merchant: Visa.** Consumers—particularly those of prosperous nations—will always be reminded that there are others in this world who are much less fortunate. Nothing comes close to the fulfillment you receive when you perform a selfless act and help those in need. With these cards, customers don't have to feel guilty when they run up a sizeable bill shopping because with every purchase, a donation is made to help their charity or organization of choice. If you are a morally conscious spender, you can give back to your school or help out a charity without actually being there or taking time away from your busy schedule—quite literally being "everywhere you want to be." With this card:

    You are socially conscious, moral, altruistic, caring.

    You want to relieve, improve, assist, lend a hand, facilitate, give back, share, help.

- **The Rebel Merchant: Discover.** Discover truly strives to live up to its name. If you can personalize your hair, your clothes, your home—why not personalize your credit card? By allowing members to select from over 150 designs, Discover Card encourages its customers to express their own unique personality. On its Web site, Discover further evokes the feeling of freedom as it urges: Go paperless; faster than mailing your bill. There's no need to be tied down with paperwork with this card in your wallet. So, with this card:

You are unique, colorful, eccentric, active, spirited, creative.

You want to "march to the beat of your own drummer," personalize, express yourself.

- **The Chic Merchant: American Express.** Advertising campaigns? Oh, that's sooooo last season. Luckily for American Express, some things just never go out of style. As long as mankind strives to achieve and succeed, there will always be a desire to have the best. American Express has brilliantly channeled this fundamental desire with the creation of its black card—so exclusive and chic that its notoriety has spread throughout the globe without a dime spent on advertising. This mythical card has become a badge of honor to the particularly wealthy, showing off their superlative purchasing power. With this card:

  You are distinctive, elite, noticed, proud, valued, worthy, important.

  You want to indulge, be spoiled, pampered.

- **The Vigilant Merchant: MasterCard.** Feeling safe and secure are innate, fundamental needs. In this age of digital shopping and e-purchases, it's reassuring to know that your credit card is actively protecting you. Many people have worked hard to establish good credit history—without which taking out loans or purchasing a house would be nearly impossible—why risk throwing that all away? Identity theft is becoming a major concern among consumers, prompting some to take a much more vigilant and cautious stance when dealing with their credit. MasterCard realizes its customers' need to protect their finances and assures them that they are in good hands. With its card:

  You are principled, honorable, decent, reliable, respectable, dignified.

  You want to depend, rely, be protected.

CUSTOMIZATION THROUGH EMOTIONAL DISCOVERY

The emotional customization answers to the longing for a unique escape, a new adventure or surprise, and a new way to build the sense of self. Apple ("customization of a music offering for you only!"); Corona beer as an "exotic" alternative to generic beers; or even the "city car," a concept sponsored by General Motors, designed by the Massachusetts Institute of Technology's Media Lab. This design proposes the ideas of miniature cars stacked up as shopping carts around the main travel hubs such as airports, subways, or train stations for your temporary use. Emotional customization also addresses the sensitive areas of our lives that we are concerned about, things like health, security, or escape.

In Japan, Natchan orange juice from Suntory smartly decided to customize its product launch by promoting the brands in toy stores. You could observe right in front of the store a salesperson dialoguing with parents and kids, introducing them to the products behind her on the shelves, including a large array of really cool back-to-school accessories. All of these are innovative ideas that push the limits of putting the product outside of its traditional context within emotional reach of people in a customized way.

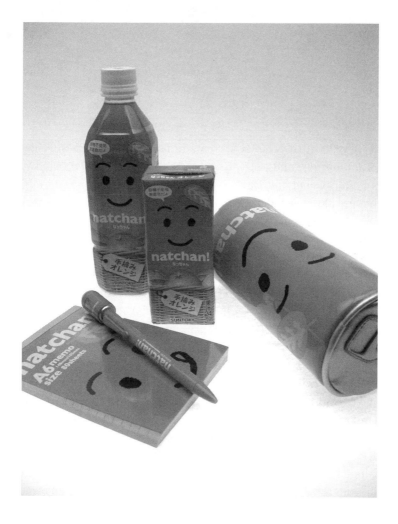

Founded in 1999, Heavy.com is a Web site featuring short-form videos, animation, racy humor, and—of course—a brilliant new trend in advertising. Creators Simon Asaad and David Carson have explained that they built this site to be more akin to a video game than a traditional Web page, as their interactive format and sparse use of text easily shows.

Once a user connects to their homepage, he is offered a plethora of free downloads, iPod videos, movie previews, and PSP (Playstation Portable) clips, to name just a few. The site is divided into "channels," including everything from "When Animals Attack" to "Gangsta Nanny 911." Aimed specifically at young men, Heavy.com has built a cult fan base nationwide and as of January 2006, boasted 10 million unique viewers monthly.

Heavy's amateur video, music, games, and parodies are all free to the audience—like many other Web pages, it generates revenue through ads placed on the site. But rather than using traditional, pre-packaged ads, Heavy.com blends its content with the advertisers' products. For example, in collaboration with Burger King, they sent out dozens of the King plastic masks to its audience and commissioned them to create their own amateur videos featuring the masked character. And the response? Amazing. Millions of people logged on to watch the Burger King character videos, and interest in the campaign spread over the Internet like wildfire, boosting sales. The Burger "King"—once an obscure character—now enjoyed national popularity, further ingraining the icon into pop culture.

Mainstream marketers were quick to follow suit. Heavy.com's roster of clients soon included companies such as Virgin, Verizon, and NBC. Sony Entertainment even partnered with Heavy.com to create a series of "branded entertainment." To promote Sony's videogame "God of War," Heavy created the concept of "Pimp My Weapon" (a nod to MTV's show "Pimp My Ride" where auto-specialists revamp and customize an unsuspecting viewer's beat-up, old car). In each episode of "Pimp My Weapon," the God of War character Kratos (an intimidating Spartan warrior) is transformed into "Ron Johnson," the host of a *How-To* show (think Bob Villa in *This Old House* or Tim "the Toolman" Taylor in *Home Improvement*), where he creates and tests weapons of mass killing practically and cheerily as if they were aluminum siding or hardwood flooring.

With the ever-expanding popularity of TiVo and DVR, it has become evident that traditional advertising needs to evolve—through customization. According to the *New York Times*, "many [companies] soon learn that less-intrusive forms of advertising can get five times the number of people to click on them . . . for advertisers, this shift means they have to alter the way they use their brands and icons."[9]

Heavy.com, MySpace, and YouTube are completely new advertising experiences—it's not a loud announcer interrupting your favorite television show to tell you which products/services you should be buying. At Heavy.com, the audience is the one who chooses which and how many ads they would like to see, empowering them with a new level of control in advertising—a trend that I predict will catch on very quickly. This unconventional format is changing the way people think about and respond to brands, icons, and advertisements. Like an eclectic video game, Heavy.com makes its advertising creative, fun, and remarkably effective.

A Personal Touch: The Designed Vacation

When Walt Disney decided to create a theme park that permitted families to step inside the movies, it was a revolutionary step in immersive design. For the first time, regular audiences could step inside the fantasy worlds that enthralled them in theaters and on TV. More recently, Francis Ford Coppola and his wife have taken this to the next level by banishing the intermediate level of the theme park derived from movies. Coppola has opened a series of Latin American resorts that themselves comprise their own original cinematic fantasies.[10] Though there are no films associated with these resorts, every destination is as finely and intricately crafted as any of Coppola's greatest works. It's not like visiting the simulacrum of a Coppola film. Instead, it's *living* the film.

Coppola's three resorts—two in Belize and one in Guatemala—are each designed to deliver a masterful experience of the like few have ever had before. Each resort was crafted according to Coppola's direction, and he and his wife have chosen almost every piece of handmade fabric, accoutrement, and furnishing that are on site. The complexes are entirely eco-friendly and native. Electronics, from cell phones to air conditioners, are absent from the premises, although a "shell phone" permits calling room service as gentle wooden fans spin overhead. Power comes from a hydroelectric generator built at Coppola's direction in nearby rivers. There's even a private airstrip permitting visitors to come and go in the director's personal airplane.

Mr. Coppola's resorts dramatize the triumph of *designed experiences* over functional and tangible commodities. Every step of the way through their stay, visitors are in the hands of a carefully tailored, coherent, and thoughtful experience.

Because being distinctive and reinforcing a customer's self-image are essential, so too, is individuality key. When John Frieda launched his hair care product line "Sheer Blonde," specifically targeted to his golden-haired customers, he enjoyed immediate and sustainable success. Soon thereafter, he was compelled to create and release "Brilliant Brunette" and "Radiant Red" for all colors of the hair spectrum. Think about it, there must be a reason why T-shirts reading "Blondes have more fun" and "Redheads do it better" are so popular: the color of a person's hair is a huge expression of individuality and pride. John Frieda was able to tap into this hair care niche and has reaped the benefits ever since. Rival hair care company Pantene quickly jumped on the bandwagon and created its own line of shampoos and conditioners specially formulated for blonde, brunette, and red hair.

Similarly, the cosmetic company Almay is exploring a customization route with their new line of makeup called "Intense i-Color" that is expertly coordinated for blue, brown, green, and hazel eyes. In Almay's series of ads featuring the fair-complexioned model Elane Irwin, they announce: "Blue Eyes. Bluer. Now you can take your eye color, and turn it up." A person's eye color is a perfect example of a personal identifier. It can even be a source of great pride as it is linked to the genetics from which we have come. Neil Young's "Behind Blue Eyes," Van Morrison's "Brown-Eyed Girl," and, most recently, American Idol winner Kelly Clarkson's hit song "Behind These Hazel Eyes" attest to the fact that the pigmentation of a person's iris can mean a lot.

Another portrayal of "customized design" is a line of modified power tools created by five interior architecture and product design students at Kansas State University. According to *U.S. Newswire*, "The students, all women and fifth-year seniors, have designed a concept for a line of tools aimed at women, the casual do-it-yourselfer or anyone who has found using tools to be intimidating or uncomfortable."[11] Dubbed "Savvy Tools," they are lighter and more ergonomic than standard bulky tools. It is most important to note how one of the designers described her product: "They aren't pink and they aren't frilly," says Alison Garry. "We wanted to make tools that are aesthetic and cohesive and more appealing to women. We think tools can be well designed and look good."[12] This clearly proves that a designer can't paint a hammer pink and market it to women—the customization of these tools is based on function, first and foremost.

CUSTOMIZATION THROUGH QUALITY CRAFTSMANSHIP
The crafts-driven customization of a product for a look and feel that is handmade, original, and considered is one of the most noticeable trends of the twenty-first century. Our need to see a human hand in the products we buy is important. Vuitton and Coach, among the luxury goods, are examples of this need, but also any products that does not feel processed, such as the Nike Considered shoe, which I talk about in Shift 6 (on judging the IDSA).

The trend against processed and unhealthy products is helping new businesses come to life with a new set of interesting offerings. In the cheese industry in America, for instance, there are 300 artisan cheesemakers, mostly in California, Wisconsin, and Vermont. "Still small and family-owned but led by their passion and love for their craft," says David Rozenberg, an executive at Bongrain USA, a global cheese manufacturer. According to David, "This type of products has grown in the United States perhaps for the same reasons that have made Whole Foods so successful as consumers are moving away from standardized tastes. They want to know the source of their food and how it is made." Healthier, higher quality products that have an identity included in their taste are more indulgent, and in the case of cheese, can lead to a shared romantic social experience, particularly when coupled with a bottle of wine.

Their Web site, ArtisanalCheese.com, takes you to a complete new world of discovery and sensual experiences that is customized to the discovery of tastes that we don't know yet but are ready to explore. The presentation of the products is beautifully designed and appeals to all your senses; it signals and reinforces the trend toward reaching out for new experiences and pleasures, far away from the banal. One could challenge that this appreciation of stronger tastes is un-American, but this is again misreading the mindset of the American consumer today and its relentless seeking toward a reconnection with a more real life and the search for authenticity. Those labor-intensive cheeses, not unlike the designer's hand that is promoted by Target, brings that extra special attention and human connection with a more powerful reality and truth.

When it comes to personalizing a product with quality, there has not been anyone more adept than Martha Stewart. Her company, Martha Stewart Living Omnimedia, Inc., encompasses magazines, TV shows, and product designs sold in stores around the globe. Her Web site, MarthaStewart.com, allows customers, the majority of whom are die-hard Martha fans, to tap into their design guru's secret recipes, gardening tips, and interior decorating expertise, and apply what they learn in their own homes. Visitors to the site are even invited to write "Dear Martha" letters, or e-mails, and these communications are never left unanswered. Stewart has not only set out examples for consumers to follow, but has also provided them with an icon to look up to and feel good about. As authors Celinda Lake and Kellyanne Conway point out in their book *What Women Really Want* (see Insight 3, "Emotional Design Is Feminized Design"), women are looking for more customized experiences that will fulfill their need for more control in their lives.[13] To turn a blind eye to this movement is to kiss your brand's future goodbye.

CUSTOMIZATION THROUGH SOCIAL REALITY

Cultural customization that celebrates people's heritage, values, and right to voice opinions is the most powerful manifestation of the postmodern global world. Cultural customization says we are all different but that there are also many people like us somewhere in the world interested in what we are interested in. Coca-Cola Black is the first attempt to add to their brand instead of diluting its message with lame flavor extensions. By bringing extracts of coffee into the mix, this new product delivers a premium emotional experience for an energy-craved market. Customers were clamoring for this product without being heard.

From red to black

The Web has indeed accelerated this process with the emergence of blogs where all buzz ideas get propagated. To listen, you need to go where people are talking as it could influence the character of brand positioning and the role of your brand outside of traditional media outlets. On a personal basis, if someone wants to brag about their private life they can; shock jock Howard Stern does it every day on his satellite radio program, and Anna Benson (wife of Orioles' pitching superstar Kris Benson) does not mind telling you all about their sex life if you ask on her blog, AnnaBenson.net ("Ask Anna Anything").

On the world stage, a new trend is taking place that brings in new voices in the media landscape. The manifestation of new cultural brands or political messages reinterpreted through new physical or virtual media is growing as well. The supremacy of the Western cultural model at its best has worked well in influencing and liberating many nations from dictatorship models to more market-driven economies. The case of Japan, Germany, Turkey, and now

Eastern Europe or China is a case in point at different levels of evolution. Through the expansion of the Western world's postmodern free-market societies, we have seen also the expansion of Western media, advertising, and brands, a situation that is now challenged by countries or cultures that want to imprint their own cultural heritage in this new world model. The new postmodern world that empowers the freedom of individuals is leading naturally also to the unforeseen but inevitable personalization of cultures.

I was born in France, but have lived in America for the past thirty years, so I can relate to the vast differences that affect both our cultures. In France, it is okay for a couple to argue in public; it is the sign of a confident and strong relationship, as a Sud-African psychologist friend of mine married to a French woman likes to mention. In America, you disagree in private and show a united face to the public. I can see that in my relationship with my French business partner; we disagree during our board meetings, and I can see the horror in the eyes of our American partners. According to my friend, when France disagreed publicly with America in the U.N., it was culturally okay for the French, but appalling for the Americans. I am sure that a lot of tension must have existed between the U.K. and the United States during the process that led to the Iraq war, but in public it was a solid front.

Those cultural nuances for brands are critical and important to understand in an emotional economy. An article in *Advertising Age*, reporting on the fortieth annual International Advertising Association World Congress, mentions how Obaid Humaid Al Taver, the Dubai Chamber of Commerce president, surprised a few delegates by saying he took offense that the Western media had created an image of an Arab as "womanizer, greedy, corrupt, lazy, illiterate, rich, anti-semitic and male chauvinist."[14] The world of branding is full of scripted and stereotyped portraits, perceptions, and consumer profiles that do not necessarily facilitate a dialogue and the pursuit of a better understanding.

The customization of thoughts can't be stopped, and the cultural voices will emerge naturally to find their voice, and most importantly, the expectation of their audiences. Al Jazeera clearly owed its success to the poorly delivered, canned Western news propagated by the Western media to the Arab world. That Al Jazeera attracts such a great following, including anchors such as Josh Rushing, a former United States marine, is the proof that this format has a future. The launch of an English version of Al Jazeera's program shows how far people will go to find the information they want and how much people want diverse information to more fully comprehend global issues. Hassan M. Fattah, in a column in the *New York Times* speaking of the channel that "inspires as much derision in the West as it does pride in the Middle East," sums up the sometimes vast divide that exists now in the media world and the limits of the "Western voice" propagated by the CNNs and BBCs of the world.[15]

Political heavyweights such as Condoleezza Rice have appeared finally on the network, and we all have seen the emotional debate of Dr. Wafa Sultan denouncing some Muslims for what she describes as their lack of reality in a modern world. Her tape has attracted hundred of thousands of people to that interview on the Web and millions more when live. Al Jazeera propagates information that is uncomfortable for the West, which is the reason why Al Jazeera was attacked by Secretary Donald Rumsfeld for its anti-Americanism. But what is the point of watching news if you feel they are not telling you the full story? The influence of the Al Jazeera model will be one of the most interesting challenges for other established networks as the new upstart knows how to "emotionalize news" for an audience. How many executives, for instance, watch Al Jazeera to get an insight not only on the Muslim world, but on the world in general, and particularly on how people truly feel in those regions? Al Jazeera is clearly now transcending the Arabic language with its new international version and fast becoming a new source of information in the Middle East and all Arab cultures worldwide. This result shows that nobody has any grip on anything anymore and that people will gravitate toward what is more relevant to them from a branding or service perspective.

The successful British play on the Iraq war, *Stuff Happens*, now in America, has its script changing according to the circumstances and evolution of the ongoing war. The play is a piece in movement, a play that continues to evolve its relevance to the audience.

Starting with an understanding of people's complex desires in the context of their real life, outside of any dogmatic perceptions and with a fair vision of reality, helps humanize brands to respond to these vast and different realities. Customization needs to include the following five components: design, service, emotion, craft, and shared voices to truly reach people. Take a small retailer such as L'Occitane; its product design is unique; its service, magic; the emotion, elevating; and the craft, fully expressed through authenticity and packaging. Through its voice, L'Occitane shares its respect of the environment and a deep connection with its guests. On Web sites such as epinions.com, you can find one of the many consumer rating sites that confirm the appeal and pleasure people have by purchasing the brand. Crafting products to fit people's needs should not overwhelm them.

Assuming One's Own Identity: We Do Not Live in a "One-Size-Fits-All" World

The challenge is that customization requires one-on-one marketing and a selective message. The "one-idea-fits-all" approach, relying mostly on traditional broadcast communication, needs to be enhanced and expanded with promising experiential messages that reach people in an emotional, sensorial, and personal way. This is when the role of design can be leveraged at its best as a form of personal identification, or an emotional badge. A consumer-driven revolution in the 1990s and early twenty-first century witnessed scores of consumers coming out of the woodwork to design it themselves, personalizing everything from Levi's jeans to posh country homes. As consumer desire and new technologies of personalization coalesced, savvy brands responded with new lines and offerings tailored to the new design drive.

However, the same trend has also whittled away some big brands' de facto dominance: in "do-it-yourself" times, the brand is in danger of becoming an unwanted middleman. With technologies offering more and more ways to "do it yourself," some people may claim that brands (especially large brands) can no longer have much of an impact.

I think they are wrong. In fact, this phenomenon is an invitation for capturing new opportunities. This need for individuality can best be fulfilled by innovative design and offerings, providing artists' vision and touch to otherwise mundane commodities. Anyone can open an Internet portal, but it takes a trained and committed designer to make that portal touching. In the earliest days of Internet access, Prodigy and America Online acted as portals that offered carefully designed communities and experiences allied with user-friendly, attractive design that gave novices the courage to enter cyberspace. However, as the market expanded, these companies lost their ability to offer up compellingly designed experiences, and they had to rethink their format.

As long as brands can offer superior and responsive "designed messages," they will retain an added valuable, sought-after commodity. However, as more consumers find out they can "do it themselves," this will raise the design bar ever higher for the brand. Anything less than brilliant design will be inadequate.

If a large, powerful brand sticks to a "one-size-fits-all" dogma, it will not survive. The easiest way to customize a brand is creating a personal brand experience has proven to be highly effective in creating a customized bond with the customer.

There are now apparel lines with customized messages. It's impossible not to notice the rise in popularity of personalized apparel as celebrities, fans, and many others choose to express their own unique message using their clothing as a blank canvas. The company Customized World runs a multitude of ads offering their services as they proclaim: "Confess your love or show your attitude with a custom-printed tee! We customize shirts, panties, shorts, hats, bikinis, and much more with anything you want." Be it a political commentary, personal motto, nickname, or inside joke, these message-clad items define the people who wear them, making them stand out among all others.

Customization has nothing to do with line extension or multiple flavors, a top-down, tightly researched, directed process that follows vague consumer information to deliver hopeful new winners. Customization is about putting all of the possibilities together and letting the people do the mixing and the wearing. It's like owning an ice cream parlor and letting your customers create their own flavor rather than simply asking them what prefabricated flavor to choose. Customization is the "freedom" flavor, the belief that anything is possible, opening up the brand to be more flexible and fun.

Customization is about putting all of the possibilities together and letting the people do the mixing and the wearing.

Unfortunately, customization is definitely not an infallible solution for branding all products. We have all seen many failed attempts in the marketplace, particularly when they were not emotionally driven. For example, in an effort to customize the "diet cola experience," customers were presented with Diet Vanilla Coke, Diet Pepsi Vanilla, Diet Cherry Coke, Diet Wild Cherry Pepsi, Diet Pepsi Twist, Diet Coke with Lime, Diet Coke with Splenda, not to mention Coca-Cola Zero, C2, and Pepsi ONE. Is this a math equation or an effective brand concept? I say neither.

Is this customization for shelf space or consumer taste?

What this means: *Consumers are looking for that customized design, that one experience that will suit their particular lifestyle and celebrate their cherished individuality. People from all walks of life have innumerable differences; yet they all share a need to feel special, unique, and "one of a kind." The concept of customization is precisely how companies can channel and cater to this need. Honestly, who wants to believe that she is just a faceless member of a mass consumer market? I certainly don't.*

The Brandjam Center

Brands, like jazz musicians, need to indulge in some serious jam sessions, bringing together all the players to humanize the brands. Consumers, marketers, branding professionals, research organizations, and creative visionaries need to work in unison to connect brands with people emotionally. We need to pull together all those groups and disciplines around new techniques that integrate the science of branding with its creative and inspirational spirit. By bridging the gap, we reconcile both the logical and the emotional aspects of a brand message. We have to get to the point where the design process is recognized as strategic thinking and bring out the "inner designer" in businesspeople to challenge the way we create and communicate brands. We need to create incubators for new ideas, "innovation labs"—ways to look at branding strategies in a more intuitive fashion. I call these labs "brandjam centers."

There are working models already in existence that can provide inspiration. Through the process of writing this book, I have discovered new and truly inspiring ways people can brandjam with leading manufacturers and retailers, and vice versa. At Desgrippes Gobé, we have transformed our company into a brandjam center where we invite clients and consumers to participate in the creative process along with us. We are not the only ones. Smart advertising has an example in TBWA's creation of a "Media Arts Lab" for their iconic Apple account, which *Advertising Age* calls a "glimpse of the future."[1] As you have read in this book, many corporations are realizing how critical it is to get their management involved in the creative process in a richer way to support innovation and bring new ideas to life.

In the brandjam centers I have been most impressed with, at GM or Herman Miller, I discovered the following:

1. Brandjam centers advance the theory that the creative process is stronger when it is part of the corporate process and thrives when supported by top management.

2. Brandjam centers encourage the process of brand innovation on an ongoing, long-term basis. The brandjam center also stimulates and energizes a company.

3. Through a participative process, brandjam centers become training centers and bonding places for executives willing to make change and ideation an important part of their jobs.

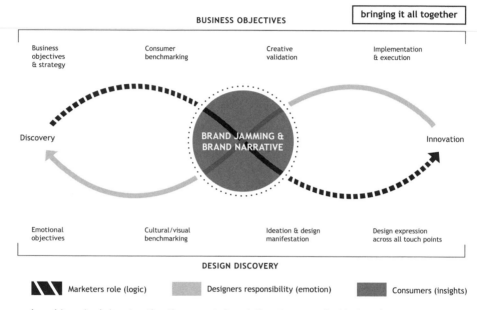

BUSINESS OBJECTIVES

bringing it all together

Business objectives & strategy

Consumer benchmarking

Creative validation

Implementation & execution

Discovery

BRAND JAMMING & BRAND NARRATIVE

Innovation

Emotional objectives

Cultural/visual benchmarking

Ideation & design manifestation

Design expression across all touch points

DESIGN DISCOVERY

Marketers role (logic)   Designers responsibility (emotion)   Consumers (insights)

brand jamming brings together the separate brand silos, the strength of logic and consumers insight around the process of innovation in a participative way.

Brandjam centers help to foster consistency and longevity in the management of brand innovation. Anne Asensio, herself the greatest proponent of General Motors design centers (see Shift 6), talked to me about the importance of cultivating the right environment for willing CEOs to take part in the creative process in the long run. For those initiatives to work, it is important to keep on brandjamming so those ideas that might not be right at a certain point in time can still be on the table a few months later, when the market is right, and the ideas seem more compelling. When I talked to Anne, I mentioned to her that her approach at GM would be invaluable for corporations to emulate, but she was quick to respond that, unfortunately, there is no set formula and that each company has to create its own innovative methodology. I am afraid that it will disappoint some of the readers who were expecting to find something like a new formula to use for their brands.

I still think that Anne's approach is a powerful model, but I agree that it can't be put into a bottle. Brandjamming is intuitive, participative, inventive, and does not abide by any formula. Anne Asensio believes that each firm needs to find its own voice and process in building innovation on an ongoing basis. "This is like tending a garden," says Anne, "the soil is the important thing; cut flowers, like fast ideas, have a short life, but a well-tended soil can breed many beautiful flowers year after year."

Those who are frustrated by the existing short-term research and innovation models in brand building and brand creation, realize that, unfortunately, the marketing world operates on a project-to-project basis, without stepping back to look at the total brand picture. It seems that critical insights from an emotional perspective and futuristic ideas just die with the completion of each project. When those Coke cans landed on John Galliano's runway, Desgrippes Gobé got an opportunity to analyze what that meant from a brand perspective. If companies don't take advantage of those opportunities and search for that "why," they miss out on the chance to learn more fundamental truths about a brand's impact on society.

In the brandjam center, you set up the foundation of ongoing brand research and development, monitoring all of the events that happen in consumer interaction with the brand before, during, and always. A complete information cycle can provide, on an ongoing basis, an accurate picture of the brand's evolving emotional status and future possibilities. From a design perspective, the brandjam center is about the manifestation of ideas and a place to bring creative people from all walks of life together. And this includes consumers and marketers. It also must be based around these six fundamental beliefs.

1. The designer is only as good as his broad supporting team and the culture of a company that privileges innovation in the long term.

2. The creative process can only come from a permanent tension that provokes and stimulates people's minds by challenging a formal context, forcing everyone to see the world from different angles.

3. Expose the work. Don't make the creative and innovative process an out-of-the-mainstream silo. Creativity needs to be connected to the rest of the organization so great ideas can be endorsed and launched with everyone's support.

4. Protect the creative teams and give them leverage and access to influence more cross-disciplinary functions such as marketing. Money should be diverted from advertising to design innovation.

5. Everything is subject to change. The market changes; so should your methodologies and discovery techniques. Jazz is about all those instruments and the continuous manifestation of new sounds. A brandjamming approach never gets stale.

6. You need a physical, permanent place or places where you can monitor innovation through consumers' behavior and emotional states, a place where you can explore, through the lens of intuition, designs that bring new ideas to life.

But the brandjam center is not an isolated event. Companies must not create exclusive brandjam centers, where elite designers and executives make decisions, cut off from the company as a whole and from the public. Creativity can become stale very quickly if not nurtured, and like good soil, it needs continuously to be revitalized by outside input and stimuli. The world has changed; new challenges have bred fear and insecurity. The narrowing of the gap between people's self consciousness and the impact of the corporate world on their lives is a factor in creating brand reputation.

It's Time to Start Jamming

I hope that I have made my case for design as the filter that will capture the moods of consumers and the process that will envision and create innovation. Visual stimuli provide the best route to innovation, as they express the manifestation of an idea and open doors to others. It is time to brandjam, and brandjamming begins with an inspiring CEO. It starts at the top so that the courage to invent can be felt and supported throughout a company. Brandjamming creates a sense of accomplishment, as teams collaborate for the same goals, change paradigms, and break new grounds, all in harmony.

Much as with jazz, each band needs a stage and each brand needs a theater. Brand communication is still operating with the belief that we process communication as individuals, when in fact communication is shared, evaluated, and discussed, thanks to technology. Younger generations are looking for messages that bring them back together, not separate them, and the corporate culture needs to reflect this new reality. Design is a new way to humanize brands by bringing a fresher, more real perspective that makes happiness and pleasure the core delivery of its offering.

In his book *Les particules elementaires*, the French writer Michel Houellebecq mentions a lonely character who finds emotional reassurance in mail-order catalogs. The reliability of mail-order delivery is, for this character, proof of a stable world. I found this observation fascinating as it shows that people connect emotionally to brands in a much more profound way than we have previously imagined.

Brandjam offers a new way to consider and explore connections with people, design being the most potent method of all. I challenge marketers to reconsider how they process and evaluate innovation by relying more on gut instinct and their creative subconscious, the same way designers do. I have interviewed and been inspired by many leaders and brand activists who are revolutionizing the way we do business and the way we understand people in their everyday lives: they are the ones at the forefront of humanizing brands.

If you want to appeal to those consumers, you will have to speak a new language born out of a passionate dialogue between marketers, consumers, and creative people.

On to brandjamming!

Acknowledgments

This book was informed by the incredible availability and time generously given by some of the most important visionaries in the business of building and humanizing brands. Some of them were marketers such as Dove's Silvia Lagnado, some were writers and columnists such as Lauren Foster who, through her interview for the *Financial Times* brought out of me the concept of humanizing brands, some were designers such as Tommy Hilfiger and his life achievement, Yves Behar who volunteered to write the foreword, or Deborah Adler, a young upcoming product designer motivated to use design to create a better world.

Anne Asensio, the lead designer for General Motors, and Chris Bangle from BMW brought to life for me the participative power and challenge of collaborative work to anticipate market expectations, given that the lead time for a car company to launch new products is so much greater than with other brands. I was also privileged to speak with Les Ateliers Champenois, designers of the Statue of Liberty torch and bearers of a centuries-old tradition of craftsmanship.

In the world of fragrances, I spoke with Veronique Gabai of Estee Lauder, who successfully translates into fragrance the genius of some of the most iconic fashion brands, such as Donna Karan or Armani. I spent time with fragrance houses and was enthralled by the work done by such firms as IFF in uncovering the hidden sentiments revealed by fragrances. At Herman Miller I discovered a culture of design that is an integral part of the business and its competitive edge.

Then there are the books that I discovered, sometimes by chance, such as Kaplan's *The Design of Herman Miller*, on founder D.J. De Pree and design greats George Nelson, Charles Eames, Robert Propst, Gilbert Rohde and Alexander Girard, all of whose careers were linked to Herman Miller. There was also a rare copy of *Leo*, written in 1971 in commemoration of Leo Burnett's legacy, given to me by ARF President & CEO and former Leo Burnett executive, Bob Barocci. In the process I was also able to discover the life-transforming philosophies of Baruch Spinoza, thanks to Antonio Damasio's book, *Looking for Spinoza*, and Carl Jung's huge impact on research and design. Further inspiration came from authors and artists such as Susan Sontag, Michel Houellebecq, Alexis de Tocqueville, and Antoine de St. Exupéry, not to mention the most inspirational figure of all, "the Duke," Duke Ellington.

Then there are the passionate collaborators who help me with research, writing, focus and inspiration. Anne Hellman, who patiently supported all my efforts with her mastery of words and knack for crystallizing complex concepts into powerful sentences. Bernie Geoghan, already part of the team while in college, now a PhD student. Finally, my former assistants Jackie Wosilius and Valerie Le Deroff, and now Joyce Hughes, who managed this book to completion. At Allworth Press, I want to thank my editor Tad Crawford, always supportive of my ideas, as well as Nicole Potter and Monica Lugo, who helped tighten the book for better reading and understanding.

I also have to thank clients and former clients or professional partners for their input, such as Steve Crawford, former Coca-Cola Global Brand Manager, and Joe Plummer, now the Chief Marketing Officer at ARF, on the sensitive topic of branding and advertising. Thom Lockwood of DMI, the most prestigious design organization, as he volunteered to co-publish this book with Allworth, as well as Jeff Glueck of Travelocity with his personal insight on branding, and Russ Natoce of AOL. Christophe Fauconnier of the Censydiam Synovate Group also gave me such a new insight on psychological research and the art of knowing why people buy what they buy. My meeting with the founder of the Brazilian company Natura was so compelling as it proved to me that the business world could be a human world that creates value and opportunities for people.

Then there are those influential figures whom I have had the privilege to meet and work with, who had the most impact on my early thinking, branding titans such as Sergio Zyman, Les Wexner, and Leonard Lauder. I acknowledge the continuing inspiration I draw from such brands as Coca-Cola, Target, Starbucks, Apple, Cirque du Soleil, and the Rolling Stones, that keep on bringing magic into my life. Finally, there are all the true believers in brands as a form of societal progress from Asia, Europe, and the Americas who have offered me such energy and have encouraged me to do "what's right" to create meaningful brands that have an impact on society.

I cannot neglect to thank my French partner and co-founder of the firm, Joël Desgrippes, for his unique imagination, immense talent and design vision. I also want to recognize Judd Harner, president of Desgrippes Gobé New York, with his relentless belief in emotional branding and design, and David Israel, our creative director, for encouraging and bringing the most amazing designs to life.

Emotional branding was my personal perception of the branding world: intuitive, passionate, and focused on people's unmet emotional needs. Brandjam is about looking out for the collaborative process that is at the heart of imagining the best ideas. Brandjam is the theory that helps jazz up and humanize a brand through design; brandjam relies on all those talents that have uncovered the unique emotional connection between brands and people. With brandjam, I also share with you some of the techniques that we have developed since my first book to better comprehend the emotional process and the power of collaborative creation.

For the past two years, writing this book has been a personal voyage into the best of our branding world and the consumer world, a voyage that has left me with a great feeling that brands can have a positive impact on our lives. A discovery that creativity is a talent that all of us have but just a few know how to bring to life.

This book was my answer. The rest is for you to imagine.

Notes

Preface

1. Anonymous, "Lafley's Love Affair With Design," *Advertising Age*, July/August 2005.

Insight 1: Postmodern Dreams

1. Paola Antonelli, *Objects of Design* (New York: Museum of Modern Art, 2003).
2. Ibid.
3. Nicolai Ouroussoff, "Where MOMA Has Lost Its Edge," *New York Times*, February 4, 2005.
4. Richard Lapper, "Beautiful, Brutal: but What about the People?" *Financial Times*, December 10, 2004.
5. Ibid.
6. Mark Taylor, Op-ed, *New York Times*, October 14, 2004.

Insight 2: Innovation Comes from the Margins

1. Tom Wolfe, "Pleasure Principles," *New York Times*, June 12, 2005.
2. Robin Pogrebin, "Impact of a Stadium: A Look at Other Cities," *New York Times*, May 7, 2005.

Insight 3: Emotional Design Is Feminized Design

1. Valerie Seckler, "Women's Wishes: Control, Security and Peace," *WWD*, December 28, 2005.
2. Ibid.
3. Ibid.
4. *www.kimptonhotels.com* (accessed August 15, 2005).
5. Hilary Stout, "Letting It All Hang Out: Pregnant Women Pose for a New Type of Family Portrait," *Wall Street Journal*, August 11, 2005.
6. Rich Thomaselli, "Beauty's New, Er, Face," *Advertising Age*, August 15, 2005.
7. Ibid.
8. Marianne Rohrlich, "Is 2 1/2 Too Old to Be a V.P. for Design?" *New York Times*, March 31, 2005.
9. Ibid.
10. Marcia Biederman, "Self-Service Printing Is Redefining the Camera Store, and Even the Maternity Ward," *New York Times*, March 17, 2005.

11. Steve Lohr, "How Much Is Too Much?" *New York Times*, May 4, 2005.
12. Ibid.
13. Jewel Gopwani, "Women Suggest Friendly Auto Design, Features," January 12, 2005, *www.freep.com/money/autoshow/2005/* (accessed August 19, 2005).
14. "Your Concept Car: An Interview with the All-Women Volvo Design Team," *www.dmi.org/dmi/html/conference/europe05/sp_holmberg_interview.htm* (accessed August 19, 2005).
15. John Gartner, "Women Drive Changes in Car Design," April 10, 2004, *www.wired.com/news/autotech/* (accessed August 19, 2005).

Insight 4: Welcome to the Twenty-first Sensory

1. David Rocks, "China Design," *Business Week*, November 21, 2005.

Insight 5: Design Democracy

1. A. G. Lafley, "What P&G Knows about the Power of Design," interview by Jennifer Reingold, *Fast Company*, June 2005, 56–57.
2. Jennifer Reingold, "The Interpreter," *Fast Company*, June 2005, 59–61.
3. A. G. Lafley, "What P&G Knows about the Power of Design," interview by Jennifer Reingold, *Fast Company*, June 2005, 56–57.

Shift 1: Think Emotional Identity

1. Screenshots on page 99 © Google Inc. and are reproduced with permission.
2. John Markoff and Vikas Bajaj, "14,159,265 Slices of Rich Technology," *New York Times*, August 19, 2005.

Shift 2: Think Brand Iconography

1. Richard Milne, "Adidas Hits Back after Ruling on Stripes," *Financial Times*, April 26, 2006.

Shift 3: Think Advertising as "Experiences"

1. Joseph Nocera, "Chicken Hawker," *New York Times Magazine*, December 25, 2005.
2. *www.adage.com* (accessed January 6, 2006).

3. Brooks Barnes, "As TV Networks Use Web, Affiliates Seek Piece of the Action," *Wall Street Journal*, February 1, 2006.

4. David Kiley and Tom Lowry, "The End of TV (As You Know It)," *Business Week*, November 21, 2005.

5. Brian Steinberg and Suzanne Vranica, "As the 30-Second Spot Fades," *Wall Street Journal*, January 3, 2006.

6. Gary Silverman, "How May I Help You?" *Financial Times*, February 5, 2006.

7. Valerie Seckler, "Some Ads Sing Louder Than the Brands," *WWD*, May 17, 2006, 7.

8. Bill Huey and Jeremy Garlington, "Why Roy Disney Got it Right," *Brandweek*, April 5, 2004, 24.

9. Stuart Elliott, "For the Olympics, Commercials for Screens of All Sizes," *New York Times*, February 9, 2006.

10. TNS Media Intelligence, reported for 2005.

11. Joe Plummer, personal communication, May 2006.

12. Andrew Edgecliffe-Johnson and Paul Taylor, "Sony Chief Unveils Vision of the Future," *Financial Times*, January 6, 2006.

13. Christina Cheddar Berk, "Retailer Finds a Shortcut on QVC," *Wall Street Journal*, January 17, 2006.

14. Leslie Blodgett, "The Human Touch," *Global Cosmetic Industry*, March 2006.

15. Molly Prior, "Bath & Body Works Turns to Infomercials," *WWD*, April 28, 2006.

16. Stuart Elliott, "No More Same-Old," *New York Times*, May 23, 2005; and James Arndorfer and Jean Halliday, "GM Signals New Marketing Era," *Advertising Age*, May 16, 2005.

17. www.AdAge.com (accessed December 1, 2005).

18. Stuart Elliott, "At a Four A's Meeting, Warnings Galore That Madison Avenue Needs to Be Nimble about Changing," *New York Times*, May 6, 2005.

19. R. Craig Endicott, "100 Leading National Advertisers," *Advertising Age*, June 28, 2004.

20. Gary Levin, "Ad Glut Turns Off Viewers," *USA Today*, October 12, 2005.

21. Jonathan Cheng, "China Demands Concrete Proof of Ad Claims," *Wall Street Journal*, July 8, 2005.

22. Anonymous, "Word on the Street," *Advertising Age*, September 27, 2004.

23. Thomas Friedman, "G.M.—Again," *New York Times*, June 14, 2006.

24. Scott Bowles, "For Hollywood, Not Enough Good Cheer," *USA Today*, January 3, 2006.

25. Eric Pfanner and Stuart Elliott, "At Bartle Bogle, a Week to Remember," *New York Times*, October 20, 2005.

26. Jean Halliday, "The Gospel According to Martin and John," *Advertising Age*, May 16, 2005.

27. Julie Naughton and Pete Born, "In the Nude: Ford's First Lineup for Lauder," *WWD*, September 9, 2005.

28. Nat Ives, "Unauthorized Campaigns Used by Unauthorized Creators to Show Their Creativity Become a Trend," *New York Times*, December 23, 2004.

29. Rachel Tiplady, "From Faux to Fortune," *Business Week*, November 14, 2005.

30. Gary Silverman, "Unilever Sets Up In-House Advertising Teams," *Financial Times*, March 14, 2006.

31. Walter Mossberg, "iPod's Latest Siblings," *Wall Street Journal*, September 8, 2005.

32. Vanessa O'Connell, "How Gallo Got Front-Row Seats at Fashion Week," *Wall Street Journal*, February 8, 2006.

33. Ibid.

34. Rob Walker, "Soap Opera," *New York Times Magazine*, April 3, 2005.

35. *Leo Burnett* (Chicago: Leo Burnett Company, Inc., 1971).

Shift 4: Think Retail as "Advertising"

1. Chad Chang, "Defining Speech," *Metropolis*, November 2004, 98.

2. Linda Tischler, "Blowing Out Advertising's Walls," *Fast Company*, June 2005, 63–65.

3. Ibid, 63.

4. Teri Karush Rogers, "A Coffee Themeland, Temporary by Design," *New York Times*, October 23, 2005.

5. Robin Pogrebin, "Bilbao? Please, That Was So Eight Years Ago," *New York Times*, December 11, 2005.

6. Elaine Sciolino, "Above the Clouds, the French Glimpse the Old Grandeur," *New York Times*, December 17, 2004.

7. Nicolai Ouroussoff, "A Vision of a Mobile Society Rolls Off the Assembly Line," *New York Times*, December 25, 2005.

8. Susan Sontag, quoted in Charles McGrath, "No Hard Books, or Easy Deaths," *New York Times*, January 2, 2005.

9. Deborah Desilets, *Morris Lapidus* (New York: Assouline, 2005).

10. Theresa Howard, "Ikea Builds on Furnishings Success," *USA Today*, December 29, 2004.
11. Kerry Capell, Ariane Sains, Cristina Lindblad, and Ann Therese Palmer, "Ikea," *Business Week*, November 14, 2005.
12. Anonymous, "It's an IKEA World After All," *Advertising Age*, December 2005.
13. Jean Palmieri, "Delivering on Imagination at Apple," *WWD*, November 16, 2005.
14. Mya Frazier, "The Bigger Apple," *Advertising Age*, February 13, 2006.
15. Stephen Power, "Threatened by Rivals, German Car Makers Race to Erect Museums," *Wall Street Journal*, April 13, 2005.
16. Nicolai Ouroussoff, "The Assembly Line Becomes a Catwalk," *New York Times*, May 22, 2005.
17. Amy S. Choi and Meredith Derby, "Flagship Redux: Banking on Stores as Showcases," *WWD*, November 3, 2005.
18. Sharon Edelson, "LVMH Redefines Shopping Club," *WWD*, March 31, 2005.
19. Gary McWilliams and Steven Gray, "Slimming Down Stores," *Wall Street Journal*, April 29, 2005.
20. Tracie Rozhon, "No Longer the Belles of the Mall, Department Stores Try Makeovers," *New York Times*, March 1, 2005.
21. Ibid.

Shift 5: Think Design Research

1. Kerry A. Dolan, "The Soda with Buzz," *Forbes*, March 28, 2005.
2. David Kiley, "Shoot the Focus Group," *Business Week*, November 14, 2005.
3. Joseph Guinto, "You Ever Heard of Sidney Frank?" *American Way*, August 15, 2005.
4. Chuck Salter, "Moto's Mojo," *Fast Company*, April 2006.
5. Sandra Blakeslee, "Say the Right Name and They Light Up," *New York Times*, December 7, 2004.
6. Jan Callebaut, et al., *The Naked Consumer Today: Or an Overview of Why Consumers Really Buy Things, and What This Means for Marketing* (Antwerp: Censydiam & Garant Publishers, 2002).
7. Michael Solomon, personal communication, July 2006.
8. Andrew Grove, *Only the Paranoid Survive* (New York: Doubleday, 1996).
9. Estée Lauder, *Estée, a Success Story* (New York: Random House, 1985).

10. Olivia Fox Cabane, personal communication, June 2006.
11. Samantha Conti, "Burberry's IT Bounce," *WWD*, July 13, 2005.
12. Franco Lodato, personal communication, February 2006.
13. Neil Buckley, "The Power of Original Thinking," *Financial Times*, January 14, 2005.
14. Ibid.
15. Dorothy Kalins, "Going Home with the Customer," *Newsweek*, May 23, 2005.
16. Andy Goldsworthy, *Andy Goldsworthy: A Collaboration with Nature* (New York: H.N. Abrams, 1990).
17. Carol Hymowitz, "Rewarding Competitors over Collaborators No Longer Makes Sense," *Wall Street Journal*, February 13, 2006.
18. James P. Womack, "Why Toyota Won," *Wall Street Journal*, February 13, 2006.

Shift 6: Think Commodity to Design (Not!)

1. David Rocks, "China Design," *Business Week*, Asian edition, November 21, 2005.
2. Quote from Deepak Advani in his speech given at "Innovative Marketing Conference," Columbia University, June 9, 2006.
3. David Rocks, "China Design," *Business Week*, November 21, 2005.
4. Jamie Lincoln Kitman, "Life in the Green Lane," Op-ed, *New York Times*, April 16, 2006.
5. Gardiner Harris, "Report Finds a Heavy Toll From Medication Errors," *New York Times*, July 21, 2006.
6. Diane Cardwell, "City Backs Makeover for Decaying Brooklyn Waterfront," *New York Times*, May 3, 2005.
7. Harvard promotional literature.
8. Sharon Reier, "When Looks Count the Most," *International Herald Tribune*, September 18–19, 2004.
9. Lisa Sanders and Matthew Creamer, "Marketers Close in on Consumer-By Design," *Advertising Age*, November 8, 2004.
10. *The Wall Street Journal*, December 14, 2004.
11. Phil Patton, "A Wild West Shootout for Car Designers," *New York Times*, January 10, 2005.
12. Ralph Caplan, *The Design of Herman Miller*, (New York: Whitney Library of Design, 1976).
13. Ibid.
14. Clark Malcolm, personal communication, March 2006.

Shift 7: Think Emotional Customization

1. Allan J. Magrath, "Managing in the Age of Design," *Across the Board*, September/October 2005.
2. Julie Hertenstein, Marjorie Platt, and Robert Veryzer, "The Impact of Industrial Design Effectiveness on Corporate Financial Performance," *Journal of Product Innovation Management*, January 2005.
3. Jean Halliday, "The Drive for Design," *Advertising Age*, July 18, 2005.
4. Matthew Egol, Karla Martin, and Leslie Moeller, "Custom Fit: One Size Does Not Fit All," *Advertising Age*, September 2005.
5. Nirmalya Kumar, "Marketing's Drive to Recapture the Imagination," *Financial Times*, Monday, August 15, 2005.
6. According to hoovers.com.
7. Valerie Seckler, "Stressed Shoppers Grab for the Controls," *WWD*, November 2, 2005.
8. Ayesha Court, "Hotels Try to Make Your Stay Personal," *USA Today*, October 25, 2005.
9. Saul Hansell, "A Web Site So Hip It Gets Laddies to Watch the Ads," *New York Times*, March 27, 2006.
10. Claire Wrathall, "You've Seen His Films and Drunk His Wine, Now Go Stay in His Houses," *The Guardian*, May 22, 2004.
11. Valerie Seckler, "Women's Wishes: Control, Security, and Peace," *WWD*, December 28, 2005.
12. "Kansas State University Students Design Hand and Power Tools for Women," *U.S. Newswire*, May 12, 2005, http://releases.usnewswire.com.
13. Ibid.
14. Rance Crain, "IAA Host Blasts Western Media—From His Own Publishing Pulpit," *Advertising Age*, April 3, 2006.
15. Hassan M. Fattah, "The Middle East Watches Itself," *New York Times*, March 26, 2006.

Conclusion: The Brandjam Center

1. Scott Donaton, "TBWA's Media Lab Offers (Limited) Glimpse at the Future," *Advertising Age*, October 29, 2006.

Index

head graphics, 118
heart graphics, 118–119
Heavy.com, 292
Hershey, 173
humanistic, design, viii

iconography, 116
IFF (International Flavors & Fragrances), 45–51
IKEA, 183–184
Ilasse, John Edward, ix
imagination, 282
industrial age, 275
The Industrial Design Society of America (IDSA), 235, 238
inertia, 103
innovation
  bad design penalizing, 235
  brandjamming as, 94
  captain of, 221
  commitment for, 260
  core of, 257
  cost-cutting over, 228
  courageous, 222–223, 266
  creativity leading, 218
  design as tool of, xxxii
  gut instinct of, 307
  individuality through, 300
  open freeway for, 254
  origin of, 17–18
  people-driven, 264
  strategies for, 255
  unpredictability of, 259
integrated model of communication, 101
International Flavors & Fragrance. See IFF
internet
  commercial on, 152
  marketing on, 292–293
  viewer recognition of, 141–142
iPod, 14

Japanese youth, 215–218
jazz, 1
Jazz, the First Century (Ilasse), ix
jazzing up
  brand design, 3
  creativity being, 233–234
  department stores, 195
  design elements, 34
  power of, 6–7
  service industry, 29
  talent, 252
Jung, Carl, 208, 230

Karan, Donna, 245–248

Lagnado, Silvia, 240–243
Les Metalliers Champenois, 258–260
logo
  desirability of, 123

emotional identity
  expressed in, 81
  expressing v. signifying, 85
  reflecting brand in, 80
  transient nature of, 84
logo design
  abstraction in, 109–110
  emotional ingredients of, 79–81
  inspiring brand language with, 91
  transparency of, 86–87
Lois, George, 20
luxury brand retailing
  moxie of, 189–191
  unrealistic expectations of, 241

makeover, 270
manufacturing, 274
market economy, 134
market research, xxvii, 194, 200–201
marketing
  amateur consumer, 153–154
  ambush approach to, 197
  baby boomer, 32
  brand retailing as, 171
  brandjamming from, 142–144
  changing landscape of, 158
  consumer democracy from, 133–134
  consumer representation by, 250
  content creation in, 146–147
  coup, 58
  creating free, 170
  creative flirting in, xxii–xxiii
  design as, 107
  emotional customization evolving, 293
  exceeding, 156
  expenditure chart of, 140
  experiences as, 133
  fixed v. motion models of, 136
  functioning without fear in, 150–151
  fusion model of, 175–177
  future of, 101
  guerilla style, 242
  internet, 292–293
  inverse proportions of, 139
  ivory-tower, 247
  lost faith in, 147–148
  as message of promise, 163
  mismatched, 145–146
  modern v. postmodern, 15–16
  multinationalism in, 59
  negative emotion in, 74
  new beginnings in, 158–161
  non-stereotypical, 168
  nurturing voice of, 103
  out of step with consumer, 135–136
  participatory, 211–213

product-focused approach to, 110–111
  spending shift in, 69–70
  television, 133–134
  traditional, 300
  trusting gut feelings in, 204
  truthful, 241
  tunnel vision of, 305
marketplace
  ad dollar spending shift of, 136
  contradictory nature of, 76–77
  differentiating in, 223
  gay, xiii
  unconscious collective of, 47
mass marketing, 230, 275
MasterCard, 290
merchant, 289–290
metrosexual, 55
Miller, Herman, 279–282
modernism, 9–13
MOMA. See Museum of Modern Art
Moses, Robert, 23–24
Museum of Modern Art, 9
music culture, 21–22

naming, 88
narrative, xxi
Natchan, 291
Natura, 267–269
The Natural Billboard, 174–175
New York, 23
New York Times, 128–130, 177
Nike, 31

Ogilvy & Mather, 242
organization, 90
original thinking, 271

Paris, 181
people
  activism among, 67–68
  art impacting, 177
  brand perception of, xxi, 51
  brand resonance with, xi–xii
  brands division from, 137–138
  building trust in, 65–67, 77–79
  catering to, 288
  connecting emotionally with, 72
  connecting sensorially with, 44–45
  cultural relevancy to, 57
  design behind, 276
  destabilizing, 256
  emotional benefits for, 94
  emotional engagement of, 114
  emotional experiences for, 51
  emotional perception of, 21–22